# Forced Labour in Colonial Africa

## A. T. Nzula, I. I. Potekhin and A. Z. Zusmanovich

Edited and Introduced
by Robin Cohen

# Forced Labour in Colonial Africa

**A.T. Nzula,
I. I. Potekhin and
A.Z. Zusmanovich**

# Forced Labour in Colonial Africa

## A. T. Nzula, I. I. Potekhin and A. Z. Zusmanovich

Edited and Introduced by
Robin Cohen

Translated by
Hugh Jenkins

Being a new edition and translation of *The Working Class Movement and Forced Labour in Negro Africa* by Ivan I. Potekhin, Aleksander Z. Zusmanovich and Albert Nzula (alias Tom Jackson), first published in Russian in Moscow (1933), together with a new Introduction, Notes and Appendices containing other writings by Albert Nzula.

Zed Press, 57 Caledonian Road, London N1 9DN.

*Forced Labour in Colonial Africa* was originally published in Russian by Profizdat, U.S.S.R., 1933. First published in English by Zed Press, 57 Caledonian Road, London N1 9DN in April 1979.

ISBN Hb 0 905762 30 4
      Pb  0 905762 31 2

Printed in Great Britain by
Redwood Burn Ltd., Trowbridge and Esher.
Typeset by Lyn Caldwell
Designed by An Dekker
Cover Design by Mayblin/Shaw
Cover photograph courtesy of Camera Press, London

# PREFACE AND
# ACKNOWLEDGEMENTS

This book had its birth more by accident than by conscious design. My interest in African labour history had drawn me to read number of issues of *African Communist,* the official publication of the South African Communist Party. There, I came across an article by 'Historicus' (*African Communist,* Second Quarter, 1976) about Albert Nzula, the first black General Secretary of the Communist Party — a figure who, despite his prominent official role, seemed to have attracted very little attention, even by sympathetic historians of the period. A rather cryptic reference, providing no publication details, referred to Nzula having co-authored a book with Ivan Potekhin and Aleksander Zusmanovich during his period in Moscow.

The bulk of this book (Chapters 1 to 8) comprises a translation of the Moscow manuscript, published in Russian in 1933, under the title *The Working Class Movement and Forced Labour in Negro Africa.* From internal evidence in the text, it appears that the book was written in 1932 and early 1933. According to a printer's note at the end of the original, the book was printed between 4th August, 1933 and 28th September, 1933.

For three major reasons, I have chosen to re-title the book. First, the original title seemed long and clumsy and did not accurately convey the contents of the original. The book represents a generalised and trenchant critique of colonialism, where this was possible, from the point of view of workers *and* peasants themselves. The stress on the working class movement in the original title therefore seemed misplaced. Also, as the book was written for a contemporary audience, the period it covered was not indicated in the title. Now, however, it seems necessary to indicate that the authors were writing in the midst of the colonial period.

Second, it was necessary to take certain liberties with, and make some additions to, the original text. For example, it was not always possible to resolve difficulties in rendering names of places or people into English. Occasionally names and short passages were elided, and sentences altered to ensure greater readability and comprehension. The tables were redrawn, or compiled for the first time, from information presented in the text. The Notes at the end of the chapters were all provided either by myself or the translator, Hugh Jenkins. In addition, certain chapters were retitled, or in one case, split into two, while many of the sub-headings have been added by the editor. Chapter 2, originally entitled *The Economic Oppression of the Native Population*, is now called *The Economic Oppression of the Peasantry*, while Chapter 3 has been separated from its original place, as part of Chapter 2, and given a separate heading. The present Chapters 4 and 8 have been given more explicit titles than their originals. While every effort has been made to preserve the spirit and style of the original work by Nzula, Potekhin, and Zusmanovich, the reader should bear in mind that the text printed here is not always a word for word translation from the original.

Thirdly and finally, both the publishers of the present edition and myself were concerned that Albert Nzula's distinctive contribution to the book should emerge. While it is difficult to separate the precise contribution of each author to a multi-authored book, there is no doubt that the Southern African sections — which are a substantial proportion of the book — were drafted or written by Nzula, while certain other sections concerning the work of the International Trade Union Committee of Negro Workers (I.T.U.C.-N.W.) would also seem to have emanated from his pen. In addition to giving Nzula the full credit he deserves for participating directly in the authorship of the book and, indeed, for providing the kind of first-hand information that made it possible for serious Soviet scholarship on Africa even to begin (see Introduction), there are now more present and compelling reasons for securing a full understanding of Nzula's views. I refer, of course, to the present state of the revolutionary movement in South Africa. Already, in the last few years, we have seen dramatic political changes in Angola and Mozambique, while the pace of events favourable to nationalist struggles in Zimbabwe and Namibia accelerates daily. Only in South Africa, which Nzula last saw as a stowaway on a ship leaving from Cape Town in 1931, do the forces of local and international capital, in alliance with the most virulent brand of racism the world has witnessed since the rise of the Nazis, appear to be on the increase. But even that is precarious, for the shock waves of events like the Soweto riots, beginning in 1976, have not yet been fully absorbed. There is now less assurance and certainly far less credibility in the Canute-like statements of the South African government. Now, more than ever, it is necessary to examine the roots of the ideology of apartheid, the roots, that is to say, in the production and reproduction of cheap labour power. This system, as Nzula's writings demonstrate, was already fully developed in the 1920s and 1930s. But, in addition to looking at how cheap labour power was exploited, Nzula also had pertinent and interesting opinions on the character and limitations of the African nationalist leadership, the balance between economic and political struggle in the trade unions and what is now termed the race/class question. These views can be found both in his contribution to *The Working Class Movement and Forced Labour in Negro Africa* and in his hitherto inaccessible writings in *The Negro Worker*.

# CONTENTS

It is now possible to secure virtually a complete set of his writings outside South Africa. A full bibliography of Nzula's writings plus all his major articles have been reprinted here as appendices (see Appendices A-K). I have also devoted the major part of the Introduction to an attempt to rescue Nzula's life and work from historical obscurity, a veil of ignorance that has only been previously lifted to some degree for a Russian reader-ship in the works of A.B. Davidson.

To summarise, because the authors' original title seemed too restrictive, because it proved necessary to make certain changes in the text and finally because of the need to highlight Nzula's views by the inclusion of further material by him, a new title, *Forced Labour in Colonial Africa*, has been adopted. While the book has now been expanded beyond its original form, the core of the book is still derived from *The Working Class Movement and Forced Labour in Negro Africa*. For help in procuring that book, I wish to thank the anonymous librarians who operate the International Inter-Library loans system. After I had searched every possible index and more or less given up in despair, a poorly bound and badly printed paperback arrived on my desk — courtesy of the University of Birmingham Library and the Lenin Library, Moscow. This stroke of luck proved auspicious. Hugh Jenkins, then conducting research at the Centre of Russian and East European Studies, Birmingham, undertook to provide a translation, despite the difficulties the text provided (see Translator's Note). An article by the Soviet Union's leading scholar on South Africa, A.B. Davidson, provided invaluable information in filling out some bio-graphical gaps in Nzula's life (see his 'Albert Nzula' in *The Working Class and the Modern World* (6), 1975). Efficient librarians at the Marx Memorial Library, London, tracked down a few copies of the *Negro Worker*, a critical journal of the period, that has now become a biblio-graphical rarity. I must also warmly thank Robert Hill, Editor of the *Marcus Garvey Papers*, University of California, Los Angeles, who referred me to the Washington Archives and obtained a number of missing issues of the *Negro Worker*. While on a visit to Trinidad, the veteran Marxist, C.L.R. James, who has personal knowledge of the personalities of the period this book covers, supplied some remarkable information about the circumstances of Nzula's death (see Introduction). Roger van Zwanenberg and Robert Molteno, of Zed Press, provided useful suggestions, and showed considerable patience at the long delays occasioned by a difficult translation and the editor's inaccessibility in a far-off island.

Finally, my gratitude and affection go to Selina Cohen for spending long hours with gazetteers and maps identifying nearly all the strange African names that emerged from the Cyrillic script. In this, and other ways, she helped nurture the book from its rebirth, through its periodic sicknesses, into good health.

Robin Cohen
Trinidad, June, 1978.

# TRANSLATOR'S NOTE

Due to certain defects and peculiarities from which the original Russian text of this work suffers, there are aspects of the present translation which should be treated with caution by the reader. These are discussed below.

Names of persons and places, both African and English have proved particularly difficult to translate accurately and reliably from Russian to English. This is because there exist vowels and consonants in English which cannot be faithfully transcribed into Cyrillic script (notable examples are *w*, *h*, and *qu*) and also because a Russian transliteration of an English name can often be retransliterated with equal validity in two or more ways. (*Johnson* becomes *Dzhonson* in Russian; this could be rendered in English as Johnson or Jonson, there being nothing in the Russian spelling from which the *h* can be inferred.) Research by the editor of the present volume has resolved most of the consequent ambiguities; where spellings remain open to doubt they are marked with an asterisk.

It will be evident to the reader that the authors made little attempt to document their sources. All notes that appear are written either by the present editor or translator. It has usually been impossible to verify the accuracy of quotations translated by the authors into Russian and now retranslated back into their original language. Further, there is some evidence that certain English sources have been poorly translated into Russian. Lastly, a number of quotation marks are missing from the original Russian, as a result of which the precise substance of certain quotations must remain a matter of inference and speculation. From the foregoing it follows that quotations in the present English version should, in most cases, be considered at best a close approximation to their English originals. No attempt has been made to reproduce the original texts of quotations from French and Belgian sources.

That their work might be read by anyone other than their immediate contemporaries would seem not to have occurred to the authors. This is suggested by the frequency in the text of such expressions as 'last year', 'in recent months' and so on. Such phrases obviously present a problem to the modern reader. It is known that work on the original began at some time during 1932, and that the book was printed in the latter half of 1933. Lacking more precise data on the authors' activities during 1932-33, the present translator has refrained from expressing these vague indications of time as specific years. To have done so would have risked the introduction of unnecessary errors into an already idiosyncratic chronology.

Certain prices and wage rates cited in the present English version are of somewhat dubious accuracy, due to the fact that they are given in roubles in the original without any overt indication of the rate used to convert sterling to Soviet currency. Calculations derived from equivalents given elsewhere in the text suggest that the conversion rate used by the authors was £1 = R9.36. Where figures are given in roubles only in the original, the above conversion rate is applied in the translation.

Those unaccustomed to the rhetoric of Soviet political writing will doubtless find the style of this work at times somewhat repetitive. It is arguable that many of the ritualistic epithets as 'imperialist' and 'reformist' could have been omitted from the English version. We have chosen to retain them on the grounds that the work, as a whole, bears witness to the authors' strong political commitment to their subject. To have partially concealed this aspect of the book would have been to alter the authors' original intentions. The style of the work has, therefore, been changed as little as possible.

Hugh Jenkins
London
February, 1978

# INTRODUCTION

## THE SETTING

The authors of this book, Albert T. Nzula, Ivan I. Potekhin, and Aleksander Zusmanovich, were writing this work at a moment of considerable excitement in the international communist movement. The capitalist world was in the midst of the Great Depression, a depression which many contemporary leftists interpreted as the major rupture Marx had held endemic to the capitalist mode of production. For the authors, 'the crisis' of the capitalist world was a visible and looming reality — as their comments, particularly in Chapter 4, make evident. This was a time for witnessing to both the hardship and suffering that retrenchment and the decline in international trade was causing the workers and peasants entrapped in the Western commodity market, and for looking to the revolutionary possibilities that such a crisis might occasion.

For the Soviet Union, the preoccupation with building 'socialism in one country' could be supplemented by a concern with events on a more distant horizon. First, a new series of initiatives were undertaken in the Comintern and Profintern, then firmly under Soviet, and some might say, Stalin's control. Second, the new policy-making initiatives of the Soviet Union had to be based on a greater familiarity with nationalist and anticolonial struggles in far-off places. This gave a strong fillip to Soviet studies of Asia and Africa, and students and revolutionaries from these continents soon filled the classrooms and corridors of the newly established Research Association for National and Colonial Problems (N.I.A.K.P.) and Eastern Workers Communist University (K.U.T.V.U.).

The shifts in policy within the Comintern were mainly related to 'The National Question', an issue that Lenin first raised in 1920. As far as the African continent was concerned, however, the major shift in focus came in September, 1928 with the adoption of the slogan — an 'Independent Native Republic for South Africa'. Within the restricted national terms of debate on the South African left, this slogan has often been held to be inexplicable: it was certainly very divisive both within the South African Communist Party (S.A.C.P.) and in the wider liberation movement, The policy may have been ill-founded or unwise in the South African case, but it is far from inexplicable if one examines the context of successive

Comintern debates, which were about China, India, Ireland, Indonesia, Blacks in the U.S., the Philippines, Persia and Afghanistan (among others), and only very marginally about South Africa. It is more than plausible to argue that the discussants correctly perceived that, in each of these cases, the revolutionary movement would collapse unless it allied itself with the national and anti-colonial struggle often led by non-working class elements. (For a summary of the discussion and extracts from the 1928 theses, see Degres, 1971: 526-548.) This question shall be considered more fully later: here it is only necessary to note that the period during which this book was written, and when Nzula was reaching political maturity, coincided with a broad shift in the international movement, from appeals based solely on class solidarity to an acceptance of the revolutionary importance of oppressed national and ethnic solidarities. The trade union section of the Comintern, the Profintern (Red International of Labour Unions) at its fourth congress in Moscow (1928), had also devoted considerable attention to the national, and, in particular, 'the Negro question'. The major consequence of this discussion was the establishment of the International Trade Union Committee of Negro Workers (I.T.U.C.-N.W.) within R.I.L.U. The I.T.U.C.-N.W. was to gain its greatest organizational coherence in July, 1930 when it convened the First International Conference of Negro Workers at Hamburg. Albert Nzula, among four black leaders 'imprisoned or waiting conviction for activities connected with struggles of Negro toilers', was elected as an honorary member of the Presidium (I.T.U.C.-N.W. Report, 1930:3). The journal of the organization, *The Negro Worker*, despite its checkered career (see Hooker, 1967: 18-32), was a significant organ of expression and was later to provide Nzula with an outlet for his views on the major issues confronting black South African workers. There is some evidence, too, that Zusmanovich was connected with the work of the I.T.U.C.-N.W. (Hooker, *Ibid*).

As regards the establishment and growth of Soviet studies of Africa and the related task of recruiting black activists and students to the Soviet Union, one need only relate the names of prominent black nationalist revolutionaries who were trained in Moscow during the late twenties and early thirties. Often Comintern agents and trainees adopted false names either as a revolutionary posture, or so they could be sent back to their countries with greater ease. The Trinidadian, Malcolm Nurse (alias George Padmore), who had already served his apprenticeship in the Communist Party, U.S.A., was lauded by the Soviets and even elected as a representative on the Moscow City Council. I.T.A. Wallace-Johnson (alias E.A. Richards) drifted into and out of the Eastern Workers Communist University (K.U.T.V.U.) as did Johnstone (Jomo) Kenyatta. The South African contingent included J.B. Marks (later chairman of the South African Communist Party), Moses M. Kotane (later General Secretary, S.A.C.P.), Edwin Mofututsanyana (alias Greenwood), and an obscure figure, Nickin (alias Hilton) (see Rytov, 1973: 95). One of the earliest arrivals was Albert T. Nzula (alias Tom Jackson), our principal subject, who had travelled a long road from Rouxville, Orange Free State (South Africa), where he was born on November 16, 1905, to Moscow, where he died, apparently of pneumonia, on January 7, 1934. It is to this journey that we now turn.

## ALBERT NZULA: HIS SOUTH AFRICAN PERIOD

In Nzula's short life (he was not yet 29 when he died), he only had a brief period of political activism — from 1928 onwards. Yet his career within the South African liberation movement was meteoric and spanned such important events as the decline and virtual collapse of the Industrial and Commercial Union (I.C.U.), the attempt by the S.A.C.P. to move away from its character as a small white-dominated party to a mass organization, the adoption by the Party at its conference in Inchcape Hall, Johannesburg (December 28, 1928 to January 1, 1929) of the controversial Native Republic slogan, a major fight within the African National Congress (one of many to come) in April 1930 between the 'radicals' and 'conservatives' and the first of the mass demonstrations against the pass system.

A detailed examination of Nzula's life can do much to illuminate the political cross-currents, domestic and international. In addition to his formal role as general secretary of the South African Communist Party (the first black to hold that position), after 1929 he was acting editor of *Umsebenzi* ('Worker' in Xhosa), then joint secretary, with Eddie Roux, of the League of African Rights and a leading activist and speaker for the African Federation of Trade Unions and the African National Congress. Unfortunately the biographical information in the conventional sources is sparse, where it is not contradictory, even on such prosaic matters as the dates of his birth and death (most sources, for example, Simons & Simons, 1969: 414, are wrong), and his home language — was he a Zulu as his name would suggest, or Basotho as Wolton oddly maintains (Wolton, 1947: 68). Fortunately, these accounts can be supplemented by two apparently reliable sources: the first by 'Historicus' in the S.A.C.P.'s *The African Communist* (Historicus, 1976); the second by the Moscow historian, A.B. Davidson (Davidson, 1975). Nzula's own writings in *Umsebenzi* and *The Negro Worker* together, of course, with the information one can piece together from the present book, now that it has been translated, provide additional sources of biographical information.

The two major personal memoirs of the period agree that Nzula was a man of exceptional talent. Wolton, who was Nzula's sponsor and patron within the S.A.C.P., is positively lavish in his praise:

> (Nzula) . . . very soon showed remarkable powers of leadership and great aptitude for organizing work . . . (He) soon developed a brilliant knowledge of socialism and particularly of the national

question and the relations of the various peoples in South Africa. With great courage and skill he exposed the faults and shortcomings of the socialism of the Europeans ... Albert Nzula will rank as one of the pioneers in the fight for African freedom, and his personal courage, devotion and outstanding ability contributed tremendously to the creation of that independent initiative which enabled the new group of Bantu leaders to assert themselves against the powerful tradition and established position of most of the European socialists ... he was rapidly becoming a writer of outstanding merit.
(Wolton, 1977: 68, 69)

Wolton's characterization of Nzula is so extravagant that it suggests that he saw Nzula as the principal means whereby he could Africanize and 'Bolshevize' the party, the task, one source asserts, that had been assigned to Wolton by the Comintern (Karis & Carter, eds., 1977: 163). Roux, who had worked together with Nzula in the League of African Rights and knew him well from other party activities, is somewhat less overawed. In *Time Longer Than Rope*, he writes briefly that 'Nzula was an African of outstanding ability, though he had grave faults of character that were later to prove his undoing' (Roux, 1964: 215). This cryptic picture is slightly amplified in Roux's posthumously published autobiography *Rebel Pity* (Roux & Roux, 1970). Here the Rouxs are largely concerned with Nzula's capacities as a public speaker and only pass a general judgement as an aside:

Nzula was a natural orator whose talents were used not only in location meetings among Africans, but also in our Sunday evening meetings on the City Hall steps where he impressed white audiences ... Nzula spoke as ever with assurance and competence and his easy control of English. No hecklers ever took him on ... Brilliant but unreliable in his personal life he was addicted to drink, and vodka was to prove the cause of his death ...
(Roux & Roux, 1970: 81, 129, 152)

The question of Nzula's death is considered again in the final section of this Introduction. But it appears that Roux had good cause to bemoan Nzula's penchant for alcohol. His fondness for drink is again emphasized by the Party's narrator, Historicus, who adds for good measure that drink is 'an instrument of personal destruction which has at times caused severe damage in the ranks of the liberation movement over the years' (Historicus, 1976: 98). Roux's additional claim that Nzula was not a good organizer is repeated by Historicus, though this assertion is totally at variance with Wolton's views and does not square with Nzula's central role in organizing the Dingaan's Day demonstrations in December, 1930 and the May Day procession of 1931. In each case, however, Nzula was more prominent as a pamphleteer, orator and a leader in the streets. It may well be that he was indifferent to, or incapable of, fully involving himself in day-to-day routine administration.

According to the accounts provided by Historicus and A.B. Davidson, Nzula's early career was remarkable only for his persistence in self-improvement. His father, described as 'a worker', imposed a religious world-view which presumed that one should accept white domination with Christian humility. Nzula rejected this quiescent attitude and sought to improve himself. He was educated at Bensonvale, Herschel and Lovedale where he qualified as a teacher. He then moved to Aliwal North to take up his first teaching post, earning some additional money by acting as an interpreter at the local magistrate's court. The I.C.U. was still highly active and Nzula gained some political experience by becoming a secretary of the local branch in Aliwal. He moved from there to Evaton in the Transvaal where he taught at the African Methodist Episcopate (A.M.E.) Mission School at Wilberforce.

The way in which Nzula was recruited into the Party is described in a typescript memoir written by Douglas Wolton in 1974, cited by Historicus (Historicus, 1976: 92-93). According to Wolton:

> ... in 1928 a Communist meeting was held at Evaton, Transvaal ... A group of African teachers had asked me to address a meeting to explain the Native Republic ... despite the rain that fell, the audience did not disperse, but remained until the end. After the meeting a young teenage (*sic*) African came forward to ask for further information which resulted in his joining the Party. His name was Albert Nzula and he was a teacher in the local school.

Roux notes that a month after the Evaton meeting Nzula wrote to *Umsebenzi* that after reading Bishop Brown's *Communism and Christianism* (a book that sought to reconcile the views of Marx, Jesus and Darwin, no less), he was 'convinced that no halfway measures will solve the problem'. Capitalist literature was unable to explain working class misery. Nzula 'was prepared to do his little bit to enlighten his countrymen on this point.' (Roux, 1974: 216).

Nzula either abandoned, or was dismissed (Davidson, 1975), from his post at Evaton and became a constant visitor to the Party headquarters at 41a Fox Street, Johannesburg. He became an avid reader in the Party library and, once a member, pressed insistently for a greater participation of Africans in positions of meaningful responsibility. His public baptism was as a speaker on the traditionally 'whites-only' steps of the Johannesburg Town Hall. In Wolton's memoirs, this was a daring success, but the occasion was not repeated (Historicus, 1976: 93). The Rouxs, by contrast, suggest that a speech from Nzula at the Party's weekly meeting was a more regular occurrence (Roux & Roux, 1970: 81). Nzula's ready tongue, this time at a Party night school in February, 1929, was sufficient to get him prosecuted for incitement to racial hostility. Two of the ubiquitous African police spies were in the audience and claimed Nzula had, in attacking General Hertzog's Native Bills, urged his audience to 'hate the enemy' and 'fight the white man' (Historicus, 1976: 94). He was found guilty and fined £10 or one month's imprisonment with hard labour. This relatively mild harassment by the authorities was the only occasion he was arrested, despite the rather more overblown halo of martyrdom that was conferred on Nzula by the 1930 Hamburg Conference on the occasion of his election to the Presidium of that body.

From the night school incident in February, 1929 to his departure for Moscow around mid-1931, Nzula was a dedicated activist. He wrote for *Umsebenzi*, rose within the Party to the rank of General Secretary, learnt his marxism from Bunting, and possibly Wolton, while remaining true to his initial impetus to Africanize the Party. Of his various activities, it is instructive to highlight three involvements: with the A.N.C., with the pass-burning demonstrations on the Dingaan's Days of 1929 and 1930, and with the African Federation of Trade Unions (A.F.T.U.).

Nzula was one of the fifty-odd delegates to the A.N.C.'s annual conference held at Bloemfontein in April, 1930. In the formal photograph of the occasion (reproduced in Karis & Carter, eds, 1977), Nzula, with white suit and stiff collar, looks socially indistinguishable from the other delegates. Yet a fundamental rift was not slow in surfacing. J.T. Gumede gave a presidential address that the Simons describe as the most forthright yet heard at a Congress convention. Gumede, who insisted he was no communist himself, nonetheless saw the Chinese and Javanese as rising up against imperialism. It was little use petitioning Britain — one had to adopt a militant policy in the spirit of other oppressed peoples. The sting in the tail was not the plea for a militant anti-imperialism, but the unexpected praise that Gumede lavished on the Soviet Union. According to Gumede, 'Soviet Russia was the only real friend of all subjected races' (Simons and Simons, 1969: 427, 8). For such a conservative body, Gumede's statement was heresy, and pandemonium, led by the outraged delegates, followed his address. Nzula, Champion, Tonjeni, Gomas, Ndobe and other militants rallied behind Gumede but their support was insufficient to counter the conservative and right-wing elements who were to take control of the Congress (and hold it until the 1960s). Tactically, Gumede's speech was a disaster for the pro-communist elements of the A.N.C. Seme (the new president) and Thaele (the Western Cape provincial president) soon weeded out the left-wing elements, and what internal dissension could not accomplish, Oswald Pirow, the Minister of Justice, soon managed. An attempt by Bransley R. Ndobe to start a radical breakaway Independent African Nationalist Congress failed when Pirow instantly deported him to his birthplace, Basutoland. From there Ndobe wrote a bitter denunciation to the *Negro Worker*:

> We want the workers of England, America and the whole world to know that every attempt on the part of the Africans to organize for better conditions is being met with police violence and imperialist terror of the vilest form. Not only this: the government has on its side a big force of African agents and reformist lackeys, whom the officials call 'good boys'. These black traitors are paid by the capitalists to side-track the masses from following a revolutionary way out of their misery.
> (Ndobe, 1932: 15)

Unlike Ndobe, Nzula appears to have wanted to continue some form of co-operation with the official A.N.C., largely in connection with the anti-pass movement he was organizing (see later). Not that Nzula was on occasion above venting his own spleen on the black bourgeoisie. Take, for example, his sarcastic denunciation of Professor D.D.T. Jabavu's visit to the U.K. in December, 1931. Jabavu argued that British liberal opinion should support his Non-European Conference as otherwise the communists would gain public support. 'Thus by a skilful utilization of timid threats and lying insinuations our Professor hopes to gain the sympathy of his English "friends" ' (Nzula, 1932: 15). But Nzula knew his theory of class alliance too well to have scorned co-operation with the A.N.C. As he was to later write in the Moscow book:

> National reformist organizations are frequently dismissed in general statements to the effect that they are in any case incapable of achieving anything, that they have no further purpose and to deal with them is a precious waste of time . . . The need for systematic work within reformist and national reformist organizations must be explained to all politically conscious workers . . .
> (Chapter 6, below)

In short, it seems fair to conclude that the communist presence in the A.N.C. was undermined not by Nzula and his comrades, who preferred a more canny game, but by Gumede's precipitous and unnecessary defence of the Soviet Union, and also, perhaps, by those, on both sides, who sought a fight to the finish. The relationship between the A.N.C. and the S.A.C.P. has remained problematic to this day.

Turning to Nzula's role as a leader of a popular movement against passes, this started in August, 1929, with the launching of the League of African Rights, whose office-holders included Gumede (president), Bunting (chairman) and Roux and Nzula (joint secretaries). Though the League demanded a wide range of 'national rights' — for example, the retention of the Cape Franchise and its extension to other provinces, free education, freedom of speech and association — its major thrust was on the issue of passes. The League was virtually a model front organization with communists or their friends in the major positions of control but with a broad enough platform to attract office-holders, adherents and supporters from the A.N.C. and I.C.U. The League's battle song 'Mayibuye i Afrika' ('Come back Africa'), subsequently to become the best-loved song at virtually any African political gathering, embodied the often inchoate but powerful national consciousness that gripped many Africans. The League, moreover, operated in a virtual political vacuum, just at the moment that Pirow and Hertzog were launching their most repressive measures. As Legassick argues, 'The collapse of the I.C.U. into squabbling factions had left its membership without an organizational and strategic focus, while the government was pressing ahead more vigorously with prosecution of militants and implementation of pass and tax legislation' (Legassick, 1973: 17). The League's officials spoke against the Pirow bills — especially the Riotous Assemblies Act — all over the country, attempted to collect a million signatures for a petition and organized a mass meeting on November 10, 1929 in Johannesburg. Pirow retaliated four days later in what the Simons describe as 'a melodramatic show of force' (Simons & Simons, 1969: 419). He personally led 700 policemen armed with machine-guns, fixed bayonets and tear gas in a tax collecting raid in the African townships of Durban. The Party responded with discipline and restraint and sought to turn the Dingaan's Day demonstrations of December, 1929 into an even wider counter-protest under the slogan of 'Long Live the Native Republic'. Then, inexplicably, a cable arrived from Moscow, giving instructions to disband the League. Here was the most blatant example of foolish dictation from Moscow — far more blatant indeed than the Native Republic slogan which had, in any case, been the subject of many discussions and had several important advocates within the S.A.C.P. The Simons mildly suggest that the instruction was 'ill-advised'. Not so: it was disastrous. The League remained the one bridge between the C.P., the I.C.U. and the more militant members of the A.N.C. It was now exposed as a tool of the Comintern to be discarded as and when Moscow saw fit. Dingaan's Day, 1929, was nonetheless marked by a large demonstration in Johannesburg from which only the A.N.C. held aloof. Thereafter, despite the enforced demise of the League, Nzula sought to build links back to the A.N.C. and to the broader African masses on what we would nowadays term 'civil rights issues'. But when Nzula chaired an 'all-in' conference at the Trades Hall in January, 1930, it had to be under the auspices of the C.P. and not the League. As a result, all organizations, with the exception of the Garment Workers Union and the Jewish Workers Club, stayed away (Simons & Simons, 1969: 425). On October 26, 1930, Nzula was in the chair once again at an anti-pass conference held at the Inchcape Hall in Johannesburg. The controversial conference of April, 1930 had meanwhile intervened and, if it were unlikely that the A.N.C. would attend in January, it was impossible that they should attend now. Nzula pressed his anti-pass campaign forward with more and more strident speeches. 'Whether educated or uneducated, rich or poor, we are all subject to these badges of slavery . . . We are slaves as long as we think we can only beg and pray to this cruel government' (Nzula, cited in Simons & Simons, 1969: 433). Ironically, Nzula did not himself have to carry a pass, his education determined that he had instead to carry 'a pass exemption certificate'. On Dingaan's Day, 1930, he threw this document into the flames with other passes at a Johannesburg rally. Considering first, the manner in which Moscow had undercut his position in the League, second, the non-co-operation of the A.N.C. and, finally and importantly, the character of the government he opposed, the Dingaan's Day demonstration can be counted as a success. This was true particularly in Durban where 3,000 passes were burned and Johannes Nkosi, Nzula's friend and comrade, was stabbed and mutilated by the African constables deployed to try and oppose a procession by the pass-burners. Nzula wrote a stirring editorial tribute in *Umsebenzi* (reproduced in Appendix K below). Two months later Nzula's account of the Dingaan's Day demonstration was published by *The Negro Worker*. He wrote:

> The consolidation of the achievements of the campaign for the burning of passes on Dingaan's Day is proceeding at a rapid pace. Concentration groups have been and are being set up as rapidly as possible, while the nucleus of a powerful Dockers', Railwaymen's and Transport Union is already functioning. The police are as active as ever in trying to prevent the activities of the Party, but the masses are not frightened, or in any way deterred by the police from following in their hundreds the lead of the Party. The Native reformist leaders, who opposed the pass-burning campaign, are being forced by the upsurge of the revolutionary mass movement to adopt left-wing phrases and slogans, while they are at the same time looking out for the first opportunity to betray the movement. (Nzula, Appendix C, below)

Despite Nzula's optimistic scenario for the future, both the level of repression by the Government, and the level of discussion and action within the Party caused its precipitous decline during the course of 1931.

Nzula's third 'involvement', we identified earlier, was in the African Federation of Trade Unions. Nzula's role as a trade unionist was somewhat artificially thrust upon him. Weinbren, the Chairman of the Non-European Federation of Trade Unions, suddenly left Johannesburg in January, 1930, while T.W. Thibedi was expelled for mismanaging trade union funds. Nzula took his place as general secretary (Simons & Simons, 1969:424). He never showed himself particularly concerned with the routine issues of wages and economic conditions and, instead, seemed to have rather fallen in with Wolton's line of emphasizing the political content of unionism — labour day rallies, marches of the unemployed, etc. Nzula ultimately chose to split off a body more firmly under his own control, which became known as the African Federation of Trade Unions. His judgement on the work of the Non-European Federation of Trade Unions (of which, after all, he was General Secretary) seems both ungenerous and unfair. According to Nzula, in the Moscow book:

> (The Federation of Non-European Trade Unions) was a narrow organization uniting black and white workers in Johannesburg. From the moment of its foundation, the Non-European Federation limited its practical activities to fixing wage rates and concluding agreements and contracts. This narrow activity undermined the Union's militant character and the mood of the black workers. It ultimately became a purely reformist trade union organization. (Chapter 6, below)

This same union was in fact responsible for organizing a notable strike of black and white clothing workers in Germiston (the first major example of inter-racial co-operation amongst South African workers) and had a reasonably large number of members and affiliates organizing both black and white workers. By contrast, under the secretaryship of Nzula, only four white unions affiliated to the African Federation of Trade Unions.

This modest achievement was hailed by Wolton as 'the rapid radicalization of the workforce' (Simons & Simons, 1969: 445). Two years later, writing from Moscow, Nzula passed a more sober judgement on the success of the A.F.T.U. He acknowledged that the 4,000 black, 'coloured' and white members of the A.F.T.U. (1932) had declined to 851 members four months later. The Union's 'ideological influence', he ingeniously explains, 'is substantially greater than its growth in numerical terms' (Chapter 6, below). The fact was that the A.F.T.U.'s poor performance was primarily due, not to the union's radicalism nor its inter-racial programme (to which other union centres also formally adhered), but its inability to respond meaningfully to shop-floor grievances. Nzula's attack on the Non-European Federation of Trade Unions should also be seen in the light of the expulsion of Weinbren and other white trade unionists from the Communist Party for reformist tendencies in September, 1931. One cannot escape the conclusion that Nzula, while in Moscow, thought it politic to distance himself from the work of the Non-European Federation with which he himself was associated. It should also be remembered that, though Nzula had left South Africa a couple of months before the September expulsions, it is likely, given his desire to Africanize the Party, that he would have approved of the purge.

The expulsions, nonetheless, caused the Party to lose a number of veteran and respected trade unionists (in addition to Weinbren, E.S. Sachs, C.B. Tyler, W.H. Andrews and Fanny Klenerman were expelled). Their loss and Nzula's earlier departure, meant that the new leaders of the A.F.T.U. were in no position to respond to rank and file demands. Nzula's own disdain for bread and butter issues, seems to indicate that he was a better orator and 'politico' than trade unionist.

Nzula's last major act within South Africa was to organize a large rally of some 2,000 Africans, mainly unemployed elements, for May Day, 1931. His group joined up with some 1,000 white workers led by Issy Diamond (a veteran communist barber). They attacked the Carlton Hotel and caused scuffles outside the Rand Club 'to the consternation of its habitues whose apprehensive faces were glued to the windows' (Historicus, 1976: 97). Issy Diamond was sentenced to 12 months hard labour while — surprisingly — Nzula escaped scot free.

Wolton had been instructed, while in Moscow, to send militants for training and it seemed an opportune moment for Nzula to leave. Under the unlikely — but real — name of Conan Doyle Modiakgotla (a former I.C.U. leader), Nzula boarded a ship in Cape Town and arrived in Moscow on August 25, 1931. He was to spend the last 2½ years of his life there.

## NZULA, POTEKHIN AND ZUSMANOVICH AND THE AFRICAN BUREAU

When Nzula finally arrived in Moscow he was attached principally to the

Research Association for National and Colonial Problems (N.I.A.N.K.P.)
of the Eastern Workers' Communist University (K.U.T.V.U.). As Hooker
explains, this was one of four Party schools: viz, Lenin University — which
served students from the West, Sun Yat-Sen University — for Chinese
studies, K.U.T.V.U. — for the rest of Asia and Africa, and The Academy
of Red Professors — which trained staff for the other three and for Party
work (Hooker, 1967: 12-17).

The establishment of African Studies in the Soviet Union was greatly
helped by the presence in Moscow, at the time, of Andre Shiik (his name
is sometimes rendered into English as Endre Sik), a Hungarian marxist,
born in 1891, who lived in the Soviet Union from 1915-45. Shiik is
considered by Soviet scholars to be the principal founder of Marxist
African Studies. (The third and fourth volumes of Shiik's monumental
*History of Africa* have only recently been published.) The importance of
Shiik and the newly-established universities, in promoting marxist studies
of Africa, has been missed by at least one Western scholar, Milton D.
Morris, who, while purporting to describe the development of African
Studies in the Soviet Union, completely omits mention of N.I.A.N.K.P.
and K.U.T.V.U. (Morris, 1973). A more recent American study by
Edward Wilson is much more satisfactory. According to Wilson, Shiik
presented the first detailed plan for a Soviet programme of black African
studies in April, 1929. It was premised on 'the enormous importance' of
Africa both to the imperialist powers and to the forces of world revolution. The 'completely new' marxist science of Black Africa would
involve two tasks. First, mendacious bourgeois literature would have to be
exposed for not revealing the 'truth' about 'hundreds of millions' of black
toilers, and the existence of an international proletariat. Second, if, as the
Sixth Congress of the Comintern maintained, it was possible for regions
such as colonial Africa to achieve a non-capitalist road to revolution, what
revolutionary agent could be substituted for the advanced proletariat of
Russia and Western Europe? Shiik further stressed the importance of
approaching the history, economics and sociology of the area from the
perspective of Africa's black inhabitants, and of the enormous amount of
institutional and organizational activity that would be necessary even to
begin the struggle for liberation (Wilson, 1976: 186-188). Shiik's plan met
with a positive response and a permanent 'African Bureau' was established
in N.I.A.N.K.P.

Obviously for the history, economics and sociology of Africa to be
approached from the point of view of Africans, suitable African revolutionaries and scholars had to be found to collaborate in this enterprise. This
is where Nzula came in. The presence of Nzula (and his fellow students)
was indispensable to the work of the African Bureau, and Nzula even
worked informally with other scholars not attached to the Bureau.
I.I. Snegirev, for example, learnt his Zulu under Nzula's tuition, and it
improved sufficiently for him to translate Zulu fairy tales into Russian

for publication. In his preface to *Zulu Folk Tales*, Snegirev wtites that he 'considers it his duty to mention as his teacher, the late A.T. Nzula, under whose direct assistance and consultation a major part of the present translation was written'. The book was dedicated to 'the memory of an ardent revolutionary and a leading fighter for the cause of the liberation of Negro toilers' (Davidson, 1975).

Among the scholars to be attracted to Shiik's African Bureau were Ivan Potekhin who was, until his death in 1964 (tragically from a disease contracted in post-independence Ghana during his first visit to Africa) the doyen of Soviet African Studies, and A.Z. Zusmanovich who was also to become a prominent authority. Ivan Izosimovich Potekhin's achievements are summarized in the biographical sketch that appeared in a posthumous volume collecting some of his major articles:

> Ivan Potekhin (1903-1964) eminent Soviet scientist who studied African history, ethnology and contemporary economic, social and political problems, was the author of the books *Formation of the National Community of the South African Bantus, Ghana Today, Africa Looks Ahead,* and many articles. He was one of the contributors and editors of the fundamental *Peoples of Africa.* A number of his books and articles were translated and published abroad during his lifetime . . . Professor Potekhin was the founder and first director of the Institute of Africa, USSR Academy of Sciences, and the first President of the Soviet Association for Friendship with the Peoples of Africa.
> (Cover in Potekhin, 1968)

Potekhin's tombstone in Novodevichye cemetery, Moscow, shows a profile relief in Soviet realism. A dignified, intelligent face looks towards an unknown object on the horizon, while one hand fondles a Sherlock Holmes pipe and the other rests on a pile of books. But the avuncular image came later. When Nzula met Potekhin in 1931, Potekhin was, in J.B. Marks' recollection, 'a vigorous young scholar, a born hard-working teacher, who never missed a chance to learn himself while teaching us' (Rytov, 1975: 95). Amongst the subjects Potekhin taught Marks in 1934 were Russian history and British colonial policy in South Africa. His research interests and writings also included material on the I.C.U. and A.N.C. in South Africa. We can assume that much of his knowledge and awareness of South Africa was derived from his early collaboration with Nzula. Potekhin's other major area of long-standing academic interest was West Africa, particularly English-speaking West Africa. It is probably the case that, as far as the present book is concerned, the West African sections were written by Potekhin.

The final author of the trio is Aleksander Z. Zusmanovich (1902-1965), born three years before Nzula and one year before his compatriot. Moses Kotane recollects Zusmanovich as being a more senior figure at the Lenin School in Vorovsky Street than Potekhin (Rytov, 1973: 98), though clearly this could hardly have been a marked seniority. Like Potekhin, Zusmanovich was a distinguished academic mainly specializing in the

Congo and, later, Liberia. It can be assumed that he drafted the sections of the book on the Congo. In fact, by scholarly standards, these sections often seem the best researched and the most detailed accounts in the book. The use of the Belgian Communist Party's newspaper, *Drapeau Rouge*, to supplement conventional sources, is of particular interest. A fuller biography of Zusmanovich appears in his obituary in the Soviet periodical, *Peoples of Asia and Africa*, though it wasn't possible to consult the relevant issue for present purposes. As far as Western scholars are concerned, Zusmanovich is (to the writer's knowledge) mentioned only once by Hooker, who assigned him a rather more sinister role than that of a mere scholar and (wrongly) assumed him to be still alive at the time of Hooker's writing (1967). Hooker describes him as being 'on mission' to Hamburg in 1930, presumably in connection with the work of the International Trade Union Committee of Negro Workers, which had its base there. Hooker quotes Rolf Italiaander, in *Schwarze Haut in Roten Griff*, as a Comintern defector, saying that Zusmanovich ascribed part of 'the operation' to him. According to Italiaander, whose language still smacks of the Cold War, Zusmanovich described the *Negro Worker* (the I.T.U.C.-N.W.'s journal) in these terms. '. . . It was the very first international journal for the Negro in all continents, which was concerned with his troubles, needs and pains. What he had been dreaming of, an international platform for discussion, we communists established for him' (Hooker, 1967: 19).

The fortuitous presence of these three young men, all still in their twenties, led to the collaborative work translated in the present volume. In many ways the writing of *The Working Class Movement and Forced Labour in Negro Africa* was a remarkable achievement. Nzula had no Russian, the other two little English, and all were remote from the major sources of African scholarship and policy-making. The book may in fact be the first written on Africa in Moscow (with the exception of a number of works on Pushkin's African origins). Its merit has been recognized by one Western scholar, Edward Wilson, who comments that the book is remarkable for the depth in which it probed the questions initally posed by Shiik and for the extent to which it used indigenous African source material. The book showed that the Soviet Africanists 'were endeavouring to base their findings upon direct sources of information from the field' (Wilson, 1976: 190). Wilson is obviously bemused by the third author, 'Tom Jackson', for he doesn't mention his contribution. Little does he realize how direct was the source of information from the field. A more detailed review of the contents of the book must await later discussion. For the moment, we shall return to Albert Nzula's activities and ultimate fate.

## NZULA AND THE I.T.U.C.-N.W.

Nzula's writings and activities in Moscow are paralleled by his increasing involvement in the affairs of the I.T.U.C.-N.W. and its journal, *The Negro Worker.* He had, as was pointed out earlier, already been elected an Honorary Member in the Presidium of the I.T.U.C.-N.W. at the 1930 Hamburg Conference. Later, according to Davidson, he was on the Executive Council (apparently a working body) as well as the Central Council of the Profintern (a high honour indeed). He also served as an editor of *The Negro Worker.* As much of his writings were published there and because of his intimate connection with the journal, it is necessary to devote some consideration to its beginnings. The journal started either in the 'late twenties' (Davidson, 1975), December, 1929 (Wilson, 1976: 213) or as the *International Negro Workers Review* in January, 1930 (Hooker, 1967: 18). It was published from Hamburg where the C.P.'s control of the civic authorities extended to the police force, thus saving the Party political embarrassment and allowing the journal to operate in a western seaport from where sailors could easily distribute copies. With the rise to power of Hitler in 1933, and the jailing of *The Negro Worker's* extraordinary Trinidadian editor, George Padmore, the journal was moved to Copenhagen, Brussels, Harlem (for one issue only in Oct.-Nov. 1934), back to Copenhagen and finally to Paris (1936-37) where it met its demise. With Padmore's expulsion from the Party, the quality of the journal declined, and its frequent changes of locale and editors has meant that a full set of issues is a bibliographical rarity. To complicate matters, Davidson tells us (Davidson, 1975) that to facilitate distribution in Africa some of the issues appeared in a cover bearing a cross and the title, *The Missionaries' Voice, The Path of the Cross, Organ of the African Methodist Episcopate of the London Missionary Society.* The second page carried the inscription 'Hearken ye that are oppressed and afflicted by manifold tribulations', while the puzzled reader had to wait for the third page to read the more familiar slogan 'Proletarians of all Countries, Unite'. Considering that Nzula taught at an A.M.E. school in Wilberforce, it is tempting to speculate that the disguise was his tongue-in-cheek response from the land of the godless.

Nzula's writing for *The Negro Worker* was often more reflective and scholarly than in his more strident days. For example, the articles on the 'International Labour Defence' (see Appendix G) and on 'South Africa and the Imperialist War' (Appendix E) show an impressive ability to command an argument outside of his immediate experience. The posthumous material published in *The Negro Worker* is also thought by Davidson to show his best qualities as a writer (see Appendix A and I for a full list of references). While the I.T.U.C.-N.W. brought together a number of remarkable personalities, Nzula is bound to have been influenced by George Padmore, who was secretary of the Committee and for a time editor of the *Negro Worker*. Though Padmore's stature has been recognized by many scholars and black activists, his name should be recalled in this context for his book, *The Life and Struggles of Negro Toilers*, first published by the Red International of Labour Unions for the I.T.U.C.-N.W. in London in 1931 (Padmore, 1971). In its scope, ambition and subject-matter, Padmore's book clearly provided a strong inspiration for Nzula, Potekhin and Zusmanovich, though Padmore's subsequent disgrace and expulsion has meant that there are no direct citations from his text by the three authors who only show by occasional allusion, that they are familiar with his work.

## NZULA'S DEATH AND HIS SIGNIFICANCE

Nzula was, so the Rouxs maintain, a victim of his liking for vodka. He fell down one night in a frozen street and lay there for some hours. After being taken to a Moscow hospital, he died of pneumonia on January 14, 1934 (Roux & Roux, 1970: 152). Davidson notes merely that he died of pneumonia, was given an obituary in *Pravda*, while members of the International Workers' Movement, party workers and academics gathered at the Palace of Labour and the Moscow Crematorium to pay their respects (Davidson, 1975). These accounts of Nzula's death are certainly credible, yet one cannot help but wonder at the surrounding circumstances. If Nzula was to be sent back as an agent, 2½ years was an unusually long training period (the S.A.C.P. was not banned until 1950 and there is no indication that Nzula could not return). Had Nzula begun to question some of the orthodoxies established by Comintern decisions? What was his reaction to Padmore's expulsion? Would his return to South Africa have exacerbated factional conflicts in the Party involving his closest friends and associates? These questions have fuelled a rumour long held by some South African leftists (especially Trotskyists) that Nzula was killed on instructions from the Comintern. While a scholar should be rightly cautious about accepting such unverifiable rumours without question, this version of Nzula's death was given some support by C.L.R. James, the veteran marxist and close friend of several of the personalities involved in the I.T.U.C.-N.W., in an interview with the present editor (Trinidad, January 1978). According to C.L.R. James, Nzula was forcibly removed from a meeting in Moscow, in full view of the participants, by two men working for the Soviet security services. He was never seen again. Jame's informant was Jomo Kenyatta, later to become President of Kenya, who further claimed that his own desertion from the Communist camp was because of the 'treatment' that had been meted out to Nzula. On the other hand, Kenyatta's testimony must be evaluated in the light of his highly conservative political views, which emerged after his country's independence.

Whatever the truth of these rival stories, they do not detract from Nzula's stature. The partial knowledge we have of him suggests a tantalizing first blooming of his talents, and an even greater potential flowering that was cut short by his early death. He seemed to have had the ability to remain within the eye of the storm within the Party — Bunting, Wolton and Roux, who bickered furiously with one another, all according him their respect. He also showed a political sophistication that the populist leaders of the I.C.U. (Kadalie, Champion) lacked, and a flair for oratory and street processions that the parsons and professionals (as the communists contemptuously dismissed them) of the post-1930 A.N.C. could not emulate. There is little doubt that, had he survived Moscow, he could have been in a unique position to combine a powerful nationalist and popular appeal with a trained revolutionary's appreciation of the character of class struggle and an unassailable organizational base within the S.A.C.P. No other black leader within South Africa would have had such a commanding position. Alas, history is not about 'what could have been.'

## THE MAIN THEMES OF THE BOOK

The book that is printed below is written, for the most part, in a simple and easily comprehensible style. Readers will no doubt address its contents for different purposes. For South African historians, the sections on the Party and South African trade unions of the 1920s, together with the light thrown on Nzula's life itself will no doubt be of great interest. For labour specialists of other parts of Africa, the continental sweep of the authors' indictment of colonial labour policies commands attention. For marxists, there are many interesting passages which explore the old questions of the balance between economism and revolutionary trade unionism, the political role of the party and of activists, and the theory of class alliances, particularly between worker and peasant, but also between these two classes and the local bourgeoisie (identified in the text as 'national-reformists'). For Pan-Africanists, the sections on national struggles and on the national question will be of some interest, though the authors are firmly wedded to a class rather than a race or national line. Finally, for Sovietologists, or for those Western politicians casting a wary eye at Soviet intentions in the Southern part of the continent today, this book provides evidence of a close attention to African affairs by the Soviets at a very early stage.

The selection of themes, therefore, has to be something of an arbitrary exercise. The discussion that follows simply reflects the issues that the present editor found of greatest interest. In the opening chapter, the authors seek to update Lenin's theory of imperialism. Using Lenin, but also some unlikely sources such as Henry Ford, they argue a case for a theory of uneven development that anticipates, in many essentials, the current concern with 'dependency theory' and 'metropolitan-satellite' relations. They lay their emphasis not so much on the search for markets and on raw materials *per se* but on the possession and retention of strategic *war* materials — Firestone's acquisition of a large slice of Liberia is cited as a prime example of the need for this kind of expansion.

In Chapter 2, the effect of colonial policies on the indigenous population is stressed. Nzula, Potekhin and Zusmanovich argue against (what is still) the conventional view that it was climatic conditions which affected where Europeans settled in the African continent. Rather, they argue, that it was the level of the productive forces and the level of political organization they encountered that were the determining factors. Despite the extensive privatization of land and the changing patterns of land distribution which they document, they argue that the pre-capitalist mode of peasant farming was somewhat preserved as a means of reproducing labour power cheaply. Once again this predates a modern marxist argument concerning the articulation of modes of production (Cf. Wolpe, 1972). The Boer farmer and the British mining industrialist, as they put it, wanted neither slave nor proletarian.

In Chapter 3, the authors look at the question of forced labour. The chapter includes a powerful refutation of the idea of Africans preferring leisure to income ( the *idee fixe* of the colonial officers which produced the so-called theory of the backward-bending supply curve of labour). The problem is not that there were no labourers available but that the wages and conditions in the compounds and plantations were so appalling. The destructive effect of the penetration of European capitalism into the Congo is graphically recalled in the words of a French journalist: 'We are tree fellers in a forest of human beings'.

Chapter 4 is a brief and rather poorly developed analysis of the effects of the Great Depression on Africa. The major argument advanced is that colonial interests had managed to shift the burden of the crisis on to the backs of the peasants and workers. The next chapter, 5, by contrast, adopts a micro-focus in examining the extent and nature of 'peasant uprisings'. The section on the Congo is particularly well argued and the authors are not slow to make the internationalist point that some Belgian workers acted in support of their Congolese brothers. Other shorter sections cover uprisings in South Africa, Rhodesia, Kenya, and Togoland.

In Chapter 6 the initiatives undertaken by organized workers are considered, the information coming from the Gambia, Ghana, Sierra Leone and (most notably) South Africa. Nothing is reported from major countries like Kenya and Nigeria and the authors fail also to describe the important strikes in Sierra Leone in 1919. However, the centre-piece of the chapter is Nzula's (it is clearly his) analysis of the four major central trade union bodies in South Africa, their activities, character and ideology.

Particular strikes in the chemical and clothing industries of South Africa as well as strikes in other parts of Africa are the subject of Chapter 8, while the final chapter summarizes some principal themes of the book and opens a substantially new discussion on the limits of national-reformism.

The formulations expressed in this chapter are of interest in two respects. Firstly, the authors strongly indict the nationalist movement for its utterly bourgeois character. In this respect Nzula, Potekhin and Zusmanovich are closer to a contemporary radical African and independent marxist position than to the Soviet Union's present position which accepts the primacy of the 'national democratic revolution'. Secondly, and by way of corollary, the authors insist on the leading role of the proletariat, but make the point in opposition to what Fanon was later to argue, that: 'due to the specific nature of the colonial economy this proletarian body is intimately and directly linked to the peasantry'.

There follow a number of Appendices designed to provide the reader with direct access to Albert Nzula's other, previously inaccesible, writings mainly in the *Negro Worker*. The last Appendix, however, comes not from the *Negro Worker* but from an obituary Nzula wrote in *Umsebenzi* for a friend, Johannes Nkosi, who was killed by police at a Dingaan's Day demonstration Nzula helped to organize. A line in Nzula's obituary captures the spirit of dedication that marks his own political life: 'A thousand Africans must take his place'.

## REFERENCES

Davidson, A.B., 'Albert Nzula: One of the First African Communists', *The Working Class and the Modern World* (Rabochi Klass i Sovremennyi Mir (6), 1975). (MS copy translated by H.J., thus no page references.)

Degres, J. ed., *The Communist International 1919-1943 Documents Vol. II 1923-1928*, Frank Cass & Co. (London, 1971).

'Historicus', 'Albert Nzula: Our First African General Secretary' *The African Communist* (65), Second Quarter 1976, 90-102.

Hooker, J.R., *Black Revolutionary: George Padmore's Path from Communism to Pan-Africanism*, Pall Mall Press, (London, 1967).

I.T.U.C.-N.W. Report, *Report of the Proceedings and Decisions of the First International Conference of Negro Workers*, International Trade Union Committee for Negro Workers, (Hamburg, 1930).

Karis, T. and Carter, G.M. eds., *From Protest to Challenge: A Documentary History of African Politics in South Africa 1882-1964*, Vol.IV, *Political Profiles*, (Volume editors Gail M. Gerhart and Thomas Karis) Hoover Institution Press, (Stanford, 1977).

Legassick, M., *Class and Nationalism in South African Protest: the South African Communist Party and the 'Native' Republic, 1928-1934*, Syracuse NY: Eastern African Studies Program, XV, (1973).

Morris, M.D., 'The Soviet Africa Institute and the Development of African Studies', *Journal of Modern African Studies* 11 (2): 247-65, (1973).

Ndobe, B.R., 'Capitalism Terror in South Africa', *The Negro Worker* 2 (4) April: 15-19, (1931).

Padmore, G, *The Life and Struggles of Negro Toilers*, Sun Dance Press, (Hollywood, California, 1971). First published by RILU Magazine for the I.T.U.C.-N.W. in Lonodn, 1931.

Potekhin, I.I., *African Problems*, Nauka Publishing House, (Moscow, 1968).

Roux, E., *Time Longer Than Rope*, University of Wisconsin Press, (Madison, 1964).

Roux, E. & W., *Rebel Pity: the Life of Eddie Roux*, Penguin, (Harmondsworth, 1970).

Rytov, L., 'Ivan Potekhin: a Great Africanist', *African Communist* (54), Third Quarter 1973, 95-99.

Simons, J.J. & R.E., *Class and Colour in South Africa, 1850-1950*, Penguin, (Harmondsworth, 1969).

Wilson, E.T., *Russia and Black Africa Before World War II*, Holmes & Meier, (York, 1976).

Wolpe, H., 'Capitalism and Cheap Labour-Power in South Africa: From Segregation to Apartheid', *Economy and Society* 1 (4), (1972).

Wolton, D.G., *Whither South Africa*, Lawrence & Wishart, (London, 1947).

# 1

# BLACK AFRICA'S ROLE IN THE WORLD ECONOMIC SYSTEM

Black Africa occupies almost an entire continent of 30,106,000 square kilometres, which could contain within itself 120 imperialist states the size of Britain.[1] Its population is approximately 150,000,000. Economically and politically, Africa is a highly intricate complex of various economic formations, created by European capitalist countries in the furtherance of their imperialistic ends.

European capitalism's first acquaintance with Black Africa began with the latter's transformation into what Marx called a 'black game reserve'. In 1562, the first cargo of African slaves was shipped out on the English vessel *Jesus*. The voyage of the *Jesus* marks the beginning of an age unparalleled in the cruelty with which colonies were plundered, blacks hunted down, and millions of them enslaved by 'civilized' colonizers. To this day, the subsequent history of Black Africa has been written in the blood of the millions of blacks who perished in the mines in California, the North American cotton plantations, the rubber plantations of the Congo, the Transvaal diamond mines, and so forth. In the nineteenth century the slave trade was officially banned. This, however, merely intensified the enslavement of blacks within Africa itself. A division of Africa was begun by the imperialists: in 1850 the imperialists had colonized only 7.5% of the total area of the continent; by 1870 they had colonized 11.7%, 12.1% by 1880, 90% by 1900, reaching 100% in 1928. The table below shows Black Africa's division among the separate imperialist states:

TABLE 1.1

TERRITORIAL SHARES OF AFRICA BY THE IMPERIALIST POWER

|  | sq. kms |
|---|---|
| Britain | 9,000.000 |
| France | 8,000,000 |
| Belgium | 2,410,000 |
| Portugal | 2,100,000 |
| Italy | 1,590,000 |
| Spain | 310,000 |
| U.S.A. | 100,000 |

## AFRICA — IMPERIALISM'S RAW MATERIAL SUPPLIER

One of the central problems of modern imperialism and international politics in general is that of raw materials and raw material markets. It is also the subject of official and secret world agreements and various conferences (particularly numerous in recent years). An immense and savage struggle is evolving before us — a struggle both diplomatic and military, bloody and bloodless — for the 'food' of industry, raw materials. During the 1920s, capitalism has generated a colossal increase in industrial output. This expansion, with which capitalism can no longer cope, has confronted each imperialist state with the full severity of the raw material problem. The sources of raw materials are distributed far from evenly throughout the world, and far from proportionally to the needs of each imperialist state and group of capitalists. In some cases, raw materials occur in the metropoles, and can be extracted in sufficient quantity. But the uneven development of the separate sectors of capitalist production, the relative backwardness of agriculture and the high price of domestic raw materials stemming from high ground rents, have led capitalists to prefer the import of cheaper raw materials from the colonies. Britain, in particular, which is a potential sheep-breeding country, prefers to import wool from Australia and South Africa.

Suffice it to say that the U.S.A., which consumes 75% of world rubber production, does not produce rubber at all. France and Germany have no oil, cotton, rubber, etc. The development of industry increases both the demand for raw materials, and the dependence of industrial nations on foreign sources of raw materials. We need only cite the fact that Britain imported £172,000,000 of foreign raw materials in 1900, and £400,000,000 in 1924. Hence each imperialist power and group of capitalists seeks to ensure its own source of raw materials, and to become independent of other imperialist powers and groups of capitalists. In his book *Today and Yesterday*, Henry Ford wrote:[2]

> 'An enterprise cannot by itself meet all its needs. It must also purchase a considerable amount from outside, and its stocks of raw materials are constantly threatened with exhaustion.'

In order to overcome dependence on the supplier,

> 'the entrepreneur must, to the extent that he can afford it, start producing his own raw materials and semi-manufactured articles. He must gradually become involved in obtaining his own raw materials and semi-manufactured articles, and in the many areas of business connected with this.'

And so Henry Ford established his own rubber plantations. Modern capitalism is monopolistic. The monopolies play a decisive role in the economy and politics of the world. The struggle for raw materials is a struggle for monopolistic and exclusive possession of their source. A monopoly of raw material, i.e. the capture of its source, is the most stable form of monopoly rule. To capture raw materials is to dictate one's will to the consumer, and to make possible colossal profits through arbitrary price increases. Powerful national and international associations were set up on this basis, monopolizing various types of raw materials. Suffice it to say that world rubber production is 79% controlled by British capital organized within the Rubber Growers Association, and that just two companies, Standard Oil of America and the British company, Royal Dutch Shell, have monopolized the entire production of oil. A tiny proportion of these powerful associations, having coalesced with an imperialist state, have the entire forces of that state at their own disposal, and have shared out all the world's sources of raw materials among themselves. The present period of capitalism indicates that certain relationships rooted in the economic division of the world develop between alliances of capitalists, and that, linked with this process, there simultaneously develop certain relations rooted in the territorial division of the world, namely the fight for colonies and the 'fight for economic territory'. A final division is typical of the present period, final not in the sense that no further redivision is possible — it is, on the contrary, possible and inevitable — but in the sense that the colonial policy of the capitalist countries has completed the capture of this planet's unoccupied land. The world, once divided up, can only be redivided. Lenin emphasizes that this division of the world is not final, and that the uneven development of capitalist countries leads inevitably to further redivisions. The uneven development of certain sectors of capitalist production and of some capitalist states is a necessary law of capitalism, particularly in its imperilist phase. Development is such that first one and then another capitalist country develops faster than the rest, overtaking them in the process. The best example is competition between Britain and the U.S.A. This uneven development leads to a change in the relation of forces and demands, the previous division of the world no longer matching the new balance of forces. A redivision now becomes essential. In this we have one of the fundamental causes of imperialist wars.

The problem of raw materials is made considerably more complicated by the growth of that inevitable attendant of imperialism, militarism. General staffs are no less concerned with raw materials than are capitalist corporations. The place of oil in modern military technology, with its aeroplanes, tanks and lorries, is common knowledge. In 1917, at the height of the First World War, Clemenceau, at that time the French Prime Minister, wrote as follows to U.S. President Wilson:

> 'Any shortage of petrol would swiftly paralyse our armies and oblige us to sue for peace on terms unacceptable to the allies. If the allies do not wish to lose the war, they must make sure that at the hour of the decisive onslaught, fighting France receives petrol, which is as vital to her as blood in the battles to come.'

Since the First World War, military technology has made great advances, and oil has acquired still greater importance. Nor can a modern war be waged without rubber. Without rubber, motorised transport and aircraft are useless, nor without it can the soldier of today's army be equipped with a gas mask etc., leaving aside such types of raw material as iron, non-ferrous metals and so forth.

Black Africa is a rich source of raw materials. It is, of course, for this very reason the greatest source of conflict between capitalists.

Let us take minerals, for example. Little study has been made of African deposits, but even so, practially every type of mineral is at present mined in Africa. In the British colony of Rhodesia, for instance, gold, silver, copper, lead, vanadium, zinc, iron and other minerals are mined. The Union of South Africa produces arsenic, asbestos, coal, copper, corundum, diamonds, gold, graphite, iron ore, manganese ore, magnesite, mica, platinum, silver, soda and tin. More than half the gold, and almost 70% of the diamonds produced throughout the world originate in South Africa. British West Africa mines gold, diamonds, platinum, tin and coal. Turning to primary products, Black Africa has cocoa (the Gold Coast alone produces about half the world's cocoa crop), oil palm derivatives, rubber, wool, maize, rice, coffee, precious woods, and so on. This incalculable wealth is a further attraction to capitalists. Nowadays blacks are no longer shipped to America and forced to work under the lash on the cotton plantations. They are now exploited at home, and forced to mine gold and copper, to gather rubber and grow coffee.

## The Case of Rubber

The development of the motor industry created a demand for rubber. In 1879, Stanley, an agent of Belgian capitalism, discovered rubber trees in the heart of Africa, the Congo. The vast Congo basin (the area of the Belgian Congo is eighty times that of Belgium) is covered with rubber trees. Belgian capitalists arrived, escorted by Belgian army detachments. Blacks were enslaved and driven into the jungle to gather rubber. Woe betide anyone refusing, or showing insufficient effort by failing to gather his quota. Whole villages were burnt down and every villager beaten. As the concessionaries wrote to their agents, 'You should not forget that the machine gun is an important factor in the procurement of rubber'. Aided by armed detachments, the generously paid agents wrung everything that they could out of the blacks. In a private letter, one officer wrote:

> 'We whites have to close our eyes to avoid the sight of horrifying corpses, those who curse us as they die, the wounded begging for mercy, the crying women and starving children. We have to block our ears to silence the groans, sobbing and curses from every bush and inch of land.'

The concessionaries cut off the hands of a black man called 'Oyo' for an unsatisfactory performance in a lesson on harvesting rubber. Not for nothing did the blacks adopt the saying 'Rubber is death'. Initial studies of the Congo put its population at 30-40 million. The latest handbooks give the population of the Belgian Congo as 8,500,000. The difference is the price of rubber. Meanwhile, the Anglo-Belgian India Rubber Company (A.B.I.R.)[3] made a profit of 400% on the capital invested in this concern in the first six years.

Let us turn to recent years and the twentieth century. World rubber consumption has been rising. America supplies the world with motor vehicles and tractors, consumes 70% of the world crop, but has no rubber of its own. Britain has a monopoly of rubber, which it produces on the islands of Malaya and Ceylon, in Burma and in Southern India. In November, 1922, the Stephenson scheme[4] raised rubber prices. By 1925 the price of rubber had risen to four shillings per pound, compared with tenpence in 1922. In 1925 British rubber companies made a profit of £57,000,000, and their dividends reached 100%. America raised a howl of protest. Henry Firestone, a personal friend of Henry Ford, advanced the slogan 'America must have its own rubber'. Rubber trees were discovered in the independent black republic of Liberia. With the assistance of Hoover, the then Minister of Trade, he drew up an ambitious plan for turning Liberia into the rubber plantation of America. Liberia was given a 7% loan of $5,000,000, with which it was to expand railway and road construction and rebuild Monrovia, the capital. Firestone obtained a concession on 1,000,000 acres at sixpence per acre from the Liberian government. A qualified assessment indicates that the new trees on this land would, when mature, yield 250,000 tons of rubber, or 30% of present world consumption. Thus America's answer to the rubber problem is to turn Liberia into a rubber plantation and expropriate 1,000,000 acres of peasant land.[5]   At the same time, Ford also obtained a concession on 3,700,000 acres in Brazil. However, America's appetites for Africa's riches are not confined to Liberia. Its hand is now reaching far into the heart of Africa, the Congo. On January 17, 1932, the influential *New York Herald Tribune* published an article by an American professor, which, in its cynicism, far surpassed much of what had been written by the pen-pushers of imperialism:

'All Europe is in debt to the United States. Instead of money, why shouldn't they give us the Congo basin, for instance — an area of 1,500,000 square miles rich in rubber trees and all kinds of other tropical plants, which could meet the needs of the American people for many years to come. The Congo is rich in minerals: copper, tin and gold. Belgium has owned two thirds of the Congo basin since 1908. The white population of this vast area is 15,000. Belgium is quite unable to develop the country — it lacks the capital, the ships and the workers. The river Congo and its tributaries are navigable for 6,000 miles. The United States must take in hand the development of this vast area with American money, American machines, American brains and above all, the hands of American workers. The United States is the only country with any quantity of labour. Where is this to come from, you may ask? From American negroes, of course.

They come from the Congo, and its climate, though deadly to the white man, is natural to them. The Congolese native doesn't want to work — you have to beat him. But the American negro has six generations of labour behind him and he knows how to work. Six generations ago, Congolese natives were taken from West Africa on slave ships — six generations of labour and tears. And now they will be returning, thousands of workers armed with the white man's knowledge and sense of purpose, able to show their lost African brothers what to do with their country. No dream could be more inspiring — the children of slaves returning to establish the United States of Africa under American leadership. Let's get down to business! All we need is a new convening of Congress to control the question of debts and reparations on the principle of territorial sovereignty. The Belgians could be excused their debts to Britain and the United States. We might even pay off their internal debts totalling a billion dollars. It would do France no harm to leave the Congo, and the British people are hardly aware that they own part of it. As for the natives — they don't care. They're used to everything, be it gathering rubber or slavery.'

## The Case of Palm Oil and Groundnuts

Let us turn now to a different sort of primary product — palm oil and nuts. The nineteenth century was the century of industrial revolution in all European countries. The growth of the urban population brought with it an increased demand for vegetable oil, for industrial use and for soap manufacture. The palm tree was capable of satisfying a substantial part of that demand. Palm trees grow prolifically in West Africa, particularly in Nigeria and Sierra Leone. But the peasant had either no desire to produce palm produce for sale, or produced it in totally inadequate volume. They had to be forced to do so. To achieve this the entire country had to be turned into a colony. In 1862, under the pretext of combating the Nigerian coastal slave trade, the first British settlement in Nigeria was established, and in 1885 Nigeria was declared a British protectorate. In 1807, the British Sierra Leone Company was founded, and, in 1808, Sierra Leone was declared a British colony.

By a variety of commercial, financial and fiscal machinations and direct compulsion, the black peasant population was forced to produce palm products and to sell them to the European trading companies. The pumping of palm nuts and oil out of West Africa had begun. Whilst 1,100 tons of palm produce were exported from West Africa in 1810, by 1850 this figure had reached 40,000 tons. Today 65,000 tons of palm produce are exported from Sierra Leone alone, and 425,000 tons from Nigeria. In order to supply itself with this commodity, British imperialism turned Sierra Leone into a mono-producer of palm produce, the latter constituting 80% of the country's total exports.

In order to provide itself with groundnuts, which, like palm nuts, are a substitute for animal fats, Britain turned a further black country, the

Gambia, into a mono-producer of groundnuts, which now make up 97% of the country's exports. To show what this sort of monoculture means for the peasant, let us quote one of British imperialism's apologists and an expert on West Africa, Allan McPhee.[6] He writes:

'The Nigerian groundnut crop is more dependent on price fluctuations than that of the Gambia. The reason for this is that the Nigerian peasant has more than one source of income. If groundnut prices are unfavourable, they can grow other cash crops. In the Gambia the peasant has little choice. He can either grow or decide not to grow groundnuts. The result of this situation is that the Gambian peasant continues to grow groundnuts despite the fall in price, and although he does not like the low profit (evidently the imperialists do — authors) anything is better than nothing. Accordingly in 1922 (a year of low prices), Nigerian exports of groundnuts fell from a previous annual figure of 51,000 tons to 24,000 tons, whilst exports from the Gambia remained stable at 64,000 tons.'

## The Case of Cocoa

A third British colony, the Gold Coast, has been turned into a cocoa mono-producer by imperialism. Exports of cocoa account for 82.4% of the country's total. It is of some interest in this case to examine the process of the Gold Coast's conversion into a cocoa country by comparing the export of two basic crops:

TABLE 1.2

COCOA AND PALM OIL PRODUCTION IN THE GOLD COAST

| Year | Cocoa (Tons) | Palm Oil (Tons) |
|------|------|------|
| 1900 | 586 | 15,138 |
| 1906 | 8,975 | 7,654 |
| 1912 | 38,647 | 5,159 |
| 1914 | 52,888 | 1,771 |
| 1921 | 133,195 | 241 |

On the one hand, British imperialism imposed cocoa upon the Gold Coast and reduced the palm oil crop to zero, and on the other it turned the whole of Sierra Leone into a palm plantation.

## The Case of Gold

Let us take gold as an example of mineral 'raw materials'. The place of gold in today's capitalist economy is well known. One need only witness the immeasurable increase in the demand for gold that has accompanied the onset of the present economic crisis.

Only yesterday the bourgeois, intoxicated with the flowering of industry and seeing money through the haze of enlightenment philosophy, delcared it an empty illusion. 'The only money is commodities.' Today the same bourgeois wails that 'the only commodity is money' from every corner of the world market. As pants the hart for cooling streams, so now thirsts the bourgeois for that unique source of wealth, money.[7] Gold is found in many African countries, but as already mentioned above, the bulk of it is mined in South Africa. These gold deposits were discovered in 1886 in the Transvaal, the then Boer Republic. A landslide of British capitalists descended upon South Africa. The Africans were driven from their lands and forced to work in the mines.

Under the present pressure of economic crisis the imperialists are stepping up the search for new deposits of gold. At the end of the last century, gold was discovered in the Kavirondo region of Kenya, which had a dense black peasant population. A gold rush began. The result was, on one hand, a massive influx of capitalists and the organization of new companies; on the other, the bitter tragedy of the peasantry. Here British capitalism repeated what it had done to the blacks of South Africa with the mass expropriation of their land. They were simply driven from the land which they and their ancestors had farmed for centuries. Hundreds of thousands of peasants were made landless and forced either to starve or to find work underground, mining gold for British imperialists. At the other end of Africa, in Sierra Leone, British imperialism has been intensifying gold prospecting for the last two years. The first favourable results of those searches augur ill for the indigenous population. The same fate awaits them as was in the past meted out to the peasants of the Transvaal and at present to the Kenyan peasants in Kavirondo.

## AFRICA AS A CONSUMER OF EUROPEAN GOODS: THE CONTRADICTIONS

Black Africa's importance to the imperialists is by no means just a matter of raw materials. The programme of French imperialism elaborated by the Governor of French West Africa in his speech of January, 1932, clearly emphasized the indigenous people's role as consumers of European goods.

'As a producer, the native deserves our attention and care, since his labour is virtually the sole source of the trade which enriches the colony. He is, moreover, a purchaser of imported goods. The normal development of this dual role, the creation of products for export and the consumption of imported goods, determines the entire economic life of the federation. But one should remember that the native can purchase goods only to the extent of what he produces, and the price he is able to obtain for that produce. We too must be guided by this principle in our policy toward the natives. We must

strive for a qualitative and quantitative improvement in native production and for adherence to the correct ratio between export and
import prices. In doing so we must not forget that the native's wages
must be high enough to guarantee an essential living minimum. Only
on this condition will the native's will to work be preserved, and
trade steadily improve. The programme for colonial exploitation
initiated by Governor Carde and implemented by myself is financed
by loans, the amounts outstanding on which must be repaid by French
West Africa. We must therefore ensure strict observance of justice
in the apportionment of the benefits and duties which stem from
this situation. Producers, administrators and merchants must each
receive a share of the profits, corresponding to the ultimate utility
of their labour.'

Thus the programme is clear. The black peasant must: (1) generate and
produce raw materials for export and (2) purchase French imported goods;
the colonial authorities will (3) care for him to the extent that he fulfils
his 'dual' function (just how they care for him will be shown below) and
(4) finance this 'dual' function by loans, subsequently repaid with interest
by the black peasants.

It should be noted that this dual function is developing unevenly. The
imperialists have been successful in forcing the African to produce raw
materials, but are utterly failing to make him a reliable consumer. This is
because imperialism leaves blacks nothing with which to buy the necessary
goods. Owing to brutal exploitation and miserly wages, their purchasing
power is extremely low. Because of these circumstances, the role of Black
Africa as a market, despite its immense potential, is negligible. Britain sells
only 7.2% of its exported goods to Africa, the U.S.A. 2.2%, Germany 2.4%.
Of France's total exports,14.8% are sold to its colonies, of which French
West Africa's share is quite small. In 1928, imports into French West Africa
totalled Fr. 1,513 million. The population is 13.5 million, and imports
per head are therefore Fr. 112 per annum. Here it should be borne in mind
that there is a complete absence of any sort of manufacturing industry. In
1933 imports to France itself were Fr. 274 per head of population, despite
France's well developed industry. In 1928 imports into Sierra Leone
totalled £2,054,000, an average of £1. 5s. 8d. per head. In 1930 imports
into Nigeria totalled £12,700,000, or 11s 7d. per head. British imports in
1927 averaged 5s. 5d. per head, despite the enormous size of Britain's
industry. The situation is similar in the other colonies. Only in the Gold
Coast and South Africa is the level of imports somewhat higher. Imports
to all colonies are low, but even here the imperialists earn considerable
sums, since goods are sold in the colonies at prices considerably higher than
those prevailing in Europe.

What do they import into the colonies? The basic import commodity is
textiles, which account for 60% of exports to Nigeria and Sierra Leone,
followed by foodstuffs, alcohol and tobacco, which make up between
20% and 25% of total imports. There is not a single colony in West, East
or Central Africa into which machinery and industrial equipment is

imported (with the exception of motor vehicles, railway and post equipment, and mining machinery). This is natural, since there is no manufacturing industry, and the imperialists have no intention of creating any: the blacks' dual function consists of producing raw materials and purchasing European manufactured goods. The British Dominion of the Union of South Africa is something of an exception in this respect. Given the existence of towns, a large European urban population and an extensive mining industry, it is simply impossible to do without bakeries, confectionery and clothing factories, breweries etc. Taking the annual output value of South Africa's processing industry, excluding maintenance workshops and railway depots, the percentage breakdown is as follows:

TABLE 1.3

SOUTH AFRICAN INDUSTRIES BY OUTPUT VALUE

|  | (%) |
| --- | --- |
| Flour mills, bakeries and confectionery production | 60 |
| Printing | 12 |
| Tobacco | 7 |
| Footwear manufacture | 7 |
| Breweries | 4.5 |
| Butter and cheese production | 4.5 |

The South African footwear industry's total production amounts to £2,237,000, which represents an annual *per capita* value of 6s. 4d. Thus, even in this most developed part of Africa, there is no manufacturing industry in the proper sense of the word. Over 40% of the country's textiles, wine and foodstuffs is imported. Taking imports into Africa as a whole, it is quite obvious that they are by nature almost exclusively consumption-oriented.

Though all the capitalist countries trade with Africa, as can be seen in Table 1.4, Britain and France occupy the leading position:

TABLE 1.4

SHARE OF IMPORTS INTO AFRICA BY COUNTRY (%)

|  | French West Africa | South Africa (1928) | Kenya |
| --- | --- | --- | --- |
| Britain (+ Dominions for Kenya) | 20.0 | 42.8 | 62.0 |
| France | 60.0 | — | — |
| USA | 6.0 | 15.3 | 11.3 |
| Holland | 3.7 | — | 5.4 |
| Belgium | 3.2 | — | — |
| Germany | 2.5 | 6.4 | 4.4 |
| Japan | — | 1.7 | 4.6 |

## Impact of the World Capitalist Crisis

The African market, as shown above, is small, but the same struggle as we may witness in every other corner of the globe is developing over it. Today, in capitalism's most bitter crisis, this struggle is intensifying still further. This is natural enough, since capitalists, in seeking a way out of the crisis, are striving to enlarge and monopolize their markets in order to ensure their ruling position within them. In these days of crisis, the struggle for consumer markets has been even more intense than for raw material markets. So far this struggle has not reached the stage of open warfare and redivision of the world, and imperialists have adopted two basic tactics: protectionism and dumping. These devices are used to conquer colonial markets or to strengthen control over them. In East Africa, and Kenya in particular, Britain and Japan are engaged in an extensive struggle because Japan is flooding Kenya with a major part of its textile production at exceedingly low dumping prices. During the first three-quarters of last year, Kenya purchased 21,154,000 yards of textiles, of which 15,134,000 were imported from Japan. This same struggle between Britain and Japan is also raging in West Africa, and especially in Nigeria. The industrialists of Manchester are worried. One Manchester merchant drew the *Manchester Guardian's* attention to the arrival of a ship in Lagos (the capital of Nigeria) with a cargo of 1,100 bales of Japanese cloth:

> 'It would be interesting to know what our government intends to do about this matter. It transpires that we are paying taxes to keep open the African ports for Japanese dumping. Our trade keeps falling, and will vanish altogether if nothing is done. The British Government must take steps to defend our industry and markets.'

The British Government went some way towards meeting the demands of the Manchester industrialists; at the end of last year, import duties were raised in all British colonies, but with preferential rates for Britain. For example, a 15.5% duty was imposed on cotton manufactured goods imported to the Gold Coast, whereas they had previously been imported duty-free. Duty on kerosene was raised by 25%, on tobacco by 12%, and on all other articles by 20%. In South Africa, Britain and the U.S.A. are involved in a prolonged and dogged struggle. South Africa has maintained a certain degree of independence in matters of tariff policy. Here the struggle between Britain and the U.S.A. is more complicated than in the West African colonies, and it is worth noting that the U.S.A. has made some headway. The American share of South African imports grew from 8.8% in 1913 to 15.3% in 1928, or by 6.5%, whilst Britain's share during the same period declined from 50.1% to 42.8%, a fall of 7.9%. Recently, Germany has persistently demanded the restoration of African colonies lost under the Treaty of Versailles. At a meeting of the German Colonial Society, its president, Doctor Schnee announced that: 'We do not consider our former colonies lost, despite the fact that they are at present controlled by other states. The mandate system is only a temporary solution to this problem.'

Finally, Hugenberg's* last memorandum at the recent International Economic Conference suggests that the struggle is about to flare up. As Lenin argued:

'The export of commodities was typical of the old-style capitalism where free competition held sway. The export of capital has become typical of modern monopoly capitalism. The need to export capital is generated by the fact that capitalism has become 'over ripe' in some countries, and that capital (given agricultural underdevelopment and mass poverty) is short of areas for its "profitable" investment.'[8]

## THE EXPORT OF CAPITAL

Thus it is not the export of commodities, but of capital which is characteristic of modern capitalism. Capital is not exported because it is superfluous or impossible to put to productive use in capitalist countries. The backwardness of agriculture and its lack of investment are well known. But where land is an object of private property and ground rent has consequently to be paid, such investment becomes insufficiently profitable. The poverty of the working classes of capitalist countries, and their low standard of living, which could be substantially improved by the use of this 'superfluous' capital, is also well known. But what do the capitalists care for the poverty of the masses? Indeed the basic condition of their growth and enrichment is the poverty of the masses. There is thus a 'surplus' of capital in capitalist countries, which is being unloaded on less developed countries where there exist cheap raw materials, and low cost, sometimes free labour. Ground rent is extremely low, if indeed it has to be paid at all. (Firestone rented one million acres of Liberia at sixpence per acre). This all guarantees capitalists higher profits than in their own countries. One might take as an example the case of the Kaduna Company Ltd. (Nigeria) which paid a total of 435% in dividends between 1917 and 1923.

One naturally realizes that such profits are impossible in any capitalist country. The capitalists, therefore, export their surplus capital to the colonies, and to Africa in particular. The prime sectors of European capital investment in Africa are trade, agricultural plantations, mining and railway construction. As the theses at the Fourth Comintern Congress stated:

'Here the dominant influx of exported capital goes into trade, where its main application is usury, thus serving to maintain and reinforce the imperialist state's repressive apparatus in colonial countries (assisted by state loans etc.) or to establish complete control of the allegedly independent state organs of the native bourgeoisie in semi-colonial countries. Part of the capital exported to a colony for

productive purposes leads partially to accelerated industrial development, by no means in the direction of independence, however, but
towards strengthening the dependence of the colonial economy on
the finance capital of imperialist countries. Capital imported into the
colonies is generally concentrated on the capture and extraction of
raw materials or in their primary processing. It is used to develop
communications, thus easing the outflow of raw materials, and
tying the colonies still closer to the exploiting country. The favourite
kind of agricultural investment is in large plantations, the aim being
the production of cheap foodstuffs and the monopolisation of huge
sources of raw materials. The transfer to the exploiting country of
most of the surplus value wrung from the cheap labour of colonial
slaves correspondingly greatly retards economic growth and the
development of productive forces, and impedes the economic and
practical liberation of the colonies.'

From the African colony's point of view, the most parasitic of all
imported capital is the state colonial loan issued to colonial governments
by British and French banks. All the African colonies are now ensnared in
a tangle of debts. The Gold Coast's total debt is £19,000,000, Sierra
Leone's £1,729,848, Tanganyika's £3,135,446, Kenya's £13,500,000,
South Africa's £243,694,261, and so on. Colonial loans are most typically
issued below par, so that the colony has to repay a part of the loan which
it never received. In 1923, for example, Nigeria was granted a loan of
£5,700,000 on condition that it was to receive only £88 for each £100
certificate, but would be bound to repay £100. This meant that in total
Nigeria was to repay £5,700,000, having received only £5,016,000. By the
end of 1926, Nigeria's debts totalled £19,000,000, whereas it had actually
received only £17,000,000 in loans. The Gold Coast owed £11,791,000
but actually received only £11,000,000. Loan repayments and interests are
a heavy burden on the budgets of colonial governments, who in turn
transfer it to the shoulders of black workers. South Africa repays
£11,000,000 per annum in interest alone, £6,000,000 of which is paid to
London, while £2,000,000 is repaid on the principal annually. Kenya
annually pays London £707,000 in interest plus repayments on the
principal of £467,000. In 1930, the Gold Coast spent £1,000,000 in loan
repayments. In 1932, Nigeria paid £993,246 in railway loan interest alone.
In that year the net income of the Nigerian railways was only £675,725.
Thus Nigeria made a loss of £317,521 in loan interest payments, a loss
which will be collected from the blacks with the assistance of fiscal
pressure. Such are the profits on these loans to the colonies by the City of
London. The London bankers collect not only all the surplus value created
by black workers, but also a portion of the taxes collected from them in
the form of loan interest. Industrialists and merchants, as well as bankers,
grown rich on loans. The major part of British and French loans, for
instance, is spent on railway and port construction. All railways in the
black colonies are state-owned, and built by governments out of foreign
loans. Allan McPhee, who was mentioned earlier, gives the following

explanation for the absence of privately owned railways:

'It is more expedient for a government to build a railway, since it is easier for government officials than for the agents of private individuals to force natives to do this work.'

## Railway Construction

Every railway has been built by forced labour. A prerequisite, however, for railway construction is the purchase of rails, locomotives, rolling stock and depot equipment in the exploiting country. Railway construction thus means a market expansion for the home metallurgical and engineering industry. Most of a loan raised in Britain, for instance, stays there in payment for railway equipment. A lesser portion is spent on wages, which also returns to the home country through the trading companies which sell their goods on the construction sites. McPhee writes:

'Railway construction funds are either spent in Britain or in West Africa. In Britain the money is spent on a wide variety of railway materials. In West Africa it is spent on wages, which are always paid in cash, although all construction workers are recruited by political pressure. Wages are usually spent by the workers on European and, in particular, British goods. Thus everyone profits from colonial loans, bankers, industrialists and merchants, the only exception being the colonial workers, who have to repay the loans and the interest on them.'

What are the aims of colonial railway construction? [Again] McPhee writes:

'The export trade in tin, coal, cotton and groundnuts is the reason for the creation of the railways, and without them the export figures would not be what they are today. The railways, moreover, mean peace and security for all loyal subjects. Any rebellion can be quickly put down by the prompt transfer of troops to the place of its outbreak.'

The aims are quite clear: (1) the railway acts as a pipe for pumping raw materials out of the colonies; (2) the railway is necessary for crushing anti-imperialist rebellions and, the authors personally add, (3) the railway is necessary for the transport of black troops to European theatres of war. Here are two or three examples: The Nigerian main line from Lagos to Kano was built to carry groundnuts from Northern Nigeria. The line was built in 1910-1914. In 1910, exports of groundnuts totalled 1,179 tons, but by 1912 had already risen to 19,288 tons, and to 57,000 tons in 1918. In the 1890s, gold deposits were discovered near Tarkwa and Aboso in the Gold Coast. During 1898-1901 the Sekondi-Tarkwa line was built. This line simultaneously helped cocoa exports to rise from 536 tons in 1900 to 2,396 tons in 1902 and 5,112 tons in 1904. From Equatorial Africa, France exported valuable types of wood (323,000 tons in 1927), rubber, oil-palm produce, etc. There was no railway, and cargoes went by ship down the river Congo. The river is not navigable beyond Brazzaville, and cargoes were therefore transported by rail beyond this point. Up till then, France had used Belgian railway facilities. However, the throughput capacity of the line is very low, and its management gives preference to Belgian goods. The French cargoes therefore had to wait. This substantially reduced the volume of trade between France and Equatorial Africa, and made France dependent on Belgium. France therefore decided to build its own railway from Brazzaville to the Atlantic. The construction of this railway was contracted to a Parisian firm on highly original terms: the colonial administration undertook to provide an agreed quantity of labour. For every African short of this quota, the administration was to pay the compensation on the basis of the number of man-days lost. Thus the less work that was done, the more the company received. Naturally, the company took full advantage of this situation. France has also long been planning the construction of the so-called Trans-Sahara Railway. In economic terms such a railway is absolutely pointless, but it would enable France to transfer its African troops rapidly to Europe if the need arose. In Africa, the railway, far from being an instrument of economic development of the colonies, is a means for their enslavement and for the exploitation of their wealth and labour.

This situation further underlines the bankruptcy of decolonization theories. The export of capital to Africa is not intended to establish the preconditions for its economic independence, or to create local industry, but, on the contrary, is intended to transform Africa into an agrarian appendage of European imperialism, to drag it into the orbit of world imperialism, and to subject it to the interests of finance capital. Our brief survey has self-evidently demonstrated the fact that Black Africa remains, as before, 'a black game reserve', the only difference being that the blacks are no longer transported to America, but are forced to fulfil their 'dual' role by making super-profits for the imperialists in their own country.

## NOTES

1.     *Angliya* (England) in original. Translated as 'Britain' throughout.
2.     Retranslation from Russian — not therefore a verbatim reproduction of Ford's original words. Where it has not been possible to check the original in other quotations, we have not footnoted the retranslation.
3.     The leading spirit of A.B.I.R., founded in 1892, was said to have been a British colonel, who was a personal friend of King Leopold. Nzula, Potekhin and Zusmanovich are correct in their assertion that this company made massive profits. With the Compagnie Anversoise du Commerce au Congo, founded in the same year, A.B.I.R. agents were even entitled to wear official uniforms of the Congo Free State. Ivory valued at Fr. 3,500,000 and rubber to the value of Fr. 1,000,000 were sold in Antwerp by these companies in the years 1892-24. Naval

Intelligence Division, British Admiralty, *The Belgian Congo*, Geographical Handbook Series, BR 522 Restricted Access, (London, April, 1944), p.200.

4.  Essentially this was a British-controlled cartel.

5.  For later assessments of Firestone's role in Liberia, see McLaughlin, R. U., *Foreign Investment and Development in Liberia*, (New York, 1966) and Taylor W.C., *The Firestone Operations in Liberia*, (Washington, 1956).

6.  The authors are referring to McPhee, A., *The Economic Revolution in British West Africa*, (London, 1926), which they rely on considerably for their West African data. The book, with a new Introduction by A.G. Hopkins, was reprinted in 1971.

7.  The reference to the protestant liturgy is inferred by the present translator — the literal Russian is somewhat more prosaic.

8.  This quote seems to be a 'quilt' quotation from Lenin's *Imperialism* ... It has been possible to find the first part of the quote in Lenin, V.I., *Imperialism: The Highest Stage of Capitalism*, (Peking, 1965) p.72.

# 2

# THE ECONOMIC OPPRESSION OF THE PEASANTRY

As we have argued in Chapter 1, the imperialists have attempted to make Africa their own satellite and market for agricultural and mineral raw materials. Those imperialists who had divided up Black Africa were faced first of all with the task of increasing the production of cocoa, palm oil, and nuts, rubber, maize, copper, gold and other raw materials. There were two ways of solving this problem: either by expropriating the land of the African peasantry and establishing large plantations there, or by subordinating small peasant farming to the interests of the imperialist economy. From this point of view, Black Africa as a whole can be divided into three distinct groups: British and French West Africa, the Belgian Congo and French Equatorial Africa, and South and East Africa.

## THREE ZONES OF EXPLOITATION

The fundamental distinctions between these parts of Africa derive from the manner in which the imperialists have settled the question of land. In the first group of colonies, the amount of African peasant land expropriated by the imperialists is negligible, and large capitalist plantations are few in number. At present small peasant farming takes first place in agricultural production. In the second group of countries the imperialists expropriated all the peasants' land immediately after annexation, and, having destroyed small peasant farming, established large plantation farming. In the third group of countries both the systems referred to above are intricately interwoven with a number of specific features. A large part of the land was expropriated with the creation of plantations. A smaller part remained in the hands of the black peasantry.

Various forms of exploitation of the indigenous population derive from the solutions to the land question in each individual group of countries. In the first group the toiling black masses are exploited as peasants and small commodity producers. Their economic activity is totally subject to the interests of finance capital (fiscal and tariff policy, non-equivalent exchange, control of production and sale of locally grown produce by the trading companies, who also monopolize such sales). A mere fraction of the population of this part of Africa are exploited as workers in the mines and on the railways and the few plantations that exist. In the second group, the indigenous population has been reduced to semi-slavery, and almost all of them are exploited by open and non-economic forms of coercion on the plantations and in the mines. In the third group of countries, both forms of exploitation operate. Part of the working population, herded on to the so-called 'native reserves', engages in small peasant farming. Their position, however, differs from that of the peasantry in the first group of countries, where there is not such a shortage of land. For this reason they live only partially by their own farming, and are obliged to engage in outside work on a European farm. Part of the population has been driven on to European farms and plantations and tied to them as 'serfs'.[1] The position of these serfs does not coincide with that of the peasantry of the second group of countries. They are not yet slaves; to some extent they still own their means of production, and still to some extent dispose of their own labour during a part of the year. Part of the population has been prolet-arianized, and already constitutes a fairly numerous urban working class, exploited through the capitalist mode of production (although in the hiring of labour a number of the features of slavery survive). All these groups have much in common, but this by no means erases the differences between them. What accounts for this difference in forms and methods of exploitation, and what determines it? The most frequently encountered explanation attributes it essentially to variations in climatic conditions. For example, a modern author who goes under the pseudonym of 'Yug',[2] and has already written several books, writes as follows in *Imperialism on the Black Continent:*

> 'The moulds in which the control of the colonies of African and the equatorial countries as a whole is cast are to a certain extent shaped by climatic conditions. The colonies may be subdivided into two completely different types: Firstly, those areas where the white population is able to settle permanently, and secondly, colonies whose climate does not benefit the prolonged residence of whites.'

This statement he repeats several times and leaves it at that. Let us hear from a bourgeois author on this question. McPhee writes:

> 'The reason for the virtually complete absence of European plant-ations in West Africa lies in the climatic conditions, which have dashed all the efforts of British capitalists to establish themselves in that country.'

No doubt climatic conditions play some part, but to restrict oneself in the examination of this question only to appeals to geography would be to abandon any real explanation, for geography alone explains nothing.

To begin with, the climate of the West Coast is only marginally worse than that of Southern Africa. Europeans live successfully in both areas. When America needed rubber, the climate did not stop Firestone seizing one million acres in Liberia and establishing rubber plantations there. Secondly, the climate of the West Coast is a good deal better than that of the Belgian Congo or French Equatorial Africa. Clearly therefore, other causes are at work.

Turning to the state of African production in East and West Africa at the moment of arrival of the white imperialists, it can be seen that the imperialist invasion found it at varying stages of development. By the nineteenth century the local peasant economy in West Africa was already to a considerable degree a commodity economy. The peasants produced a number of commodity crops, including coffee, groundnuts and ginger, and had done a brisk trade with Europe for some time. This enabled the imperialists to subordinate local farming to their own interests by monopolizing the trading and marketing operations of the Africans. Without interfering directly in the productive activity of the local economy, the imperialists were able to channel the development of African production in the desired direction through trade and customs policies, the fiscal system and the appropriate arrangement of credit, and to make the Africans produce in the required quantity what European industry needed. We can now state the direct outcome of this imperialist policy. The imperialists forced the peasants of the Gold Coast to produce cocoa and made their economy monocultural and highly commodity-oriented.

The situation is different in East Africa. At the time of the imperialist invasion, African peasant production constituted a mainly closed and natural economy. A substantial number of tribes led a nomadic existence. Trade with Europe was only weakly developed, and carried on through Arab merchants. Here it was impossible to subjugate the local economy by appropriate trade and fiscal policies, or to influence the market and steer the local economy in the required direction. In order to obtain raw materials of the necessary type and quantity, intervention was needed. A solution was needed to the same problem as in West Africa, but in this case it could only be solved by expropriating the land, organizing European plantations and turning the local population into workers on those plantations. What basically determined land policy and the various forms in which the African population was exploited by the imperialists was the level of development of the country's productive forces and the nature of indigenous production at the time when the imperialists arrived.

Let us take another aspect of African society: their degree of political organization and their consequent strength of opposition to imperialist designs. In the Gold Coast, for example, the entire central area of the present colony was inhabited by the Ashanti. By the beginning of the nineteenth century this tribe had already reached a fairly high level of economic, political and cultural development, and was already trading with Europe on a large scale. This highly centralized state, was led by a king and had a fairly strong military organization. The Ashanti in fact ruled the weaker tribes of the Gold Coast. They were aware of their complete independence and forced Britain to respect their sovereign rights by repeated rebuffs to her designs. Britain fought six wars with the

Ashanti (in 1803, 1822, 1826, 1863, 1873 and 1896) and it was only during the last war that Britain finally succeeded in defeating the Ashanti king, who had been exhausted by continual British-inspired wars with neighbouring tribes.

Thereafter, Britain frequently met with stiff resistance from the African population, and was more than once forced to accept a retreat, and then achieve her aims by indirect means. In 1852, a law on poll tax was passed by the Governor of the Gold Coast. The Africans unanimously refused to pay the tax. All efforts by the Government to collect the tax ended in failure, and the law had to be repealed. In 1897 a land law was passed, placing all lands at the sole disposal of the Government. The African population organized a mass protest campaign, and the law was repealed. In 1911, a law on forests was passed by the Government, entitling it to set up forest reservations. Once more a strong protest campaign ensued, and once more the law was repealed. This, of course, does not mean that Britain had failed to enforce its policies in this country, but it does demonstrate considerable local resistance, which has forced Britain to manoeuvre and use roundabout methods of achieving her aims.

A completely different situation existed in the Belgian Congo. Here there were no strong states of the Ashanti type, the development of indigenous statehood being at a lower level. Divided into hundreds of tribes, they were unable to resist the depredations of the imperialists on a united front. This situation was similar to that in French Equatorial Africa. The dates of French penetration of the country are as follows: in 1893, a treaty for the establishment of a French Protectorate was signed with King Denis*, in 1842 a treaty with King Louis*, a series of treaties with the Gabon chiefs in 1845, a further series with the coastal chiefs during 1842-62, a treaty with the Makoko (King) of the Bateke in 1880, with the King at Loango in 1883, and so on. There is no need to explain what sort of treaties these were, signed as they were by chiefs who could not read. However, France subjugated the whole country by this system of piecemeal bribery. Stanley, the first agent of Belgian imperialism, made over two hundred treaties with local chiefs in the Belgian Congo.

Finally, the third question — what brought the imperialists to a particular colony, and what were their expectations? British imperialism finally subdued South Africa after the discovery of gold and diamonds in that country. Gold and diamonds are what determined the policy of British imperialism in South Africa. But to mine the gold and diamonds it was first necessary to drive the peasants from the land and expropriate it. The mines needed labour. But, given sufficient land, the African population would support themselves by their own farming, and would not go to work in the mines. They would need to be dispossessed of their land. The British imperialists could not, therefore, leave the land in the hands of the peasants, and would have to confiscate it. In the Belgian Congo, the policy of the imperialists was initially determined by rubber. To make the Africans gather rubber, it was necessary to confiscate their land and drive them into the jungle by force.

The imperialists came to West Africa for those raw materials which could be successfully produced by the local farming system, and which were already being produced. The African population alone could not mine diamonds, since capital would be required, but they could grow cocoa and gather groundnuts. The only requirement was a 'rational' policy of making the peasants specialize in the production of specific types of raw materials. It was these factors, rather than geography, which constituted the main reasons for the varied forms of exploitation in the different parts of Black Africa.

## SMALL PEASANT PRODUCTION IN WEST AFRICA

British West Africa is the classic example of the imperialist use of small peasant farming to exploit the colony, subordination of peasant farming to the interest of finance capital, the coalescence of imperialism with local feudal strata and their employment as a means of domination and exploitation. We shall therefore dwell in some detail on this part of Africa. (For basic information, see Table 2.1 below.) We shall then examine the position of small peasant farming on the native reserves in the Union of South Africa, where its development is affected by substantially different conditions.

TABLE 2.1

BRITISH WEST AFRICA: AREA, POPULATION, CAPITAL CITIES

| Colony | Area (in sq. miles) | African Population | Capital City |
|---|---|---|---|
| Nigeria | 372,674 | 19,923,171 | Lagos |
| Gold Coast | 80,000 | 3,125,000 | Accra |
| Gambia | 4,134 | 210,500 | Bathurst |
| Sierra Leone | 27,000 | 1,542,348 | Freetown |
| Total | 483,808 | 24,806,049 | |

## Colonial Political Strategy — Manipulation of Chiefs

The British invasion of West Africa found the African population at the tribal stage of social organization. The basic unit of social and economic life was the extended family. A number of these families formed a tribe. The tribe was led by a chief, whose title was primarily passed on by inheritance. The chief was first of all a military leader who personally led the tribe in wars against its neighbours. The chief was manager of the tribal land. The land was considered to be the property of a god or of the spirits of deceased ancestors, the chief being their representative managing the land in their name. The chief was the principal judicial authority of the tribe, passing judgement and sentence in accordance with the indigenous legal system. The chief owned a large farm which was worked by fellow tribesmen and slaves. The chief was also the tribe's leading merchant. He was, in short, a feudal lord at the initial stage of feudalism's development.[3] In a wider context, there also existed a hierarchy of chiefs. The tribe was divided into a number of clans led by local chiefs, who were vassals of the tribe's supreme chief. In several places still larger groupings were found in the form of tribal federations led by kings, emirs and sultans.

Having seized West Africa, the British imperialists did not destroy the established feudal system of chiefs. The chief had immense authority in the eyes of the African population, and the British thought it profitable to use the chiefs as an instrument for dominating and controlling them. For this reason, the British did not demolish tribal organization and the institution of the chief, but turned these elements of feudalism into a social support for their oppression of the people.

Each colony is ruled by a Governor General, who is appointed by the British King. In the Gold Coast, the Legislative Council is made up of 15 senior colonial officials and 14 other members with a consultative role, three of whom are appointed by the Governor General, and one each by the Chambers of Mining and Commerce. Three are drawn from the large towns of Accra, Cape Coast and Sekondi, and six are African chiefs elected by the provincial councils. A colony is divided into a number of provinces, which in turn are divided into several districts. To administer each province the Governor General appoints a European official, for whose assistance a provincial council made up of European officials and African chiefs is created. However, in Nigeria, for instance, several provinces, for example Kano, have been turned into 'independent' native states or emirates. In this case the province is ruled by the emir with his own council and staff of European officials. The emir possesses his police force, law court, prison and other attributes of statehood. The emir of such emirates as Kano, Sokoto and Shekhu of Bornu are paid a salary of £600 by their treasuries. A district is administered by a European official appointed by the Provincial Governor. He deals with all matters concerning the indigenous population through the supreme chief of the district, to whom clan and village chiefs are subject. The functions of a village chief consist of collecting taxes from the population, sending them to perform compulsory public works, distributing the land, and responsibility for the political condition of his village community. He is in short a typical official of the colonial government, cloaked in the authority of a chief and the robes of hereditary democracy.

It should be noted that this democracy is being systematically eroded.

Despite the fact that a chief is elected from among a specific small group of families, as for instance is the case in the Gold Coast, his election must be approved by the Governor in order to ensure that the elected candidate is fully loyal to British imperialism. In Sierra Leone, a special school has even been opened for the training of chiefs, and has already produced its first graduates, who are now working as district and village judicial officials. The districts of Sierra Leone are not administered by a European official as they are in Nigeria or the Gold Coast. Supreme power is vested in the chief, to whom a European adviser is attached. Thus, in this case, the freedom to choose a chief is even more restricted and narrowly circumscribed. There has recently been a widespread overthrow of chiefs by the people in the Gold Coast. This is the so-called 'destoolment' (a chief's throne is known as a 'stool' in the local language of the Gold Coast). Chiefs ascend the 'stool' but can then be removed from power with lightning rapidity. The intrigues of the colonial government are behind these overthrows. Once a chief has been installed in office by the colonial government, he cannot be deposed without infringing the system of customary democracy. The colonial government therefore resorts extensively to the well proven method of intrigue. Since there are not one, but several families from which a village chief can be elected, there are always other claimants to the 'stool'. When the colonial government wishes to replace an undesirable chief, it sets other claimants against him. The issue is settled by hereditary democracy and the new chief is subsequently confirmed by the government. There is a growing discontent among the African peasantry with the policies of these chiefs enforcing the will of the colonial government, and this serves as the basis for exploiting the masses as a weapon in these intrigues. The economic penetration of the country has finally crushed the Gold Coast peasantry and has considerably sharpened class contradictions. The seething hatred of the masses, however, is being channeled by the skilled hand of the colonial government and its agents into the struggle against 'useless' chiefs. Particularly noteworthy is the fact that every re-election of a chief is accompanied by open armed conflict between the different families and supporters of the opposing candidates with the number of victims running into tens and even hundreds.

It should be noted that in all four colonies the government has imposed innumerable chiefs upon the people, considerably more than there were before the coming of the British. There were previously 40 paramount chiefs in the Gold Coast, whereas 121 'independent' states have now been established. To this number one must add a host of village chiefs.

To the colonial government this system of control has the further advantage of costing nothing. The chiefs are not paid by the colonial government, and even their emirs are paid from their own treasuries. Each paramount chief of a district has his own treasury. There are 80 such treasuries in Nigeria, 13 in Sierra Leone, and 121 in the Gold Coast. What are their sources of income? The first is taxes. The collection of taxes, levied at rates laid down by the colonial government, is carried out by the chief, who receives a percentage commission on the amount collected. One may thus understand the chief's desire to extract every penny he can, and a little extra if possible. Secondly, fines are imposed on those people sentenced by the chief: the more crimes committed, the more money the chief receives. Thirdly, licences of every type imaginable are imposed: permits for the gathering of medicinal herbs, for tapping palm trees (the sap thus gathered being made into wine), for the sale of palm wine, and levies on peasants from outside the village visiting the market and so on. Fourthly, occasional, extraordinary levies are inflicted on the peasantry for the replenishment of an empty treasury, or for some specific purpose. For example, the paramount chief of the Axim district of the Gold Coast travels to Cape Coast five to six times a year to attend conferences of the national reformist organization,[4] imposing a special levy on his subjects on each occasion. A further example: with £900 in his coffers, an Ashanti chief collected money from his subjects for a journey to the funeral of another paramount chief. In 1926-27 the combined income of the 61 treasuries of the province of Northern Nigeria was £711,446, comprising £617,347 in taxes, £37,168 from the courts, and £66,931 from other sources. Thus, by preserving the local tribal organization, the British imperialists gained a widely branching and cost-free apparatus of oppression, cloaked the real oppressors in the robes of hereditary democracy, and created their own social support in the person of the chief. Such is the face of hereditary democracy, whose preservation in West Africa the British imperialists are so given to boasting, depicting it as one of their services to the blacks.

## Land — Indigenous Systems and Capitalist Penetration

Before the coming of the British, the blacks had no conception of land as private property. The land belonged to the tribal community, and was managed by the chief. Consequently, Africans were ignorant of such European customs as renting, trading in, and mortgaging of land. Land was sometimes sold to another tribe, but only to meet a large outlay such as a war indemnity or the ransom of a chief or fellow tribesmen. There were two categories of land: tribal land and family land. A third category existed only in the Gold Coast, that of the 'stool' land, or the crown property of the chief. Family land was managed and shared out among the members of the family by its head. When a new adult member of the family appeared, he would approach the head of the family with a request for land. The head of the family would provide him with a plot from the family's existing allocation of land. If the family's land was fully occupied, the petitioner would approach the chief, who would provide a plot from the land available to the tribe as a whole. A new family group would then appear.

As we have already explained, British imperialism (in West Africa) did not expropriate the land of the African peasantry, but left it in the hands of the tribes. British rule, however, could hardly fail to influence and correspondingly alter the ownership of land. Firstly, the arrival of the British generated a demand for mining and plantation land, which was either obtained through direct agreements between industrial firms and chiefs (for example the renting of 1,000 hectares by the Ashanti Goldfields Corporation), or provided by the government. Though left in the hands of the peasantry, the land was declared crown property. This gave the colonial government the right to alienate the land it required by various plausible methods and pretexts. In Northern Nigeria, for instance, the government took land wanted by Europeans from the Africans for fixed compensation or in exchange for other plots of land. The rent from this land contributed to government income. In Southern Nigeria, the government obtains the necessary land in similar fashion, but pays the rent to the treasury of the relevant chief. In Sierra Leone, the chiefs can only lease land to Europeans and dispose of the rent with government approval. In the Gambia, the government pays no compensation whatsoever for land taken from the people, and retains the income. Only in the Gold Coast can the chiefs personally lease land to Europeans and dispose of the rent as they see fit.

With the arrival of the British, a demand arose for land for public requirements, such as railways, stations, roads, model plantations and so on. Once again the government took land from the indigenous population and herded them elsewhere. This process had a dual outcome: (1) it erased the religious overtones of land ownership, destroying the age-old conception of the land as divine property; and (2) it substantially reduced the total area of African land, thus limiting any potential enlargement of African plots and demonstrating to the people that land, like the product of their labour, had its price, and when so required could provide a means of obtaining money.

The new conception of land ownership was assimilated particularly quickly along the coastal belt, which had been the first area to be occupied by the British. For example, when Lagos was annexed, a British court was instituted, which administered justice by British law with total disregard for indigenous common law, especially in the sphere of land relations. Hence cases of confiscation and sale of a peasant's plot by court order were frequent. The old communal system of land ownership was rapidly broken down, and the alienation, sale and mortgage of plots commenced. These new concepts of land relations inevitably penetrated deep into the country.

A further process was simultaneously taking place within the black peasant community. We have already shown that imperialism has not destroyed peasant production by the expropriation of land, that agriculture is almost wholly in the hands of the small peasantry, and that capitalist plantations play virtually no part in the economy of West Africa. We shall now trace the development of peasant farming under the domination of finance capital.

Imperialist policy was aimed above all at increasing the dependency of peasant farming on the production of commodities, and at turning individual countries into specialist producers of one particular type of raw material. There was practically no cocoa crop before the end of the nineteenth century. In 1879, the first cocoa seeds were imported from Fernando Po. A series of measures were taken by the government to make the blacks raise cocoa trees through the reduction in cultivation of other crops. Before 1916 cocoa was exported duty free, whereas duty was charged on all other exported products. The trading companies (the export of agricultural produce is virtually monopolized by one large company, the African and Eastern Trade Corporation) used the above customs policy to justify raising the buying price of cocoa, lowered the prices of other agricultural products they bought, and gave large advances to cocoa growers. Credit policy was arranged accordingly. The government distributed cocoa seeds and set up plantations for demonstration and experimental purposes. The whole system was bound to steer the development of peasant farming towards specialization in cocoa. A rapid growth in the export of cocoa began:

TABLE 2.2

COCOA PRODUCTION IN THE GOLD COAST

| Year | Export of Cocoa | |
|------|---------|------|
| 1891 | 80 | lbs |
| 1900 | 536 | tons |
| 1905 | 5,093 | " |
| 1910 | 22,631 | " |
| 1915 | 77,278 | " |
| 1921 | 133,195 | " |
| 1926 | 231,000 | " |

The export of all other crops grew at considerably lower rates, in some cases not at all, but in either case their importance to peasant farming rapidly declined. Over the nine years from 1910 to 1919 exports of copra rose by only 27% from 775 to 984 tons, exports of palm oil over the same period fell by 54% from 2,044,868 gallons to 938,595 gallons, exports of palm kernels fell by 31% from 14,182 to 9,892 tons, and that of rubber fell by 60%. Thus, under the 'skilled' management of the colonial government, the Gold Coast was transformed into one large cocoa plantation. McPhee bluntly and rightly says that cocoa is the adopted son of the government of the Gold Coast.[5] A similar process took place in the Gambia, where we have the following export movements for the main crops:

TABLE 2.3

PRODUCTION OF PRIMARY PRODUCTS IN THE GAMBIA

|  | *1910* | *1917* | *1917 as % of 1910* |
|---|---|---|---|
| Groundnuts | 39,000 tons | 74,000 tons | 190.0 |
| Rubber | 43,000 lbs | 1,753 lbs | 3.8 |
| Wax | 45,500 lbs | 3,962 lbs | 8.7 |
| Palm Kernels | 255 tons | 532 tons | 200.0 |

At present, groundnuts account for 97% of the country's total exports, although they were practically unknown to Africans before the coming of the British in 1840. This process can also be seen in Sierra Leone, which specializes in the products of the oil palm. How does this specialization and increased commodity dependence in peasant farming affect the social system of the black peasantry, and what processes occur within the peasant community as a consequence of this specialization?

Lenin argued that the transformation of agriculture into a sphere of commodity production leads to a growth of capitalism in agriculture, and to an upheaval in its social character, since the process creates an internal market for capitalism, intensifies agriculture's demand for improved means of production and causes both a differentiation of the peasantry and the formation of contingents of workers. In this respect the situation in Russia was substantially similar to that in all the non-colonial countries.[6]

In West Africa, we find the same process to some degree. However, the domination of peasant farming by finance capital, and its accompanying exploitation by money lenders and feudal elements caused these processes to occur in a particularly acute and distorted form. Specialization and increased commodity dependence have not created an internal market, since exchange takes place between the metropoles and the colonies rather than between individual regions and countries within British West Africa. The growth of commodity agriculture has not generated a demand for improving the means of production. Agricultural equipment is not renewed, and to this day the peasantry work the fields with their own primitive implements. The basic reason for this technical backwardness is that small peasant farms do not have the necessary means for their own re-equipment. So many parasites have attached themselves to the small peasant farm, that the peasant is not only forced to part with his surplus produce, but often with some of the produce which he needs for himself.

## How Surplus is Extracted from the Peasantry

The peasant is firstly fleeced by his chief. We have already shown that the chief frequently collects money from the peasantry for his treasury, and takes full advantage of tax collecting and his role as judge to levy fines. Secondly, the peasant is fleeced by the trading companies and their local agents. When selling his own produce, the peasant is entirely in the hands of the trading companies and their agents. He has no choice of customer, since the purchase of the primary product he produces is usually monopolized by one company. Based in one of the posts, the company sets up a system of warehouses along the railways, area warehouses at remote points, and an extensive network of produce buyers. By monopolizing the market, the company is able to pay the peasant a lower price than on the European market. In October 1926 for example, the price per ton of cocoa (including transport costs and the middle-man's profit) was £37.18.0 at Cape Coast, and £51.0.0. at Liverpool. The price per ton for palm oil was £21.15.0 and £37.0.0 respectively, and £12.9.0 and £20.19.0 for groundnuts. The low price paid by the company is reduced still further by their agents, who buy direct from the peasants. For example, though the most recent price established by a company in Sierra Leone for palm nuts is £4.17.6, the agents paid the Africans £1.17.0. A number of secret agreements between agents have been recently discovered in the Gold Coast, concerning the purchase of cocoa at prices lower than those laid down by the company. Newspapers recently publicized the trial of a group of produce buyers who had secretly agreed between themselves to buy cocoa from the peasant at 8s 5d per basket, instead of 10/- as fixed by the company. In the boom years the buyers made a fortune from the most blatant swindling of the peasantry. R.L. Buell estimates that in 1920 some buyers made as much as £10,000 a year.[7] This robbery leaves the peasant with only enough to keep him from starving. One Sierra Leone newspaper estimates that a peasant and his family nowadays earn between 7d and 9d per week. But the peasant is also robbed by the government. We shall deal later with the peasants' duty to perform unpaid labour, and examine here the tax system of the colonial government.

There is no uniform tax system in the colonies of British West Africa. Nigeria, Gambia and Sierra Leone have a direct system of taxation. In Nigeria, income tax is charged at 10% on all peasant income, while a separate tax *(gangali)* is levied on livestock at the rate of 1s 6d per head of cattle, 6d per sheep, and 3d per goat. In Sierra Leone there is a tax on dwellings, and also in the Gambia, where it is charged at 5/- per dwelling. But the main form of taxation, and in the Gold Coast the fundamental form, is indirect, above all export and import duties. Customs duty constitutes 46% of government income in Nigeria, 61% in the Gold Coast, 64% in Sierra Leone, and 74% in the Gambia. In the latter, direct taxation yielded £11,665 in 1929, and duties £124,396. The blacks purchased

£82,715 worth of cotton manufactured goods, and paid £8,271 in duty to the government. They paid £54,917 for kola nuts used for food, paying £24,973 in duty, and £18,591 for tobacco, paying £12,264 in duty, etc. For every ton of groundnuts exported, the Gambian peasant paid £1.0.0 in duty. The situation is similar in other colonies. Consequently, the peasant is left not only with nothing with which to buy improved agricultural implements, but does not even have enough to meet his daily needs as a consumer. According to George Padmore's estimates, the average Gambian peasant sells 1½ tons of groundnuts annually at £5 per ton on the local market, thus raising £7.10.0. Out of this he buys rice for food worth £1.16.0, seed worth £1.4.0, and pays 4/- tax on his hut and 6/- poll tax. So £4 remains. Putting his daily family outlays on food and clothing at 1/-, he therefore needs £18.5.0 annually. He has only £4, however, and is thus £14.5.0 short, which obliges him to leave home to find other work.[8] In this lies the reason for the backwardness of peasant farming. All the bourgeois papers of West Africa write about this backwardness: the peasant cultivates the land badly, and picks cocoa and palm nuts when still half-ripe in order to sell them as soon as possible. The result is low quality cocoa, which fetches low prices. The Governor of the Gold Coast complains that the purity of cocoa has been falling year by year: 88.5% in 1927-28, 88.4% in 1928-29 and 87.7% in 1929-30, whereas the U.S.A. demands cocoa which is 90% pure. Peasant farming is collapsing rather than progressing. But, as is universally the case, the degradation of the main mass of the peasantry in a highly commodity-dependent economy has, as its reverse side, the differentiation of the peasantry and the evolution of a small group of prosperous peasants. A stratum of rich peasants is gradually emerging, who are beginning to use improved methods of farming and to increase capital investment, in relation to which their own plots of land soon become inadequate. A growth is taking place of an indigenous trading bourgeoisie, who are establishing their own cocoa and palm plantations. The farms of chiefs are expanding. Here it should be noted that this evolution of capitalist elements is proceeding extremely slowly and spasmodically. In this case we are dealing with the situation prior to the present world capitalist crisis. The picture has now altered sharply.

## Imperialism's Impact — the Argument Summarized

These two processes, the partial expropriation of peasant land thus destroying their former conception of land ownership, and the differentiation of the peasantry, confront the peasant with a revision of existing land relations. One should remember that the main crops of these colonies are perennial. Cocoa trees mature at twenty years, palm trees at thirty. This means that any given plot will be attached to a peasant for many years, and redistribution of land becomes impossible. Peasants who have prospered need to buy or rent additional land, whilst those who have been ruined are prepared to rent their land or to sell part of it in order to meet their need for money. As McPhee writes:

> 'The planting of cocoa prompted farmers to demand the right of private property over land. This development marked the end of communality and the authority of tribal power as such, the introduction of land as private property, and its transformation into a commodity. Thus this newly evolving society can no longer rest upon kinship relations.'

Although the indigenous system of tribal organization has not yet been destroyed and communal ownership of land persists, both are being rapidly undermined from within. The sale, leasing and mortgaging of land by the peasants are no longer fortuitous phenomena among the black community of West Africa. The community is being supplanted by private property over land. Land is following agricultural produce in becoming a commodity. However, for a revolution in the social system of agriculture, the final destruction of the community, and the economy's transformation from a simple commodity to a capitalist type, labour must likewise become a commodity. This is just what has not happened. The entire system of exploitation by feudal elements, money lenders and imperialists has not promoted, but rather retarded the peasant's conversion into a free labourer. Capitalism is growing extremely slowly in the system of agriculture in these colonies, since the rate of initial accumulation has been held down by the systematic robbery of the peasantry by the imperialists, indigenous feudal elements, and money lenders. Such accumulated capital as is available is preferentially invested in money lending and trade. There is no urban industry. We have seen that capital imported to the colonies is invested in the mining industry or in railway construction. The development of a processing industry would involve on the one hand a contradiction of sales markets, and on the other the creation of an urban proletariat. Both would contradict imperialism's root interests in the colony. Nor can the development of urban industry be financed from indigenous capital accumulation, since such industry would not survive competition with the metropolis. The only sphere for the employment of labour is the mining industry, but both the size of this industry and its demand for labour are very small. Labour surpluses, in the form of a reserve army of labour, are being developed in the countryside, but there is no demand for this labour. A ruined peasant cannot abandon his farm completely and become a proletarian, because as a proletarian he is needed by no one. This system of exploitation by imperialists, feudal elements and money lenders retards and distorts the revolution in production relations and in the social system of rural colonial areas, condemning the peasant to pauperisation, hunger and beggary. The peasant is confronted with the acute necessity for a radical and revolutionary break-up of the whole existing system of relations in the countryside, which is supported by the imperialists in alliance with the local chiefs.

## SMALL PEASANT FARMING ON THE SOUTH AFRICAN RESERVES

The Union of South Africa is a British dominion with an area of 1,223,000 sq.km. (about 9 times the size of Britain itself). It has a population of 7,895,000, of which 79% are black, and 21% white.

By the time South Africa had been brought under the domination of British imperialism, there was already a considerable amount of large-scale farming by the Boers, immigrants from Holland, who had conquered the southern part of Africa at the end of the eighteenth and beginning of the nineteenth century. British imperialism's conquest of South Africa offered new prospects for the development of farming, particularly of sheep farming, to supply the Manchester woollen industry. As already mentioned, deposits of gold and diamonds were discovered in the 1890s in the Transvaal, which was then a Boer Republic.

### British Imperialism's Three Goals

The prime requirements of farming and mining were land and labour. In tackling the land problem, and in settling the fate of the black peasantry in doing so, British imperialism was motivated by the wish to: (1) provide farming and mining with sufficient land; (2) provide farming with labour; (3) provide industrial enterprises with a constant influx of labour from the peasantry. This required the expropriation of indigenous peasant land. The total expropriation of the land would, however, merely have aggravated the problem rather than have solved it. It would have meant openly making slaves of the African population. The British, however, like the Boer imperialists, knew from personal experience, if only that of the war with the Zulu chief Dingaan, that such open enslavement of the Zulus would have involved an extremely prolonged and intense struggle with them, and the annihilation of hundreds of thousands or millions of Africans. Even a negligible quantity of labour could have been bought only at the cost of wiping out most of the indigenous population. The exploitation of the colony required the labour of the entire population, and the expanding mining industry demanded that a reserve of labour be available. But the Boer farmer and British mining industrialist wanted neither slave nor proletarian, which were expensive and not without their dangers. They wanted a peasant who was tied to the land, who would support himself when not needed to work for his European exploiters, and who could be re-engaged whenever needed. These considerations have been, and still are, the basis of British imperialism's land policy in South Africa. Having expropriated the greater part of the land, the imperialists turned the remainder into so-called native reserves, and crowded the black peasantry on to them. The entire subsequent history of imperialist rule in South Africa is one of making the black peasant landless and progressively limiting his rights. The result of this policy has been a situation in South Africa where 1½ million whites own 92% of the land, leaving a mere 7% to the 6 million blacks, or, on average, 154.5 acres per white, and 5.3 acres per member of the black population

The 1918 Report of the Commission on Native Land Use gives the following data on the distribution of Africans on the different categories of land on which they live: of a rural black population of 3,881,000, 1,930,000 live on native reserves, 95,000 live on land owned by religious missions, 123,000 on their own land, 121,000 on Crown lands, and 1,611,000 on land owned by Europeans. In other words 50% of the total rural black population (25% of the total population of the country) live on native reserves.

## The System of Native Reserves

The reserves are fairly large tracts of land located in various parts of the Union, and inhabited exclusively by blacks. They are mainly the poorest areas of land, since the right to own the better areas is the privilege of the white farmers and Boer landowners. Land is not held as private property in the reserves. The land there is considered the property of the tribes inhabiting it, and is apportioned by the tribal chiefs according to communal land usage. Here the British imperialists have preserved the indigenous system of tribal organization and have turned the chiefs into their own officials to an even greater extent than, for example, in British West Africa.

The reserves are severely overpopulated, and the peasantry therefore suffers from an acute land famine. The average area of a plot of land on a reserve is 12 acres, which, under the South African conditions of poor soil, drought-prone climate and low technical level of African agriculture, is totally inadequate. The minimum size of an average family's plot should be, according to the Transvaal Land Council, 36½ acres. In the district of the Transkei, for example, where livestock is the most important sector of African farming, experts have concluded that the land requirement is six acres per person. A further example is the Witsiehoek reserve in the Orange Free State where only 12-15,000 acres are suitable for ploughing, though its total area is 1,058,000 acres. 10,000 people live in the reserve. There are thus 1.27 acres per person, or 6.35 acres per family of five. Not only are there no unoccupied areas in the reserve, but a considerable part of the reserve's population has no plot whatsoever, and is waiting for plots to become vacant. This overcrowding of the land, and its prevailing communal use leads to the predominance of small plots, which is exceedingly backward. The peasantry of the reserves cannot yet even dream of using agricultural machinery. Even the plough is an unattainable desire for the majority of peasants, and the crude hoe remains the universal agricultural implement. The land shortage and primitive implements are the cause of the low level of productivity and income of peasant farming.

On most reserves the peasantry is not even self-sufficient in maize (the African's staple food) and other foodstuffs. Let us take the Witsiehoek reserve referred to above. 10,000 Africans live on it. In 1929, they harvested 1,300 bags of maize (1 bag = 100 kg.), or 13 kg. per person, together with 500 bags of millet. Even if the harvest is normal, the Transkei area uses maize from European farms. In 1924-25, the traders imported (less exports) more than 140,000 bags of maize. Let us take the Herschel area as a further example. Its annual maize requirement is 67,500 bags, but the harvest has never exceeded 42,000 bags in recent years. According to the figures of the Lady Grey Railway, in 1925 (a good year for the harvest) the export of grain was no more than a few bags, sent mostly as parcels, whilst a considerable quantity of maize is brought into the area every year by European merchants. Altogether, the peasants in the reserves and missionary and crown lands harvested 3.4 million bags of maize in 1929, which is two bags of 200 kg. per person for the year for 1.77 million people, or 16.5 kg. per month. According to the figures of a 1929 budget survey, average per capita maize consumption is 2.75 bags. Thus this section of the peasantry produces 1,427,500 bags of maize less than it consumes.

Let us take the average family in Mooi River in the province of Natal. They sow 4.9 acres of maize. The average yield per acre is 1.25 bags (125 kg. maximum), whereas on a European farm it is 410 kg. Their total harvest is 5.125 bags, but their requirement is 13.76 bags. The family has a deficit of 7.65 bags. The peasants of this village sow no other grain crops. This deficit does not, of course, mean that the peasants do not sell maize. They sell it to pay the taxes, but then buy it back at treble the price. There are also 4.12 head of cattle per family, 1.45 sheep and goats, 0.53 pigs and 0.48 donkeys, (the main draught animals, there being no horses) and six chickens. The average family receives an income of £3.18.6 from the sale of animals, 18/- from the sale of chickens and eggs (the family itself consumes 48 eggs per year), 2/- from selling the skins of dead domestic animals, and £1.10.0 from fruit and vegetables. The family's total sales are £6.8.0. It must now buy the maize which it lacks, which costs £5.14.4. Only 13/8 remains. From this it must buy all its other items of consumption (sugar, salt, tea, tobacco, etc.) and pay the taxes.

Let us take another average family in the Transkei reserve, where the maize harvest is higher (4 bags per acre), and where the family has a surplus of 2.25 bags of maize which it sells and does not have to buy back. Such a family has a net income of £2.12.6. Here we shall consider only taxes, leaving aside the family's miscellaneous purchases. The peasant pays an annual land tax of 10/- on his tiny plot of land. Every adult male pays an annual poll tax of £1. There is then the tax on livestock, 1/- per head of cattle, and 6d per sheep. To this must be added a further special type of tax on Africans, the charge for a pass.[9] Apart from its other purposes, the pass system is used by the government as a substantial source of income. Thus for example, in the Transvaal, where £409,000 was raised in poll tax, the pass system made £350,000 for the government. Our first average family had to pay £1.14.0 in taxes. Quite apart from absolutely essential purchases, the family needs a further £1.1.2. The tax owing by our second average family is £2.7.6. Their net residual income is 5/-. In short, most peasants are unable to pay their taxes from the income of their own farming. The taxes are usually collected at the time of the maize harvest. In terror of imprisonment for default, the family is forced to sell the maize that it has just harvested to a European merchant. At this time, large quantities of maize are coming on to the market, resulting in a sharp fall in prices. The peasants, however, hounded by the tax collectors, cannot wait for prices to rise, and sell their maize at a nominal price, only to buy it back at treble the price when they have earned some money. The buying and selling of maize is, in all, an unfortunate necessity for the peasant. Having sold his maize and paid his taxes, he is left without both his staple food and money. It is then that the money lender offers the peasant his services.

Money lending is highly developed in South Africa. Though most money lenders are Europeans, the wealthier Africans, mainly tribal chiefs, are also involved. But these are usually binding loans. In the Transkei, for instance, money lenders give loans at 100% per annum. In most cases the merchant, the money lender and the recruiting agent form a single enslaving alliance, ensnaring the peasant on every side. As one of the speakers at a recent congress of trade unions related:

> 'Immediately after the harvest, the officials demand payment of taxes, knowing quite well that the peasants have no money, and that in order to pay the taxes they will have to sell the maize they have harvested at 8/- a bag or less. To pay the government tax, they need to sell at least 4 bags, and soon after the harvest, the natives have nothing left to eat. They then have to buy back their own maize at a price 3 to 4 times higher than they sold it for. They go on buying in this way until they are utterly entangled in debts. Then the trader, who also deals in recruiting for the mines, begins to demand money from them. They are left with no other choice than to go to the mines or sell their cattle. Of the two evils, many blacks choose the former.'

The land shortage and the whole complex system of the peasant's enslavement by the government, the trader, the money lender, and finally by the tribal chief, forces him to take on outside work. He cannot find work in the reserve. The development of rural capitalism and the emergence of large peasant farms employing hired labour has been extremely weak, and highly distorted in its form. The initial accumulation of African capital is made exceedingly difficult. The Africans in the reserves are forbidden to engage in trade. In every village there is a European trader's shop, which buys up all the marketable produce of the local peasants, and sells the peasants goods from the town. The peasants are also forbidden to deal in money lending. If an African is in debt to a European trader or official, and fails to repay in time, he can be turned over to the courts and his last effects put under the hammer. If he has borrowed money from a wealthy African and has not repaid it, the latter cannot take the matter to court, since the court does not recognize him as a lender of money. This situation does not, of course, render such loans impossible, since patriarchal relations are still very strong in the villages. But it does restrict the development of indigenous money lending to a substantial degree. There is no vacant land on a reserve. Each peasant is allocated an identical amount of land, regardless of his economic circumstances. Each peasant holds land only on condition that he personally cultivates it. The land may only be cultivated by other persons for the duration of one harvest. This provision is widely exploited by the wealthier section of the peasantry. A peasant, unable to cultivate his plot, rents his land to a wealthy peasant. Prosperous peasants are thus always able to sow more land than they own, though the land is different on each occasion. Although this section of the peasantry uses the labour of others to cultivate rented land, this labour is not exploited on a hired basis. There are, as such, no hired workers on a native reserve. As a rule, work is performed as payment in labour for the loan of a plough, seeds, or horse and similar 'assistance' to a neighbour. The general result is that the use of non-family labour is very limited in peasant farming in the reserves. Free labour must be exported beyond the boundaries of the reserves. Migrant labour is hence particularly widely developed in South Africa. At the time of the 1925 census, for example, of the 200,000 adult men in the Transkei, 86,000, or 45% (in effect, all adult able-bodied men) were working outside the reserve. MacMillan is quite right when he says that 'the most important export of such areas as Herschel is labour.'[10]

Let us look at this class of the peasantry from another point of view, namely the degree to which the native reserves can be regarded as producers of primary products. In 1928, South Africa exported the following agricultural products:

TABLE 2.4

SOUTH AFRICA'S EXPORT OF PRIMARY PRODUCTS, 1928

| Agricultural Product | Tons | Value |
|---|---|---|
| Maize | 574,960 | 3,520,454 |
| Maize flour | 710.9 | 431,398 |
| Wool (raw) | 123,439 | 15,975,812 |
| Wool (cleaned) | 3,315 | 87,539 |
| Cotton | 2,222 | 203,634 |
| Sugar | 84,132 | 909,430 |
| Meat | 8,567 | 229,977 |
| Leather and skins | 44,000 | 4,580,000 |

These are the main exports. The rest are items of secondary importance such as ostrich feathers, tanning materials and goats' wool. What is the proportion of peasant produce in these exports? Since statistics do not provide a direct estimate, we shall attempt an indirect estimate.
574,960 tons of maize were exported. In the same year, European farms harvested 1,387,618 tons, which is a quantity quite sufficient to cover the exports and feed the peasantry of the reserves. Moreover, we have already seen that the peasantry of the reserves does not even grow a sufficient quantity to meet its own consumption. Turning to wool, 123,439 tons of raw wool and 3,315 of cleaned wool were exported. The European farms gathered 113,309 tons of wool, which covers almost 90% of exports. Peasant farming as a whole accounts for only 7% of total wool production, and the peasantry on the reserves for 2 to 3%. As for cotton and sugar cane, these are grown only on European farms, and the African peasantry therefore takes no part in their export. The peasantry of the reserves does play some role in the export of leather, skins and fruit, although this role is quite insignificant. Hence it is clear that the peasantry of the reserves plays virtually no role in exports, and that peasant farming at its present stage of development cannot be regarded as producing primary commodities for export.

## Reserves: Peasant Agriculture or Capitalist Reservoir of Cheap Labour?

From this brief analysis we may conclude that the native reserves are essentially a reserve stock of labour for mining and European farming. If the Africans were completely deprived of land, the imperialists would be obliged to shoulder, in some way, the cost of supporting them as a functioning or potentially functioning work force. It was impossible to make them free proletarians, since neither mining nor farming could have absorbed such a quantity of labour. The imperialists would have had to give some assistance to the unemployed or lose their labour, quite apart from the effect that this would have had on the political state of the colony. So they have allotted land to the peasants, who live out the hungry existence of paupers, though this does not enable them to become proletarians.
Thus this peasantry has a different place in the system of imperialist exploitation of Black Africa than does the peasantry of British West Africa. In British West Africa, the peasantry's function consists of producing raw materials for the metropolis and purchasing European goods. The function of the peasantry in the South African reserves amounts to acting as a labour reserve. They are taken on for work in the mines or on the farms when there is a demand for labour. When his labour ceases to become necessary, the peasant must support himself and reproduce the reserve work force.
Comrade Shiik is therefore wrong when he writes:

> 'Thus one must distinguish between two parallel sectors in the agriculture (of South Africa), the white plantation and farming sector, and the 'native sector'. (i.e. the peasantry in the reserves). This division coincides exactly with the division into *capitalist* and *peasant* agriculture.' (Shiik's italics)[11]

Thus, for Shiik there are two sectors, capitalist and peasant, each following their own path of development in parallel, and neither hindering the other. Can one say that the peasantry of the reserves constitutes a sector independent of, and parallel to, European farming? We submit that there is no justification for such a view. In British West Africa, British imperialism left small peasant farming intact in order to exploit the peasants as small-scale commodity producers, producers of raw materials and buyers of European goods, once having subjected them to its own interests. This was not the aim of British imperialism in South Africa in leaving part of the land to the peasants and permitting them to continue their small-scale farming. The peasants play virtually no role as primary commodity producers, but they would play a more important role as purchasers if they were not small peasants. By giving them land, the imperialists aimed to create a reserve of cheap labour for themselves.

> 'It is essential to establish permanent reserves within the colony, and in siting them to leave sufficient land between them as to allow Europeans to settle there. Under these circumstances every European will be in a position to obtain an adequate number of labourers from the reserve in his direct vicinity.'
> (Letter from Earl Grey to Sir Harry Smith)

The native reserve is an *appendage* of European farming, rather than a sector parallel to it, and is a reserve of labour for European farming and the mining industry. If we are to speak of the native reserves as an independent sector parallel to European farming, as the labour sector of peasant farming (contrasting it with capitalist farming), one is also bound to say that British West Africa, a peasant economy throughout, is an independent sector parallel to the world capitalist economy! Hence by analogy we would have to say that there are two parallel sectors in the system of world imperialism, the capitalist sector and the colonial sector! It is clear, however, and is clearly stated by the theses of the 6th Comintern Congress, that the colonies are satellites dominated by the world capitalist economy. Thus there is no question of parallels. If the colonies, and South Africa in particular, are the agrarian and primary producer satellites of the world capitalist system, then the South African native reserves are the satellites and reserve labour force of the mining industry and European farming.

## NOTES

1.  The term 'serfs' is obviously alien to Africa (where such terms as 'squatters', 'contract' or 'migrant labour' would be more familiar). But the Russian vocabulary, though obviously designed to find an echo in the minds of the book's readers, is not unhelpful in illustrating the social relations of production in Africa that the authors are trying to depict. For this reason the term 'serfs' has been retained.

2.  The author referred to appears to be a Russian. The pseudonym means 'South'.

3.  Potekhin, one of this book's authors,was to return to the question of 'feudalism' in later writings. See Potekhin, I.I.,'Land Relations in African Countries', *African Problems*, (Moscow, 1968). This article was also published in the first issue of *The Journal of Modern African Studies* 1 (1) (1963).

4.  This is probably a reference to the National Congress of British West Africa (1920), for a discussion of which see, *inter alia*, Coleman, J.S., *Nigeria: Background to Nationalism*, (Berkeley and Los Angeles, 1965).

5.  McPhee's interpretation of the centrality of the government's role in stimulating cocoa production, which Nzula, Potekhin and Zusmanovich accept, has been challenged by subsequent research. Polly Hill, in particular, argues that the cocoa industry was well-established *before* the colonial officials knew much about it, and that the principal innovators were migrants to Akim Abuakwa, an area of virgin land. Thus they were not a settled peasantry whose traditional crops had been forcibly driven from the market. See Hill, P., *The Migrant Cocoa Farmers of Southern Ghana*, (Cambridge, 1973). On the other hand Hill's work only covers a small section of the cocoa-growing area and it seems difficult to avoid the conclusion that the colonial government provided a crucial 'enabling' role.

6.  The reference here is almost certainly to Lenin, V.I., *The Development of Capitalism in Russia*, Various Editions, e.g. (Moscow, 1964).

7.  The reference here is to Buell, R.L., *The Native Problem in Africa*, 2 Vols, (New York, 1928), (Reprinted London, 1965).

8.  These figures are from Padmore, G., *The Life and Struggles of Negro Toilers*, Red International Labour Union Magazine for the International Trade Union Committee of Negro Workers, (London, 1931) pp.27, 28, New Edition issued by Sun Dance Press, (Hollywood, 1971). It is in fact noteworthy that Nzula, Potekhin and Zusmanovich take so little opportunity to use Padmore's book, over half of which is concerned directly with Africa, and represents the only comparative work by a sympathetic writer of their time. In fact this is the only occasion when they refer to Padmore directly, though

there are other hints throughout the book showing that Nzula, Potekhin and Zusmanovich were familiar with Padmore's work. One can only assume that Padmore's expulsion from the Party was already 'on the cards' (see Introduction to this volume) and that our authors were already treating him as *persona non grata*.

9.    'Passes' to regulate the movement and settlement of Africans and so-called 'coloured people' have a long history in South Africa, and date back to the early nineteenth century in the Cape. The defining political principles of the pass laws were established in 1921 when Col. Stallard, Chairman of the Transvaal Local Government Commission, reported that: 'The native should only be allowed to enter the urban areas, which are essentially the white man's creation, when he is willing to enter and to minister to the needs of the white man, and should depart therefrom when he ceases so to minister'. Pass law contraventions have increased from 94,300 in 1933 (the year when Nzula, Potekhin and Zusmanovich first published this book) to 621,400 in 1970. Wilson, F., *Migrant Labour in South Africa*, (Johannesburg, 1972), pp.160, 232.

10.    This is almost certainly a reference to MacMillan, W.M., *Bantu, Boer and Briton*, (Oxford, 1963). First published in 1929 by Faber and Gwyer Ltd., London.

11.    Shiik, Andre, in *Agrarye Problemy*, No. 5-6, 1932. Shiik was regarded as a founder of Soviet African studies and was a teacher of Albert Nzula (see Introduction).

# 3.

# FORCED LABOUR ON PLANTATIONS, FARMS AND MINES

[This chapter is concerned with four principal issues:] firstly, the Belgian Congo as an illustration of the exploitation of the colonies and their indigenous populations by the plantation system; secondly, the case of the Union of South Africa as an example of the exploitation of hired labour on European farms; [thirdly, the character of forced labour in the mines, paying particular regard to the case of South Africa; and finally the question of whether contract and forced labour is a special form of slavery.][1]

## THE PLANTATION SYSTEM IN THE BELGIAN CONGO

The Belgian Congo is a country unsurpassed for the cruelty with which millions of blacks have been enslaved and wiped out by the Belgian imperialists. The cruel truth about the Congo is being hidden by the social democratic ministers of the Belgian Government. We may read reports in the press on the colossal dividends of the countries exploiting the blacks of the Congo, but only the frequent rebellions which cannot be covered up, throw any light on the position of the black workers of the colony.

The Belgian Congo, lying at the very centre of the African continent, has an area of 909,654 square miles, and a population consisting of 8,500,000 blacks and 25,000 whites. Before the coming of the Europeans, the tribal organization of the Congo's black population was the same as in West Africa and most African countries, the sole difference, to the disadvantage of the black people, being that, at the time of the arrival of European capitalists, there were no large state-like groupings like the Ashanti. Such large inter-tribal groupings had been known in the history of the Congo, but these had, for a number of reasons, disintegrated by the time the Europeans arrived. As we have already shown, this fact simplified the Belgian enslavement of the Congo and the implementation of their imperialist policies.

## Belgian Manipulation of Indigenous Political Organization

Just like British imperialism in West Africa, the Belgian imperialists formally preserved the system of tribal organization, but so altered its content that in reality nothing was left of it. Present policy as regards tribal organization is based on a 1910 decree of the Belgian Government, according to which every African must belong to a specific tribe ruled by a traditional chief. But having announced this, the government radically rebuilt the entire system of tribal organization. First of all, the number of tribes was doubled during the five years following the initiation of the policy: 3,653 in 1914, and 6,095 in 1919. The fragmentation of the tribes occurred for a number of reasons. Firstly, all tribes of any significant size who had offered any resistance to the government were broken up into several individual tribes ruled by government-appointed chiefs. Secondly, the government disregarded the tribal organization of the population when establishing administrative boundaries within the colony. The tribes were adapted to fit the administrative scheme. As a result, some tribes were divided into parts located in different provinces by administrative bounaries, and the resulting parts hence received new chiefs whereas before the tribes had remained united. The breaking up of tribes eventually reached a point where, in Manyema district, there were 530 chiefs for a population of 185,000, or 530 'states', each with a population of 350. At the same time, in a number of other places, a process of amalgamation of tribes was taking place. Thus the present boundaries between tribes no longer bear any relation to the tribal divisions of the Africans before colonialism. The tribal chiefs are appointed and removed from office by the government. Each chief must obtain a special nickel medal from the government as a symbol of power, without which he is not recognized by the government as a chief. In Buta and Stanleyville the government has opened special schools for the training of chiefs. A chief of this type has nothing in common with the former elected or hereditary tribal chief, and is no more than an official of the colonial government. The duties of the chief include: informing his subjects of government decrees, informing the government of all events in his tribe, collecting taxes, assisting company agents in labour recruiting, supplying labour for government projects, carrying out various police duties, and so on.

A chief receives a salary from the government, the size of which, in each individual case, depends on the number of people in his tribe and the standard of his work. Three classes of chief have been established by the authorities: average, good, and very good. Per head of his tribe, an 'average chief' receives Fr.0.24, a 'good' chief Fr.0.36, and a 'very good' chief Fr.0.48. These rates are received whenever the work of a chief improves or deteriorates, according to which he is transferred from one class to another. He receives, in addition, a specified percentage of the taxes he collects, which gives him an incentive to collect as much tax as possible.

As in other colonies, the Belgian Congo is headed by a Governor General, appointed by the Belgian Government. He has a State Council consisting of himself as Chairman, the Vice-Governor, the Attorney-General and the heads of the various government departments. The colony as a whole is divided into four provinces, Congo-Kasai, Equatorial, Eastern, Katanga, and a further fifth province, the mandate territory of Ruanda-Urundi (a former German colony). Each province is ruled by a Governor. The provinces are divided into a total of 22 districts administered by District Commissioners, the districts being divided into a total of 179 sub-districts administered by government agents, to whom the chiefs are directly subordinate. Such is the system of political and administrative oppression of the Congolese population.

This administrative machine has a considerable army of Africans at its disposal. Unlike the other colonies, the Belgian Congo has no division of government forces into police and army. The soldiers of the indigenous army carry out routine police functions, and are also sent on punitive expeditions to put down rebellions. In January 1932, Paul Kroker*, the Belgian Colonial Minister reported to the Colonial Council that the strength of the Congolese Army was 14,319 black soldiers under the command of 313 officers. The Minister assured the Council that 'their drill and training made them the best of colonial armies'. Although volunteers are taken into the army, they account for a negligible part of it, due to the exceedingly hard conditions of service. Most soldiers are taken into the army by force, there being no formal recruiting system. The chiefs are simply instructed to send a certain number of men into the army, which, for the chief, is a convenient way of ridding himself of personal enemies. The length of service in the army is seven years, a period clearly sufficient for training good soldiers. In providing the Africans with military training, Belgium recognizes that they are not only needed for crushing rebellions in the Congo, but also that they could be used in a European theatre of war, for example in a war against the U.S.S.R. It should be noted that Belgium is not alone in this respect. Britain and France are training even larger contingents of future African armies in their colonies. This system whereby the indigenous population is politically and administratively controlled also safeguards the existing brutal system for exploiting the enslaved peasantry of the Congo.

## The Land is Expropriated

In 1879, Stanley 'discovered' the Congo and its rubber trees for Belgian imperialism. In 1885, the King of the Belgians, Leopold II, proclaimed all free land in the Congo the property of Belgium, maintaining a diplomatic silence on the question of which land was considered 'free'. Considering the fact that most peasants lived by gathering the fruits of wild plants, and, in any case, performed very little cultivation of the land, virtually all of it could be classed as free. An interpretation of the initial decree soon followed, the gist of which was that:

'The State has the right of absolute and exclusive ownership of all

> the land and its fruits. Any person gathering any fruits whatsoever
> will be punished as a thief, and any person buying such fruits, as a
> purchaser of stolen goods.'

The Africans were thus deprived of the right to gather fruit of whatever
sort in their own forests. The Belgian merchants of the Congo also lost
the right to buy anything from the Africans. They protested, however,
and the right was restored. But the peasants' right to the land was not
restored. Having thus usurped the peasant lands, the government began
trading in it, leasing concessions to European trading companies. The
quantity of land leased in concessions was not measured in hectares or
thousands of hectares, but in whole districts — the A.B.I.R. Company, for
example, gained a concession in the two river basins of the Lopori and the
Maringa. In 1901, 13 companies were established, which, in a few years,
merged to form the one giant Compagnie du Kasai, which held a concession
on virtually the whole of the Congo.

## Forced Labour Introduced

The problem was then to make the blacks gather rubber. In this vast,
sparsely populated and unexplored area, expropriation of the land was on
its own insufficient. It was necessary to force the indigenous population
to work on plantations or gather the fruits of wild trees in the forests. As
for the blacks, they showed no inclination to become the white expropriators' slaves.

To carry raw materials out of the country, roads and railways were
needed, and also black Africans as bearers where these were unavailable:

> 'The rapid expansion in the production of any industrial crop —
> cotton, for example — creates an immediate demand for a large
> number of native workers for working in the fields, cotton ginning
> factories, the construction of new roads, railways and harbours, and
> for warehouses and transport. A labour shortage immediately
> becomes a matter of Government concern.' (Ormsby Gore,
> Secretary to the British Colonial Office)

The imperialists' solution to this problem in all the colonies, particularly the Congo, was the introduction of the forced labour system.
The Belgian imperialists introduced forced labour in the earliest days
of the 'civilizing' activity in the form of a tax in kind levied on the black
population. It was the duty of each African to supply a company with
a certain number of kilogrammes of rubber. The fixing of the level of
this tax was left to the company agents, who received a bonus for
delivering extra rubber. It has already been shown how the imperialists
used this tax to make the people gather rubber. (In addition to this
tax, the people also had an obligation to supply food for company
officials and employees.)

> 'Thus the Bumba sub-district, consisting of 100 households, had to
> supply 5 sheep or pigs, 50 chickens, 60 kg of rubber, 125 baskets of

manioc, 15 kg of maize and 15 kg of sweet potatoes every month. In addition, one man in ten had to perform various types of work on the orders of the authorities, and each year one man left the village to join the colonial army. Moreover, the entire tribe had to labour on public works every four days.'[2]

## Palm Oil Plantations Replace Wild Rubber Gathering

Such were the first fruits of Belgian imperialism's 'civilizing' mission in the Congo. The problem, however, had been solved. In 1891 rubber to the value of Fr.300,000, was exported from the Congo. In 1896 the value had reached Fr.6,600,000, and by 1905, Fr.44,000,000. From 1915 onwards, however, exports of rubber systematically declined, falling to Fr.5,500,000 by 1924. The reasons for this decline were, firstly, the annihilation of most of the population (8.5 million remaining out of an original 30.4 million) thus leaving scarcely anybody to gather the rubber, and, secondly, the development of the mining industry and palm plantations. Together with rubber, palm trees are the basic wealth of the forests of the Belgian Congo. In 1911, the British soap manufacturers, Lever Bros., gained a concession on 750,000 hectares for growing palm trees. (Belgium is 2½ times smaller in area than this concession). The Colonisation Agricole au Mayumbe then obtained a concession on 20,000 hectares, and Omnium Africaine a concession on 90,000 hectares. Thus approximately 40 companies divided the entire territory of the Congo among themselves. It is typical that for the majority of companies one of the conditions of the lease is that, on its expiry, the land shall become company property.

With the establishment of palm plantations and the development of the mining industry, the problem of using African labour became more acute and altered to some extent. The African's labour was now not only required for gathering and carrying rubber, but for the most diverse functions of the imperialists' colonial economy. The labour of the black population was no longer claimed by one or two rubber companies, but by 30 to 40 different firms. Taxes in kind, in the form of gathering rubber, were no longer a solution and had to be abolished. Different measures for the coercion of Africans living on plantation lands were necessary. This section of the peasantry, landless and deprived of the right to gather fruit in the forests now owned by the companies, was forced either to go to the towns (impossible without a pass, which the local official, acting in the company's interests, would not grant them) or to obey the demands of the company. The company needed palm kernels, and the peasant was sent into the forest to gather them. This, however, did not solve the labour problem. Labour had to be engaged from other areas, and even from other colonies. What was needed were measures which would make an African from a different locality come to work on the plantations. One such measure was taxation. It was necessary to create a need for money on the part of the peasant, and on a scale such that he could not satisfy it from the produce of his own farming. This problem was to be solved by taxing him, which in addition financed the apparatus to oppress him. From Fr.30,000,000 in 1914, the colonial government's budget rose to Fr.147,000,000 in 1924 and Fr.690,000,000 in 1930.

## Taxation — Another Method to Get Forced Labour

Taxation is the prime source of government income, and takes the form of direct taxation of the indigenous population, and of imposing duties on exports and imports, which are mostly transferred to the shoulders of the African people as buyers of imported goods. In 1930, direct taxation made up 39% of total government income. Tax is levied on all Africans, and the total tax raised has grown from year to year. Fr.15,550,000 was raised in 1920, Fr.26,949,000 in 1923, Fr.45,000,000 in 1926, and finally Fr.269,000,000 in 1930, a sixfold increase in total tax revenue over four years. Distributed over the total population, including the non-working population, this total amounts to Fr.31.7 per person. If we assume, however, that only one-third of the population is self-supporting, the total tax per self-supporting taxpayer rises to an annual Fr.93.21. Here it must be remembered that the peasant, in fact, pays more than this, since the system of using the chiefs as tax collectors and the payment of commission to them, leads to a great deal of abuse by the chiefs and officials. Export and import duties account for 33.5% of total government income, amounting to Fr.231,265,000 in 1930. The European population of the country is only 25,000. Thus the bulk of imported goods is purchased by the Africans who therefore pay most of the duty collected. Imported manufactured goods, for example, carry a duty of 25% of their value. In 1923, Africans purchased manufactured goods to the value of Fr.41,000,000, thus paying over Fr.10,000,000 in duty to the government. Income tax, which is levied on trading and mining companies, makes up only 4% of the colonial government's total revenue. Here it is interesting to note a further feature of the colonial budget. In 1925, out of a budget of Fr.273,294,990, Fr.7,000,000 was spent on maintaining prisoners, Fr.33,500,000 on the army, Fr.8,000,000 on aid to African agriculture, and Fr.10,000,000 on African education. The government thus spent Fr.40,500,000 on prisons and the army, and only Fr.18,000,000 on aid to African agriculture and education. In the language of the imperialists this is known as the 'civilizing mission of the white man'. This system of taxation is a rather strong method. Before the present economic crisis, the peasant had to sell at least 128 kg of palm kernels to European merchants in order just to pay his direct taxes.

To the Russian reader it will not be quite clear what is involved in gathering 128 kg of palm kernels. One firstly needs to know that the usual height of a palm tree is 11 to 13 metres, and that the nuts grow at the very top of the tree. One needs much strength to climb a tree without branches twice a day, to say nothing of the considerable danger involved. We are told by comrades from Africa, who have gathered palm nuts themselves, that two to three months of intensive work are needed to accumulate 128 kg. To pay his taxes, the black peasant has to choose between climbing trees for nuts for two to three months, or earning the money by going to work for a European plantation owner. The majority opt for the first of these: they prefer climbing trees to slavery on the plantations, if only to retain their freedom. And in any case, apart from the bestial working conditions and treatment on the plantations, the system of wages gives the peasant no chance of earning enough to pay the taxes. The colonial government is itself aware of this. In his report for 1924, the Governor General of the Belgian Congo wrote that: 'Industry and trade meet with thousands of difficulties in obtaining workers.' This is explained by: 'the disproportion between wages and the value of agricultural produce. In a few days a peasant can earn the monthly wage of natives working for Europeans.' Hence the difficulty is not that there are no workers, or that the peasant does not want to work, but that European plantation owners and mining industrialists want cheap or almost free labour. Under such circumstances taxation, though onerous, is not enough in itself to make the peasant go to work on the plantation.

## Labour Contracts — Yet Another Device

Administrative pressure was then applied to the Africans. In 1922 the Governor General instructed his officials:

'Under no circumstances whatsoever should it be permitted to occur that a peasant, who has paid his taxes and other legally required obligations, should be left with nothing to do. The moral authority of the administrator, persuasion, encouragement and other measures should be adopted to make the native work.'

He later wrote that anyone telling an African that he need not work if he has enough money to pay his taxes, was an enemy of the colony. Private entrepreneurs are forbidden to use forced labour by the constitution of the Belgian Congo, but this does not prevent them from using it under the guise of a contract with Africans. Each company has an extensive network of agents who tour the villages making contracts with the black population. It is the duty of local officials to give every assistance to these agents. As the Governor General of the Belgian Congo wrote to his agents:

'Administrative and moral pressure on the part of the sub-districts administrator is essential to the satisfactory recruiting of labour. Every adult native must be strictly obliged to work for a certain period of time.'

And one local official wrote in his report:

'As I have already stated in my previous report, the agents make use

of the administrator's assistance in recruiting labour. They are
convinced that they have a right to such assistance, and that the
administrator's only reason for existence is to recruit labour for
them.'

The chiefs have a duty to use their authority and make their people sign
the contracts. Chiefs who are not sufficiently energetic in assisting the
agents are either transferred to a lower grade, which means a cut in salary,
or are simply replaced.

Every method has been used to make Africans sign these contracts:
taxes, low prices for their products, and straightforward coercion. Clearly
such a contract does not constitute the free hire and sale of labour. Africans
so recruited are despatched in batches of 50 to 250 on a journey, by stages,
to the place of work. Current legislation fixes the daily travelling distance
at 30 km, with one rest day every six days. Considering that some of the
Africans recruited live one to two thousand km from their place of work,
it follows that they spend approximately two months in travelling time alone.
The length of work is usually stipulated as nine months by the contract,
but since festival days, rest days and illness are not included in this period,
work usually lasts 12 to 14 months. If one adds the journey by stages in
both directions, it turns out that the worker is away from home for almost
two years. Breach of contract, or leaving work before expiry of the
contract, are regarded as criminal offences, and are punishable by two to
four months' imprisonment. After serving his sentence, during which the
African also performs work for the state or for a private individual, he is
returned to his hirer, and continues to work off the remainder of his
contract. Despite these draconian measures, 20 to 30% of all workers
recruited desert from work.

## The Plantation System

For gathering nuts, Lever Bros. organized the use of such recruited
labour as follows. Several hundred trading stations were set up in their
concession territory. Each such trading station constitutes a small village
of about 100 persons with a company agent in charge. The village has a
company store and shop where Africans buy the goods they need.
Adjoining each hut is a small garden plot of 100 square metres where the
African peasant grows his essential vegetables. Some villages have large
communal kitchen gardens. This is all the land that he possesses. Each
inhabitant of the trading station has to gather 36 'clusters'[3] per week, for
which he receives Fr.7.20, or 20 centimes per cluster, from the company
agent. A worker who has worked a complete week and fulfilled the norm
receives an extra Fr.2.10 for food and 3 kg of rice. The firm has 12
factories producing palm oil, and another 12 producing soap from this oil
— over 20,000 workers being employed in the factories and trading
stations of the concessions. Exports of palm kernels and oil from the

Belgian Congo (see Table 3.1) have risen steadily right up to the time of the present economic crisis.

TABLE 3.1

EXPORTS OF PALM KERNELS AND OIL, BELGIAN CONGO
(1900-1930)

| Palm Kernels | | | Palm Oil | |
|---|---|---|---|---|
| Year | Tons | Value (Fr.1,000) | Tons | Value (Fr.1,000) |
| 1900 | 4,776 | 1,297 | 1,505 | 738 |
| 1905 | 807 | 1,489 | 1,726 | 936 |
| 1910 | 5,436 | 1,958 | 2,005 | 1,341 |
| 1915 | 7,778 | 3,683 | 2,428 | 1,556 |
| 1920 | 39,457 | 58,990 | 7,624 | 18,511 |
| 1927 | 74,007 | 151,716 | 18,373 | 64,305 |
| 1929 | 75,388 | 154,546 | 30,296 | 98,463 |
| 1930 | 66,356 | 99,535 | 36,989 | 110,966 |

In addition to oil palm plantations, there are large plantations of coffee in Eastern province and Mayumbe district, and of rubber, cotton and other crops. But palm plantations occupy the most important place. The proportion of the various crops in agricultural exports for 1928 is shown in Table 3.2:

TABLE 3.2

AGRICULTURAL EXPORTS FROM THE BELGIAN CONGO, 1928

| | Value (Fr.1,000) | Percentage of Total Agricultural Exports |
|---|---|---|
| Oil palm products | 234,862 | 59 |
| Coffee | 5,578 | 1.4 |
| Cocoa | 8,244 | 2.7 |
| Rubber | 14,297 | 3.6 |
| Cotton | 102,498 | 26 |
| Copal | 31,943 | 7.4 |

As can be seen from Table 3.2, the products of the oil palm, the harvesting and processing of which is virtually monopolized by Lever Bros., account for the bulk of agricultural exports.

Of the remaining plantations, the Forminiere plantation in Kasai province is of considerable interest: the company has large diamond workings in the province, and about 30,000 Africans work in the mines. The problem arose of supplying food for the workers. In general, the Belgian Congo is poorly endowed with railway lines. The total length of the railway network is only 0.17 km of track per 1,000 square kilometres of land, whereas, even in British West Africa there are 0.30 km per 100 square kilometres. In Kasai province there are no railways at all, and the delivery of food from other districts is extremely difficult. Thousands of African bearers were employed, but it was still impossible to supply adequately the mining region's population with foodstuffs from outside the region. The mining companies then gave the local people small plots of land, and set up a number of plantations for cereal crops. Thus in 1922, Forminiere obtained a concession of 75,000 hectares from the government and set up a number of large plantations upon it. Labour for these plantations, like that for the mines, is recruited by coercion. The average wage of an agricultural worker on such a plantation is around Fr.30 per 30 working days. The British imperialist journal *African World*, for 9th April 1932, writes of a similar case:

> 'The Aketi-Buta railway line is at present being extended eastwards. The line will reach Titule and Zobia by the end of the year. Lienart, the railway's chief controller, has said that when the line reaches the Kilo-Moto goldfields, the company will be able to transfer to work in the mines the 3,000 natives at present bringing up food for the 22,000 native mineworkers, since the railway will provide the mines with food from the western agricultural districts. This increase of 3,000 in the workforce will raise the output of gold by 1,000 kg per year, and yield an additional profit of Fr.15,000,000.'

## Conclusions

The colonial government of the Belgian Congo is thus solving the labour problem by dispossessing the peasants of land, taxing them at extortionate rates, and finally by direct coercive means. Blacks continue to be hunted as they were in the era of the slave trade. Admittedly such hunting is now carried on by more 'civilized' methods, and in a more organized fashion, but this is of no benefit to the peasant. Just as the ancestors of today's black population were once enslaved on the plantations of North America, so have hundreds of thousands been made semi-slaves on European plantations. Hundreds of thousands more have been driven underground to mine gold, diamonds and copper for the European imperialists. 15,000 blacks have been put in uniform and made, by oppressing their brothers, to maintain 'law and order', or in other words to preserve the right of the imperialists to enslave and exploit the toiling masses of the Congo and maintain, uninterrupted, their parasitic feeding upon the enslaved population. A fourth, and quite considerable, part of the black workers of the Congo are small peasant farmers. But even they are not free. They are serfs of imperialism, paying quit rent in kind. They have to grow what they are told to by the government. In the districts of Maniema, Sankuru and

Uele, for example, the government makes every peasant grow at least one hectare of cotton. One hectare of cotton, however, requires as much labour as five hectares of grain. Given the low productivity of peasant farming and its extremely primitive implements, this is all that the peasant can cultivate. Hence all his labour is taken up growing cotton which, in this time of capitalist crisis, he now cannot sell. In the Mweru district of Tanganyika, the government has, in contrast, forbidden the peasants to sow cotton. This region has mines which must be supplied with food. The government has responded to the mining companies by making the peasants sow cereals. Thus even this small section of the peasantry has been placed directly at the service of the mining companies and the textile industry of the metropolis. In the Belgian Congo, the 'cultural and educative' role of the imperialist states in the colonies, of which so much is said by both the imperialists and their lackeys from the camp of social fascism, boils down to that of executioner.

Let us now turn again to South Africa, which is ruled by British rather than Belgian imperialism. Here, though perhaps better organized, we shall find the self-same slavery.

## FORCED LABOUR ON THE EUROPEAN FARMS OF SOUTH AFRICA

British imperialism has expropriated virtually all (93%) of the land of the indigenous peasantry in the Union of South Africa, and has set up large farms. It has tied one half of the peasantry to these European farms, and has herded the other on to reserves, turning it into a reserve pool of labour. European farming has monopolized all the most important sectors of the Union of South Africa's agriculture. It produces 98% of the total wheat harvest, 75% of the maize, and approximately 100% of the sugar cane and other industrial crops. European farmers own 90% of merino sheep, 86% of angora goats, and produce 93% of the country's wool. In short, the white farmers have captured all the commanding heights of the agricultural sector of the Union. As a rule such farming is run on a large scale, and is based on the use of hired labour (using this term of capitalist relations in a relative sense). According to the most recent census of 1929-30, there were 94,908 farms in the Union, with a total land area of 204,254,511 acres, an average of 2,152 acres per farm. They can be grouped as follows by land area: (see Table 3.3 overleaf).

The smallest three groups account for 21% of the total number of farms, but own only 0.6% of all farm land. Among these farms there are, no doubt, a considerable number which make no use of hired labour; rather most of these are suburban farms (market gardens and small holdings) run on pure capitalist lines. The rest are run on a large scale and based on semi-serfdom, and in some places complete serfdom.

TABLE 3.3

DISTRIBUTION OF LANDHOLDINGS IN SOUTH AFRICA
(ACRES) +

| Size of Farm | | No. of Farms | Total Land Area | Average Farm Size |
|---|---|---|---|---|
| 0.0 — | 10.6 | 3,585 | 17,700 | 5 |
| 10.6 — | 46.3 | 7,774 | 168,987 | 22 |
| 46.3 — | 211.7 | 8,560 | 1,058,381 | 124 |
| 211.7 — | 1,058.5 | 29,356 | 18,596,656 | 633 |
| 1,058.5 — | 2,117 | 19,154 | 29,979,309 | 1,565 |
| 2,117 — | 4,234 | 13,132 | 39,995,719 | 3,046 |
| 4,234 — | 6,351 | 4,595 | 24,430,381 | 5,338 |
| 6,351 — | 10,585 | 3,643 | 29,944,078 | 8,220 |
| 10,585 — | 21,117 | 2,175 | 32,373,087 | 14,884 |
| 21,117 and over | | 865 | 30,348,624 | 35,085 |

+ Original in morgen. Converted at 1 morgen = 2.117 acres. Certain
calculations were missing in the original and have been added here.

In 1928-29, the total sown area of industrial grain crops on European
farms was 7,551,333 acres. Maize is the largest in sown area — 74% of total
sown area in the Union, 94% in Natal, 89% in both the Transvaal and Orange
Free State, and 17% in the Cape Province. Most of the maize is concentrated
in the Transvaal and the Orange Free State. Maize constitutes 100% of
sown area in a number of districts. There are farms which sow 1,059 acres
of maize or more. Wheat is second in sown area — 11.5% of the total Union
sown area. 71% of all wheat is sown in the Cape Province. Notable industrial
crops are cotton — sown area 42,332 acres, tobacco — 24,443 acres, and
sugar — 635,100 acres. (Sugar plantations are found only in the Province
of Natal).

A further element in the agricultural production of European farmers is
livestock, in which sheep farming is predominant. There are 40,056,185
sheep and 3,402,561 goats on European farms. Sheep are bred mainly in
the Cape Province (47%) and the Orange Free State (34%). Farmers gather
10,000 tons of wool per year from these flocks.

## The White Farmers Need Cheap Labour

Technically, European farming is very backward. There are about 1,500
tractors on the 95,000 farms, viz., about 1.6% of farms have a tractor. The
farms use a total of 3,600 gas, oil and petrol engines, 1,760 steam-driven
engines, and 1,080 electrical machines, or in other words only 6.7% of
farms use power (assuming only one machine per farm). Horses and mules
are the basic source of traction. Little use is likewise made of more complex

agricultural machinery. Cheap, or even cost-free African labour provides no incentive to introduce machinery. In a letter to *The Farmer's Weekly*, a farmer compared the use of tractors in America and South Africa:

'America has a cheap tractor, cheap fuel, and expensive labour. Tractors and fuel are expensive here, but we do have cheap labour, so we are not forced to spend large sums of money to save on it.'

This is still further confirmation of Lenin's statement that:

'In economies where labour is regulated, wages are much lower than where free hired labour is used; and it is a well known fact that low wages are one of the main obstacles to the introduction of machinery.'

Here one must also bear in mind that the use of complex machinery in agriculture demands a well-developed road network and a system of repair shops and factories. South Africa has neither. Here the one thing we are concerned to establish is that such large-scale farming is founded exclusively upon manual labour, and that the problem of finding labour is of exceptional importance to the farmer-landowners. Complaints from farmers about labour shortages are of everyday occurrence in South Africa. Open any issue of *The Farmer's Weekly* and you will find two or three letters from farmers on this subject. Here is a letter from a large farmer with 1059 acres of irrigated land in the Barberton district:

'The natives of the neighbouring reserves live practically without spending any money. They have good land and harvest an adequate quantity of food from it. Therefore they do not want to go and work on the farms, even when offered £3 a month. This year the position of the farmers has been made considerably worse by the fact that the natives have had a good harvest. A further explanation of the native's refusal to work is the fact that the municipality and the railways offer higher wages for a shorter working day.'
*(The Farmer's Weekly,* 10th July, 1929)

In its report for 1930-32, the Native Economic Commission (a special commission of the government) wrote that complaints of labour shortage were a phenomenon encountered everywhere. Beggarly wages, bad food, poor living conditions and a working day lasting from sunrise to sunset, force the African to go anywhere but to the farm to look for a wage. The fact that the complicated pass system in South Africa generally hinders the influx of free labour must also be borne in mind. It is not only the farmers who complain of the labour shortage, but also the mine owners, and this at a time when a colossal reserve army of labour exists, mainly in a hidden form. This contradiction of the considerable relative over-population of the reserves and a simultaneous labour shortage is the result of the contradictions of colonial economic policy and of the policies of the white imperialists in South Africa. The imperialists' answer to this contradiction is the imposition of forced labour in all its various forms. In the case of European farming, the most widespread form of forced labour is the system of tenant workers who, in South Africa are frequently referred to as squatters and constitute the main body of farm workers.

## Tenant Workers as Forced Labour

A tenant worker is a peasant receiving a plot of land from a landowner, and having to work for the landowner for a certain amount of time in return. The economic basis of this system has already been exposed: on the one hand masses of landless African peasants, and on the other the concentration of a colossal amount of land in the hands of white landowners. Land in the hands of the white landowner is in this case a means of guaranteeing a supply of labour and of tying the peasant to his farm. This however, as we shall see below, has not proved on its own to be enough to make serfs of the peasantry. The relations developing from this system are therefore becoming incorporated in government legislation, thus turning such serfdom into a fully fledged, legally enforced system.

At present, about 1.3 million people live on European farms as tenant workers, or, taking five as the size of the average family, 260,000 peasant families. From the farmer, a family receives an area of ploughland, the right to pasture a certain number of livestock, a plot for building their hut, and building materials. In each case the area of ploughland is determined individually by agreement between the peasant and the farmer, or rather at the arbitrary decision of the farmer, since the peasant has no choice. The size of this area ranges from five acres per family in the Orange Free State to 50 acres in Natal. The African, however, who has neither the means nor the time, rarely cultivates more than five acres.

Statistics yield no information regarding how much land is sown by Africans on European farms. If, however, we take the 1928-29 harvest of maize and millet of this section of the peasantry, and divide it by the average yield of these crops on European farms, reduced by 10%, we get a sown area of 596,994 acres for maize, and 221,381 acres for millet. Apart from maize and millet, the black peasants on European farms sow virtually nothing. We thus arrive at a sown area of 818,633 acres, or 3.18 acres per family. From this area, in 1928-29 the peasants harvested 1,401,609 bags of maize, or 5.5 bags per family of five, and 418,294 bags of millet, or 1.6 bags per family. (This, incidentally, further confirms our reckoning of 3.18 acres sown per family.) The peasant has no (legal) right to the land that he cultivates, and can be evicted at any time by the farmer.

During the last decade there has been an increasing tendency to reduce the area of ploughland allocated to peasants owing to an increase in land prices and an expansion of European farming, particularly sheep farming (total flocks of long-haired sheep have risen from 11,000,000 in 1904 to 38,000,000 in 1928). In 1928-29, so-called squatters on the European farms sowed no maize in 71 districts of the Union (mainly in the Cape Province), sowed no millet in 113 districts, and sowed nothing at all in 70 districts. In most cases the peasant uses the farmer's equipment to work the land he is given. Only 48,180 families, i.e. 18% of all peasant households on European farms, have a plough. (This assumes only one plough per family.

A considerable number of peasants use a plough belonging to other peasants of their own tribe.) The majority, however, obtain a plough from the farmer. The same thing applies to draught animals. The total African agricultural population owns 170,690 horses, 133,000 donkeys, and 2,770 mules, or, assuming an even distribution of working livestock throughout the Union and throughout all sectors of the peasantry, only 39% of peasant households own a single head of working livestock. One can, of course, find better-off peasants both on European farms and especially on the reserves who have more than one horse, and who use this advantage for their own self-enrichment by exploiting peasants of their own tribe. But the average figures show that the peasant on a European farm has to use the farmer's implements and working livestock. In the Albany district, for instance, of the peasant farms surveyed by the Native Commission, 35% use the farmer's plough and working livestock, for which they pay part, or sometimes all of their milk, receiving skim-milk in exchange.

Along with ploughland, the peasant is given the right to pasture livestock. The amount of livestock is strictly limited, varying from region to region. Thus, for example, in the Albany district, on 31st August 1931, 3,500 families owned 7,126 head of cattle (or two per family), 82 pigs, and 71 sheep. In the Benoni district, 10,000 peasant families owned 32,460[4] head of cattle (or three per family), 223 pigs and 95 sheep. On average, each peasant family on a European farm owns 6 head of cattle, 0.5 pigs, 2.1 sheep, and 4.3 goats. In 27 districts the peasants have no livestock whatsoever.

In return for this land, the peasant has to work for the farmer. Until recently the duration of the period of work has varied between 90 and 180 days annually, but the latest law on peasant affairs has laid down a uniform period of 180 days on all farms. These 180 days are spread throughout the year, the farmer making use of the peasant whenever he is needed. There is no established system of wages for such work, everything depending on the arbitrary decision of the farmer. Of the 16 districts of the Cape and Natal provinces for which we have data, such work is entirely unpaid in nine of them, and is paid in the remaining seven, though not on all farms. The monthly wage ranges between 5/- in Alexandria, 10/- in Wodehouse* and 20/- in the Alfred district, and averages 10/-. In a number of places work is paid for in kind. During a period of work, the peasant is given food, and sometimes his master's discarded clothing at a reduced price.

Under such working conditions the peasant never has any money to pay his taxes or buy essential goods. It should be pointed out that the peasant's harvest from the plot which he is given (of which many have none) is rarely sufficient to feed his family, and as a rule the peasant has to buy his food as well as his manufactured goods from the farmer or from a European trader. In its report, the Native Commission notes widespread indebtedness among the peasants, which is a further means of tying them to the farm. The shortage of money forces the peasant to go to the town after his 180 days of work on the farm to earn the money he needs. The farmer usually allows the peasant three to four months leave of absence during the slack season on the farm, and issues him with a pass for that period. In certain districts, such as Bredasdorp, Africans have no right at all to leave the farm, in which case the farmer pays the £1 tax for each African, later deducting it from his wages. In many cases, peasants, particularly youths, break the pass laws and return to the farm late or not at all.

The farmers are all united in a storm of protest over the Africans' flight from the farms and the shortage of labour at times of high demand. In 1932, in response to the demands of the farming community, the government adopted a new and draconic law on African farm labour, the so-called 'Native Servant Contract Act', the basic provisions of which are as follows. (1) The peasant is obliged to perform an annual 180 days work for the farmer. The farmer is entitled to refuse him leave to earn wages in the town if he finds it profitable to do so. (2) No-one is entitled to hire a peasant if he lacks a pass certifying that he has leave from the farmer, or if that pass has expired. (3) Should a farmer sell his land, the peasant will pass to the new owner along with that land. (4) The peasant may be punished by being caned for infringing this law, impudence towards his master, or for negligence towards his work.

What, one may ask, is the difference between this draconian law and the 'good old days' of the Russian landowner Saltychikha?[5] And yet the white 'civilizers' dare to say that they have no forced labour!

In concluding this outline of the position of these tenant workers, we quote one of their own number. An old peasant told Professor Jabavu (a national-reformist leader) that:

> 'the size of his flock was extremely limited and any surplus has to be sold to his master at half price. He had to give his cream to his master in payment for the right to pasture livestock on his land. Living conditions were disgusting, especially in the rainy season. The only food consisted of boiled maize with no meat, except on the rare occasion when a cow died.'

Professor Jabavu himself writes:

> 'The landlord's rule is so unlimited and ruthless that he locks his tenant workers in the punishment cell for the most minor and trivial misunderstandings. Under the laws of 1913, they are liable to sudden and arbitrary eviction by the farmer. There are many cruel and brutish employers who use the whip and other physical methods of coercion.'[6]

These conditions, we might add, must somewhat hinder the esteemed Professor's political efforts to create harmony between the European serf-owners and the African peasantry.

## Seasonal Workers — The Essential Reserve Army

Peasant tenant workers, as already explained, make up the main body of workers on European farms. At harvest time, however, the labour of the peasant and his family is insufficient, and the farmer engages additional seasonal workers. A considerable number of European farmers, moreover, who are farming land which they have rented or purchased, cannot allot land to tenant workers, and therefore run their farms with a number of workers whom they employ throughout the year, engaging additional seasonal labour when the work load is heavy. Tobacco, cotton and sugar-cane plantations are worked predominantly by seasonal labour. In addition to the 1,200,000 serfs who occupy plots on the European farms, these 'civilized' serf owners have a further special reserve of labour, namely the native reserves, where there is always an adequate quantity of labour available, and where the majority of peasants are constantly in need of supplementary outside earnings.

But the working conditions created by the farmers are such that no one would willingly go to work on the farms. However, with the help of the colonial government, the farmers have sufficient means at their disposal to force the peasantry of the reserves to work on the farms. In constant need of money, the peasant in the reserve usually falls into the clutches of the trader or the money-lender. Once entangled in debts, he must either perform forced labour in prison, or sign a contract with a recruiting company to work on a farm or in the mines, obtain an advance, and thereby pay off his debts. Having signed a contract he cannot refuse to work, or he is threatened with forced labour and imprisonment. As in the Belgian Congo, an entire network of special organizations has been established, with an extensive system of offices and agents. These agents are issued with special licences for recruiting labour by the Department of Native Affairs. In 1930-31, 93 permits to recruit farmworkers were issued by the Department, 23 of which went to the Natal Coast Labour Recruiting Corporation, which mainly supplies seasonal workers for sugar plantations. For recruiting workers, the organization receives £2.5.0 for each contract worker from the farmer. The term of a contract is between three and six months, in most cases six.

Farm working conditions are very hard. The working day is limited only by the rising and setting of the sun. Machines are few, all basic tasks being done by hand. Labourers work throughout the day under the eye of European supervisors. The verbal abuse and beating of workers is an everyday occurrence. As the Native Commission has stated, living conditions leave a great deal to be desired. Workers live in hurriedly built huts and barracks, which become flooded after the slightest fall of rain. Although they are given food by the landowner, it consists mainly of maize in all its many forms, indeed maize is the only food on a considerable proportion of farms. On dairy farms, the workers are given skim-milk and other waste products. They receive no milk at all on arable farms. Meat is hardly ever seen. The Native Commission writes in its report that:

> 'The carcasses of sheep, goats and other animals which have died as a result of age or disease, and in some cases the heads, feet and entrails of animals slaughtered for the farmer, are given to the workers.'

The wage level of seasonal workers varies considerably. On sugar-cane plantations, the monthly wage of an adult worker varies between £1.15.0 and £2.3.0 plus food. (During the cane-cutting season there are 40,000 workers, about 15,000 being recruited as seasonal workers, on the plantations.) The monthly wage of an Indian (Indians constitute the majority of sugar plantation workers) averages £3.0.0. An African youth receives between 5/- and 7/- per month. On the Barberton cotton farms, for example, the monthly wage of an adult African worker is about £1.10.0 per month. These are considered high wages, and are accounted for by the competition from the local mines. Young girls, who form a large part of the labour force during the cotton harvest, receive an average monthly wage of 15/-. On sheep farms, shepherds receive 10/- to 15/- per month in cash, three sheep, three buckets of maize, one pound of coffee, tobacco, soles for their shoes, and clothing. Shearing is paid on a piece rate basis — in Craddock, 1½d. per sheep and 1d. per goat. A good well-trained worker can shear 16 to 25 sheep per day, thus earning 2/- to 3/- daily. Only 1d. per sheep is paid in Elliott. Seasonal workers on arable farms are also paid on a piece rate basis. In Elliott, 1/6 per hundred sheaves is paid for harvesting wheat and oats, and 2d. to 3d. per bag for harvesting maize. In over-populated areas, remote from the mining centres, wages are substantially lower. Thus in Glen Grey, for instance, a contract worker receives between three and ten shillings per month.

The worker, however, does not receive even these utterly paltry wages in full. The journey from the worker's home in the reserves to the place of work is paid for by the farmer through the recruiting organizations, and is subsequently deducted from the worker's wages. The rail journey consumes up to 40% of an entire six month's wages. Sugar plantation workers, for example, are recruited mainly in the Transkei and Pondo and assembled at Durban, and thence distributed to the farms. The cost of the journey from home to Durban is 30/- plus 30/- for the return, plus the cost of food during the journey, and of the journey from Durban to the farm. Taking the return fare to Durban alone, travelling expenses come to £3.0.0.

Taking 1/4d as the daily wage, a worker earns £12.0.0 during the 180 days of his contract. £9.0.0 remains after deduction of rail fares. A worker receives an advance of £2.0.0 upon signing the contract, which is usually spent immediately on paying off debts or taxes. Hence only £7.0.0 remains. Assuming that the fare and food for the return journey to his home cost the worker £1.0.0, the worker is left with £6.0.0 for six months' work. Considering that during these six months a worker must buy some items for personal use, such as tobacco and clothing, it becomes obvious that he has only worked for the advance which he received upon signing his contract, and which he has immediately spent in paying his taxes. The peasant's reluctance to work on the European farms is hence quite natural. And it is only the measures described above for coercion by other than economic means which are turning him into a contract (though in reality forced) seasonal labourer on the farms.

## FORCED LABOUR IN THE MINING INDUSTRY

We have established the fact that the imperialists exploit black workers either as small-scale peasant producers of commodities, or as semi-slaves and serfs on plantations and farms.

Let us now examine how imperialism exploits these same toilers as workers in the mining industry. Together with agriculture (the production of animal and vegetable raw materials), the extraction of minerals by the mining industry is a highly important factor in imperialism's policies in Black Africa. Black Africa is extremely rich in minerals, and in this respect offers abundant opportunities for capital investment and high profits. But this requires that the imperialist makes the African go down the mine to extract these minerals.

### The Labour Recruiting System

In all the countries of Black Africa the imperialists have solved this problem by the same method, that of forced labour in the form of contractual recruiting. In every single country of Black Africa, the mining industry relies on contract labour, which in actual fact again is forced labour. In all those African colonies in which the mining industry has been to any extent developed, recruiting is carried out by specially created recruiting companies, which in themselves constitute sizeable capitalist enterprises, making substantial sums of money from hunting blacks in this way. Let us consider the Union of South Africa.

At first, (1904-1911), the mining companies tried to deal with labour problems by importing workers from other countries, mainly Chinese and Indian 'coolies'. But with the development of the industry and the increase in demand for labour, this measure proved highly unprofitable, and had to be abandoned. In 1909 an agreement was signed with Portugal, under which the latter undertook the annual supply of 100,000 African workers from Mozambique. This agreement is still in force, and around 100,000 'slaves' from Mozambique are at present sent every year to the South African mines, where the capitalists use inhuman methods of exploitation in order to maximize profits. Only half of these slaves ever return to Mozambique.

This system, however, also does not satisfy the demand for labour. Entrepreneurs have introduced contractual recruiting of labour on an organized basis in South Africa itself. Several special companies with a large staff of special agents were created for this purpose. The Witwatersrand Native Labour Association (Wenela) has 75 stations in Mozambique, and employs 30 European and 250 African recruiting agents. The Native Recruiting Corporation, like the Witwatersrand Native Labour Association, also has its own agents throughout South Africa, while local and travelling commissioners are on permanent salary.[7] The Department of Native Affairs issues recruiting licences at a cost of between £1 and £50. A large number of recruiting agents are traders in the reserves. Thus they have two sources of profits: trading and recruiting. An agent receives £2 for every man recruited. The white shopkeepers in the reserves have found a quick route to riches in the recruiting system. They lend money to the peasants, not so much for the sake of the interest as for what they can make on recruiting Africans for the mines. They retrieve the money lent to the peasants, and receive commission from the mine owners and farmers. The high profits, and the favourable conditions for making them in this sphere attract not only the traders, but also numerous small private recruiting agents, not counting the Witwatersrand Native Labour Association and the Native Recruiting Corporation, which supply hundreds of men to the mines. In their pursuit of this particular class of slave, the recruiting agents are not above the practice of straightforward deception of those Africans who are reluctant to work in the mines. The agents announce that they are not recruiting for the mines, but for some other private business which pays higher rates. In so doing they sometimes give large advances and take their victims' passes, so that the Africans are in the end forced to sign the contract for work in the mines.

Mineworkers are recruited by similar means in the Belgian Congo, where three special recruiting companies have been established. In British West Africa, where the mining industry is as yet still poorly developed, and where fewer workers are thus needed, there are no special recruiting companies, and the mining companies do their own recruiting, which, of course, is of no greater benefit to the African workers.

## How The Miners Are Exploited

Those who have been herded into the mines are perhaps the most exploited and oppressed element of the population of Black Africa. Taking as our example the mines of South Africa, where the mining industry is more developed than in any other part of Black Africa, let us acquaint ourselves more closely with the material and legal position of black mine workers. The cost of living in South Africa is considerably higher than in any of the capitalist countries. Given below are comparative prices for various foods in South Africa and Britain. (The prices are pre-crisis.)

TABLE 3. 4

COMPARATIVE COST OF LIVING, SOUTH AFRICA AND
BRITAIN

|  | Britain | South Africa |
|---|---|---|
| Bread per lb. | 2d | 3½d |
| Butter | 1/1d | 2/1d |
| Bacon | 1/3d | 1/9d |
| Flour (25lbs.) | 4/4½d | 7/3d |

The wages of the black South African miner, on the other hand, are
perhaps the lowest in the capitalist world, and bear no comparison whatsoever with those of European and American miners. In 1929 the South
African mining industry employed 360,792 workers, of whom 322,615 or
90% were blacks, and the remaining 10% whites. White workers earn
several times more than black workers, even where the latter are performing
the same work as Europeans. In 1928-29 the wages of white miners ranged
between £251 and £288 per annum, whilst those of black miners never
exceeded £31. Consequently, the 10% of white miners received a total of
£10,901,318 in wages in 1929, whereas the 90% of black workers received
only £9,142,063. The wages of white South African workers are perhaps
the highest in the capitalist world — 30% higher than in Britain, and 50%
higher than in Berlin and Paris. In contrast, the wages of the blacks are the
lowest in the world. Before the crisis, the average wage of a black miner was
£2 a month (£3 to £4 in processing industries). The average daily wage of a
black miner before the present world crisis was 1/6, or £2.7.1 per month.

But the miner does not receive even this paltry wage in full. To begin
with, the cost of his journey from the reserve or country of recruitment
to the mine is deducted from his wages, and there are then monthly
stoppages of 2/- for his pass. No wages are paid for days of sickness or
temporary incapacitation, even when due to injuries sustained in the mine.
Days of sickness are not even counted against the length of contract.
Drillers are paid a piece rate of 7d per foot. A worker failing to drill three
feet in a shift has zero marked in his book, and is paid nothing. Further-
more, there is a wide variety of fines. For instance, the established
reception time for sick workers is 4.30, but if any patient presents himself
at around 5 o'clock, he is arrested for idling, imprisoned for 24 hours, and
his day's wages are kept by the company. Consequently, the miner earns
considerably less than £2.7.1 per month. His net income is even further
reduced, as a large part of his remaining pay is sent to the tribal chief or
village authorities to pay taxes. It must, moreover, be added that the black
worker can only make his necessary purchases in the company shop at the
mine, since in some diamond industry compounds the workers are not

allowed out for the entire duration of their contract, or are let out once a week, anyone returning after 9 p.m. being put in prison.

The imperialists of the Belgian Congo pay the miners even lower wages. Thus, according to the American bourgeois press, the miners of the Katanga copper mines are paid between 5.5 and 34 cents, depending upon length of service and the type of work done. In the Gold Coast, wages are just as low as they are in South Africa.

## Atrocious Working Conditions

The vast majority of South African mines work on a one or two shift basis. The working day lasts 12 to 14 hours. Working conditions underground are exceptionally hard, with suffocating heat, the miners working knee-deep in water, and experiencing appalling treatment. Mechanization is rare due to the cheapness of labour. All basic tasks such as rock drilling, loading ore and hauling tubs are done by hand. There are no effective safety measures.

An enormous number of accidents occur in the mines, and these have steadily increased in frequency during recent years. In 1924 the average number of accidents was 433, and increased to 466 in 1925, 472 in 1926, 672 in 1927, 785 in 1928, 889 in 1929, and in March 1931, 1,084. (The figures are from official statistics.) Taking the workforce as a whole, we obtain the following rate of accidents: in 1924, there were 27 per thousand workers; in 1927, 25, and in 1929, 29 per thousand workers.

It should also be noted that the number of accidents among blacks is higher than among whites. Thus in 1930 there were 24 accidents per thousand whites, and 29 per thousand black workers. In 1928, the number of fatal accidents was 742 (2 per thousand workers), 809 in 1929 (2.3 per thousand workers) and 846 in 1930 [8] (2.4 per thousand workers), whereas in the German mining industry, for example, the number of fatal accidents in 1930 was 1.7 per thousand. Despite frequent injuries, the black worker receives no injury benefits. It is true that there is a law on accident insurance, which stipulates that black workers sustaining injury at work must be compensated. The rates of compensation are ludicrously low — £1 to £20 for partial incapacitation and £30 to £50 for total incapacitation. Only those familiar with the law, however, are able to obtain compensation, and then only with the aid of a lawyer. This in effect means that black workers receive no compensation at all.

## Appalling Living Conditions

Living conditions are just as appalling as working conditions in the mines. The overwhelming majority of black workers live in compounds. Compounds are usually circular, and have one entrance which is guarded by police day and night. It is impossible to enter or leave the compound without a pass. Workers returning from work or from the town are frequently searched. Diamond mine compounds differ from the usual type by the fact that they are surrounded by thick walls, within which are located the mineworkings, factories and company shops where workers must make any necessary purchases. Once inside this camp, a worker cannot get out before his contract expires. Even after this, however, he has to spend several days in 'cleansing' quarantine, so that he cannot take with him any diamond which he may have swallowed. Workers do not sleep in separate beds in the compound, but on shared plank-beds arranged in several tiers. Forty to fifty men sleep in each room.

The living conditions of workers who live in the towns are no better. There they live in special black quarters on the outskirts of the town. In such quarters the black proletariat live in corrugated iron shacks, which are full to capacity due to the landless peasants moving to the towns, and continually swelling the population of the black quarters. Daily round-ups take place in the towns, resulting in numerous arrests of those blacks who have allowed themselves to fall asleep in the yards of factories located outside the black quarter. The interiors of the shacks inhabited by the blacks defy description — they are cold in winter and suffocatingly hot in summer. Two or three families live in a cramped, tiny room without a floor or a ceiling, with bare corrugated iron walls. Along these walls there are low shelves, arranged one above the other, on which the members of the various families sleep. Epidemics sweep through these huts as they do through the compounds. In 1918 more than 500,000 blacks, i.e. around 10% of the total population, died of influenza. In many black quarters the infant mortality rate is 900 per thousand. Rents for these shacks are extortionate. On the subject of the living conditions of black workers, the head of the Johannesburg City Department for Native Affairs wrote as follows:

'150,000 natives are employed in Johannesburg. 50,000 of them work in the mining industry, and are provided with housing, but the other 100,000 live wherever they can, paying enormous amounts of money for any slum that they can find. Things have reached the point where an enterprising individual will buy an old building, cram as many natives into it as he can, and charge them fantastic amounts for these "vice and crime-breeding" slums, in which at present 40,000 families live. Certain people are in favour of moving the natives out of town, but I consider that this would be unprofitable to Europeans from an economic point of view.'

The black workers are given food by the mine owners, who deduct its cost from their wages. We shall leave it to an actual miner to give us some idea of the quality of this food:

'The main food is *Makha*, a weak, watery soup, gruel made from spoilt maize flour, and occasionally in addition a dish made from beans or carrots. They are admittedly given meat once a week, but the pieces are so small that most workers don't even notice it. The so-called bread consists of small rolls made from maize and a negligible amount of (wheat) flour. Coffee is made from roasted maize. It is served only in the morning, and only to underground workers. For surface workers the main item of food for the duration of their contract is *makha.*'

Due to these working conditions, tuberculosis is incredibly widespread among black miners. It is an interesting fact that the health organizations look after only white miners. Thus in 1928, for example, periodic screening for tuberculosis covered 26,394 Europeans and only 108 black workers.

We shall not go into the situation of miners in the other countries of Africa, since their position in both the Belgian Congo and Rhodesia, and in the other parts of black Africa is basically the same, or at any rate no better than in South Africa.

# CONTRACT LABOUR, FORCED LABOUR AND SLAVERY

We have shown that the imperialists use African workers in the mines and on the plantations in the form of contract labour. We have seen that this labour, though formally contractual, is in actual fact forced, slave labour. The methods used by the imperialists to make the blacks sign contracts for mine or farm work are the confiscation of land and enslavement of the peasantry by the capital of traders and money-lenders, extortionate taxes, and finally direct coercion. By no means can this be considered the free hire and sale of labour. In reality, contract labour is forced labour, a specific form of slavery.

## Forced Labour and Slavery

The difference between this form of forced labour and straightforward slavery comes down to no more than the fact that, in this instance, enslavement is masked by a legal transaction: the agreement between the slave owner, designated in the contract as the hirer, and the slave, designated in the contract as the seller of labour. But this is a legal deal in which one party thereto, the black worker, is deprived of all rights, and forced into the bargain by administrative means. The bargain is a mere fiction, a fig-leaf concealing actual slavery. A further difference between forced labour and slavery is that the slave, the black African, is not the property of an individual. Imperialism, represented by its colonial governments, confronts as slave owner the toiling masses of Black Africa as slaves. The final difference between forced labour and slavery is that the depersonalized slave owner of imperialism takes no responsibility for looking after the black workers when it has no need of their labour. It merely leaves them a tiny patch of land, by the cultivation of which they maintain themselves as potential labour for the imperialists. These are the three features which distinguish forced labour from slavery in Black Africa. The slave's predicament, however, is not altered by whether or not his slavery is masked by some fictitious legal transaction. The African's position is not ameliorated by the fact that before starting work for his slave owner he has to sign a contract of slavery, or rather apply his fingerprint to a paper of whose contents he is quite ignorant. The position of the slave is not in the least improved by the fact that his owner is not an individual, but the imperialist system as a whole, as personified by colonial governments; on the contrary, this only makes his position worse. To the extent that the slave owner has a limited number of slaves, that they have been paid for, and are each one a commodity on whose sale he hopes to make a profit, the slave owner is obliged to show some concern for them. But these slaves in Africa cost the imperialists nothing, and the position of the black African slave is consequently even worse, particularly when the colonial government starts using his labour for its so-called public works.

## Mass Slave Labour for Railway Construction

The main area for the direct use of mass slave labour by colonial governments is railway construction. The aims and reasons for railway construction in Black Africa have been stated above. Let us now see how these railways were built in, for example, French Equatorial Africa and the Belgian Congo.

We have already mentioned the construction of the Brazzaville-Ocean Railway in French Equatorial Africa. The line is being laid through impenetrable virgin forest, with deep swamps teeming with poisonous snakes and lizards. The sun's rays never penetrate the undergrowth of this forest, which is consequently laden with unhealthy vapours and dense mists by night, as a result of which neither body nor clothing ever dries out. It is, moreover, a highly dissected area, with steep-faced hills, rivers and swamps. Several tunnels and a large number of bridges must be built. And so to build this railway, blacks from all parts of French Equatorial Africa have been herded together with neither their agreement nor even such fig-leaves as contracts of hire. Accompanied by soldiers, recruiting agents tour a reserve (i.e. a black settlement), and drive the inhabitants to the place of work. They are force-marched for hundreds and even thousands of kilometres. Those falling by the way are left to die. The blacks find no barracks or shelter when they reach the place of work. They live on bare ground, and eat manioc and bananas. They work, fall, and die. The same ditch is used for corpses and other purposes. In the event of a new shortage of labour, agents and armed men are sent off for further recruiting. On learning of the arrival of recruiting agents, the black population usually take refuge in the forests, leaving the villages completely empty. A round-up of the forest is then commenced, which becomes straightforward hunting. Those caught are sent off to the work-site.

Working conditions on the construction of this railway defy all description. We leave this to the French journalist, Londre,* who has visited the site, and writes as follows:

> 'I have seen how railways are built elsewhere. I have seen how special
> equipment and materials for track-laying are prepared in advance. But
> here blacks were used instead of machines and everything else. The
> Negro replaces machines, lorries and cranes, and if it were at all
> possible, he would be used as an explosive.
>
> The equipment used by Batignol Construction et Cie to load a
> 260 lb barrel of cement consists of one stick and two blacks. Here I
> came across two further highly 'improved' tools — the hammer and
> the hoe.
>
> At Mayombe we are to drive a tunnel with these tools. The blacks
> are dying like flies. Some time after arrival at Batignol*, only 5,000
> were left out of an original 8,000, then 4,000, and finally 1,700.
> New recruits must take their place. But what has been happening
> among the blacks?
>
> As soon as the whites began preparations for the construction of
> the railway, rumours about 'the machine', as the blacks refer to it,
> began to spread everywhere. The blacks knew that the whites were
> looking for labour to build the railway, and began to run away."You
> taught us yourselves"they told the missionaries, "that we must not
> commit suicide, but going to work on the 'machines' means death".
> They took refuge in the Chad Coast forests of the Belgian Congo. In
> once-inhabited areas, the recruiting agents found only chimpanzees.
> One can hardly build railways with monkeys, so we began to hunt
> the blacks, using every effort to catch them with lassoes and so on.
> We then put collars (as they are called here) on them. The human
> material thus recruited was not exactly the best. The mortality rate
> rose. "We must reckon to lose 6-8,000 men, said the Governor
> General, or do without the railways". The number who died was,
> however, much higher. Today it is over 17,000. We are tree-fellers in
> a forest of human beings.'

Another bourgeois journalist wrote in the reactionary paper *Les Temps* of
the 12th February 1929:

> 'During the first months of work in the Mayombe Hills all the natives
> were mown down, some by dysentery resulting from inadequate
> food and the lack of clean huts, others by lung infections due to
> climatic conditions, by starvation caused by the appalling organiz-
> ation of food supplies, and by exhaustion and overwork. Mortality
> on the Mayombe section of the line was over 60%. Of every 100,
> 60 die within a year. Each consignment of these slaves works for
> about two years. And how many return? So far 140 km of the line
> have been laid (work began 1929). We do not know exactly how
> many blacks perished on this section, but it was obviously at least as
> many as the number of rails laid. Some put the number of deaths at
> 18,000, i.e. 130 per kilometre.'

The same methods of railway construction are used in the Belgian
Congo. Every year hundreds of thousands are driven from every part of the
country to build railways and roads, to maintain shipping channels and
navigable rivers, and so forth. In Matadi, for instance, 14,000 Africans were
employed on railway construction in 1929. 2,000 of them were brought
from Eastern Province, 4,000 from Equatorial Province, 2,000 from

Makuyu district, 3,500 from Congo district, and 2,500 from Lower Congo. Some of them were thus driven to their place of work from districts lying over one thousand kilometres from the railway.

On 6th February 1926, the Belgian newspaper, *Information Colonial*, published in Kinshasa (Belgian Congo), reported the following facts regarding African labour on railway construction:

> 'Some natives were recently summoned by the administrator of Poko territory in the Upper Uele District, allegedly to work on a cotton farm in the area. The unsuspecting and well meaning natives responded to the Government representatives' call. A grim fate awaited them, however. As soon as they arrived at the administrative centre they were told that they must go to Leopoldville for railway construction work. They were dispatched a few days later, each one tied to the other by a rope aound the neck. It goes without saying that their wives were not allowed to accompany them. At the beginning of January, 150 natives of the Bangala tribe were in Lisala under reinforced police guard awaiting dispatch to Leopoldville. As for the conditions under which they were transported, they were simply diabolical. They travelled under scorching sun in overloaded open barges. The only food was rice without palm oil, and there were no utensils for preparing food.'

The working conditions on railway construction are no better in the Congo than they are in French Equatorial Africa. We again quote the words of a witness (a black worker's letter to the International Trade Union Committee of Negro Workers).

> 'I work on track repairs with a group of fellow villagers. Men work on one side of the track, women on the other. When a woman can't be sold or gets too old, she is made to do more work than a man. In scorching sunshine they carry large stones on their heads, level the ground and drag blocks of marble along, all to the sound of continual sad moaning. There is also a black overseer. The monotonous beating of a drum gives rhythm to the work, but when the music stops, the negro overseer brings down his whip on the shoulders of 50 or 100 male and female workers, passive, weakened and hungry. This is how we build the road to civilization. That's how progress goes. The engine's whistle blows where there was once the silence of the impenetrable forest. But the train runs on the bones of the thousands who died without even knowing what was this progress, in whose name they were made to work.'

This is also the way in which railways are built in British West Africa and other parts of Black Africa. As well as for building railways, the colonial government uses Africans to build other public works such as homes and country houses for European officials, laying urban water-pipes, building schools for European children and as porters, etc. When the European officials of Coquilhatville needed a well-made road for evening drives along the banks of the River Congo, the road was laid in four months by hundreds of blacks rounded up from surrounding villages.

## Other Forms of Slave Labour in Africa

Apart from this type of slave labour, however, there also exists the private ownership of slaves, slavery as a punishment for debt, and finally slave trading. In 1930, a book by the title of *Slavery* was published in England. Its author was Lady Simon.[9] This sentimental lady did not wish to depict the dreadful picture of slavery in Black Africa, particularly in the colonies of His Majesty the King, and she went no further than to draw to the attention of the esteemed capitalist public the fact that slavery still existed. However, despite the Lady's extreme caution, certain of her descriptions, according to the British papers, nevertheless evoked a feeling of 'cold horror'. According to Lady Simon's most cautious estimates, there are at present 6,000,000 slaves. Such is Lady Simon's estimate. But if one also considers the fact that during the present economic crisis the capitalists have been placing the brunt of it upon the shoulders of the oppressed colonial masses, and also the forms of exploitation applied to the indigenous population of the colonies, one needs to increase this figure several fold.

Slavery exists in all the colonies in one form or another. The most shameful of all forms of slavery has survived here, namely the debtor who sells himself into slavery. Thus slavery is flourishing in Africa, particularly under the British flag, despite its formal prohibition under British law. As Lady Simon says, Abyssinia leads in the development of slavery and the slave trade. Abyssinia has been a member of the League of Nations since 1932. In joining the League of Nations, Abyssinia bound itself to the eradication of slavery and the slave trade. However, it subsequently emerged that the entire budget of the Christian clergy and government is dependent upon the slave trade, the main clients of which are foreign concessionaries. The promise has remained on paper, and as before, slavery continues to flourish in Abyssinia. In October 1932, the British bourgeois papers reported that one of the reasons for the unrest in Abyssinia was the publication of proclamations announcing the emancipation of slaves without compensation. Headed by the Emperor's son, and supported by the imperialists, the Emperor's clique rebelled against the abolition of slavery under the slogan 'We will not introduce European novelties and do without our slaves'. At present the slave traders, with government permission, are organizing raids on the Abyssinian people and hunting them down like wild animals.

Arabia is the second largest slave trading country. One witness has stated that an average of no less than 5,000 men, women and children are annually delivered to Arabia for sale in the markets, a significant number of these slaves being from Britain's African colonies. The average price for an able-bodied slave varies between £80 and £100. Slave trading is officially permitted in Jiddah. A considerable proportion of the slaves are imported from Central and East Africa.

The Portuguese capitalists, however, have always held first place in the slave trade. To this day they have retained the palm of supremacy with honour. One year ago the Portuguese press announced that the colonial authorities had issued an order stating that Africans were to be forcibly sent to the island of Sao Tome, where labour is currently needed for the cocoa plantations. A system exists in the Portuguese colonies whereby workers can be put on a contract of several years' duration. An African who signs such a contract puts himself entirely at the mercy of his master. He can be beaten and even killed — so states the contract. In 1926 the Baldwin government confirmed a decree passed in a colony of His Majesty King George V, by the Southern Rhodesian authorities, on the use of African youths as slave labour, according to which the right was established to subject anyone not wishing to work to corporal punishment. In essence, this decree means that young men and women are obliged to work in the mines and on the plantations, and are whipped for refusal to do so. The Secretary of the Anti-Slavery Society has interpreted this law as being passed at the insistence of local white farmers who needed cheap labour. The 'workers' government of Ramsey MacDonald failed to repeal this law.

In another British colony in West Africa — Sierra Leone — slavery of the cruellest type has been flourishing for over 30 years. In 1926 the British Governor General decreed that every African born in, or brought into Sierra Leone must be free. This brought massive objections from the slave owners, and in 1926 the colony's Supreme Court argued that: 'None of the country's present laws can prevent a slave owner's use of force to retrieve an escaped slave.'[10]

In the 'free' Republic of Liberia slavery exists, as a correspondent of the *New York World* figuratively put it, in its classical form. In 1930 a League of Nations Commission visited this 'happy' Republic with the aim of throwing some light on the question of slavery. The picture of slavery exposed by the survey was a disquieting one, but since such surveys are confidential and not intended for the general public, the Commission decided to keep the matter quiet.[11]

Nevertheless, it emerged that among other highly respectable slave traders, a major role was played by the King of Spain himself, Alphonso XII, to whom slaves were sold by the Liberian Government for use on the Spanish-owned island of Fernando Po. In the same way the Liberian Government sold black Africans to French plantation owners on an island off the Dahomey coast. The government also forcibly recruited workers from the indigenous population for Firestone's rubber plantations in Liberia itself. The Commission, moreover, was convinced that certain tribes stole each other's members and sold them into slavery. In addition it was found that in Liberia men and women are not only sold, but are also mortgaged, and become the object of all sorts of commercial operations.

Here it is of some interest to quote from a letter by a leader of the African national reformists, in which he described his journey around Africa:

'When I visited Lobito Bay in April 1927, I saw several thousand black Africans herded into a barn rather like a corral for bulls. They had to spend several nights in that barn in the cold of the monsoon, the majority of them half naked. In just the same way they have to work under the burning rays of the sun in the hot season. When I asked who these people were, I was told that they were native slaves who had been marched from Luanda (the capital of Angola) to work on the construction of a railway. A considerable number of them had died from the intolerable working conditions, the disgusting food and the tropical heat. People may tell me that things have changed since 1927, but I visited that post again in 1929, and it emerged that the situation of the slaves had become even worse.'

Apart from the above facts and examples of slavery, the use of prison labour is widespread in the colonies of Black Africa, and is, in essence, no different from slavery. Many black workers are imprisoned for failure to pay the exorbitant taxes, for breaking the pass and other laws, for 'insulting' the prestige of the whites, and so on. In recent years there has been a significant rise in the colonial prison population. The same African national reformist leader has this to say on the slave labour of prisoners:

'We watched a detachment of a thousand prisoners go by. My friend said to me "The prisoners that you see have been handed over by the government to the white farmers and businessmen to help increase their profits". I could hardly believe this story, since up till then I had had the idea that the British Government was the most humane one of all, and anything like giving away prisoners to become slaves seemed to me a black mark on Britain's reputation. I told my friend that I would not believe this tale until I had concrete proof. And then a year later, as proof of his statement, he sent me some cuttings from the *Natal Mercury*, which ran as follows: "The system of hired prison labour has been in operation for eighteen years, yielding an annual income of £120,000. According to a statement of the Minister of Justice this sum should be doubled if possible. The minister reported that he had already issued appropriate instructions to all farmers in Bethal, and that, should he succeed in distributing a further 5,000 prisoners among them, it would be a fortunate event for the treasury. The minister went on to say that the system had so far fully justified itself, and that he had no intention of abandoning it, with or without agreement." '

It is interesting to quote, in conclusion, the official opinion of the most imperialist predators on the question of slavery. When a few years ago the League of Nations decided to deal with the question of slavery, the representatives of those states possessing colonies or mandated territories categorically objected to any tabling of such a question. As a result we have the resolution of the League of Nations Commission, which in terms of clarity could hardly be bettered: 'Slavery is the legal status of an individual to whom the property rights of another person are applied.' The objections of the representatives of the colonial imperialist states led to the question of slavery being passed to the I.L.O for examination. The I.L.O. sent all the imperialist governments a questionnaire, which asked the following question:

'Does the government deem necessary the abolition of forced or compulsory labour in all its forms, and is a transition period necessary prior to its complete abolition?'

We give below the extremely brief answers of the imperialists to this question:

> *Great Britain:* 'The Government admits that immediate abolition may not always be practicable.'
>
> *France:* 'The move to apply European labour legislation to native labour seems at present premature.'
>
> *Belgium:* 'From the factual side, it would be more appropriate to continue matters to the adoption of a draft convention, having as its sole aim the limitation or regulation of the use of forced or compulsory labour.'
>
> *Holland:* 'The abolition of forced labour is at the moment unimplementable.'
>
> *Portugal:* 'The Portuguese Government's answer to this question is negative. It is still too early to fix a final date.'
>
> *Germany:* (which at present is deprived of her colonies) expresses herself as follows: 'A transition period must be allowed for. It would be preferable not to foresee any special resolutions on this account. One could demand 90 days of forced labour from the natives. For women and minors work should be provided no further than 15 km from their permanent place of residence.

Thus the imperialist states themselves admit that in their colonies there exists forced labour and slavery, which they have no plans of relinquishing.

## NOTES

1. The sections in square brackets have been added by the present editor to improve continuity.
2. The reference is to Buell, R.L., *The Native Problem in Africa*, Vol. 2, (New York, 1928).
3. The Russian would translate as 'branches'. However, there are, more accurately, four or five 'clusters' of nuts on each tree, located immediately underneath the palm fronds. Based on the editor's observations in Trinidad it appears that each cluster has between six to ten nuts on it.
4. The original gives 3,246, but this doesn't tally with the later average figure. The figure for cattle has therefore been multiplied by ten, assuming that an 0 has been omitted in error.
5. Saltychikha, Dar'ya Ivanovna (1730-1801). Landowning noblewoman of Podolsk, famed for her brutality to her serfs. Over a period of six years she personally participated in torturing 139 serfs to death. She was condemned to death after an investigation lasting six years, but was later committed to imprisonment in a nunnery, where she

died. Her name is synonymous with the barbaric treatment of Russian serfs by the landowning gentry. (*Bol'shaya Sovetskaya Eutsiklopedia*, Vol.34, p.634.)

6. This quote almost certainly came from *Imvo Zabantsundu*, the organ that Jabavu edited from 1921 until his death. D.D.T. Jabavu was born in 1885 and educated in England, graduating from Birmingham and London Universities. He was long associated with moderate or conservative views, opposing for example the formation of the African Nationalist Congress, not to mention the Communist Party and various trade union groupings of black workers. See Simons, H.J. & R.E., *Class and Colour in South Africa, 1850-1950*, (Penguin, Harmondsworth, 1969), pp.254, 267. Nzula, whom we can assume penned this passage, was always ready to refer to Jabavu in a derogatory or sarcastic manner. Though not exactly a South African equivalent of 'Uncle Tom', Jabavu came to be associated in the minds of white administrators with 'civilized' and 'reasonable' demands by Africans.

7. Formed in 1896 under the name of the Rand Native Labour Association, Wenela was principally responsible for recruitment from Mozambique, though its activities were later extended to other African countries. The N.R.C., established in 1912, recruited mine labour from within South Africa and the British Protectorates (Basutoland, Bechuanaland and Swaziland). One might comment on Wenela's more recent situation. So important were its activities that Wenela built a 1,500 mile road from northern Botswana to Namibia in the 1960s to facilitate recruiting. With independence in Tanzania and Zambia its activities there were halted. Wilson, F., *Migrant Labour in South Africa* (Johannesburg, 1972), pp.3, 115. Miners from Angola and Mozambique will be more difficult to obtain since these two countries have attained independence. But the consolidation of underdevelopment and dependence in parts of Mozambique through generations of W.N.L.A. activities has meant that a sharp rupture by the Mozambique government is difficult. A team of researchers from the Centre of African Studies, University of Maputo, are now working on this problem.

8. 1920 in original — assumed to be a misprint.

9. Lady Kathleen Harvey Simon's book was in fact first published by Hodder & Stoughton (London) in 1929. A reprint has now been issued by the Negro Universities Press: Simon, K.H. (Lady), *Slavery*, (New York, 1969).

10. In this passage Nzula, Potekhin and Zusmanovich fail to explain that the British Colonial Government was attempting to suppress indigenous domestic slavery. It is disputable whether this was slavery 'of the cruellest type'. In any case, lest the reader be mislead, it should be made clear that 'the slave owners' concerned were not British.

11.    This is not strictly accurate. A version of the Commission's report
       was issued by the U.S. Government. *Report of the International
       Commission of Inquiry into the Existence of Slavery and Forced
       Labour in the Republic of Liberia*, (Washington Printing Office,
       1931).

# 4.

# THE EFFECTS OF THE DEPRESSION ON BLACK AFRICA

The current world economic crisis (the Great Depression — ed.) has exposed with particular clarity the parasitic nature of the exploitation of colonial Africans by modern imperialism, the colonies' dependence, as satellite agrarian sources of raw materials upon the imperialist metropoles, and the consequent fettering of the growth of their productive forces. The crisis of agricultural production began in the colonies long before the present generalized crisis of capitalism. World agriculture has been suffering from a crisis of over-production for more than a decade.

The First World War gave rise to a great demand for agricultural produce, particularly for foodstuffs to feed the armies, which numbered several million men. In those countries which were not the scene of hostilities (U.S.A., Canada, Argentina and Australia), and also in the colonies, this increased demand led to a substantial expansion in agricultural output, an increase in exports, and a rise in prices. With the ending of the War, the market for this increased agricultural output shrank considerably, due to the termination of war-time demand, and to a significant reduction in the purchasing power of the mass of the population, which had been ruined and impoverished by the War.

In the immediate post-war years, massive agricultural over-production in the Americas, Australia and the colonies was further aggravated by the gradual agricultural recovery of the combatant European countries, the industrial crisis of 1931, and the sluggish development of world industry during this period. There began the period of intensified competition, and the rapid fall in agricultural prices, which has lasted to the present day.

The current crisis of capitalism has had a catastrophic impact on colonial economies. The entire system of feudal and imperialist exploitation of the indigenous peasantry, the agrarian raw material producing character of the colonies' subjection to the metropolitan countries, the system of mono-cultural economies and dependence upon the world market have all combined to provide the preconditions for an extreme intensification of the current economic crisis in these countries. Moreover, the imperialists have transferred, and continue to transfer the burden of the crisis on to the shoulders of the toiling masses of the colonies, those of Black Africa in particular. The imperialists are attempting to make up for the lessening value of industrial production at home by lowering the prices of raw materials produced in the colonies.

## THE WORLD CAPITALIST CRISIS HITS AFRICAN AGRICULTURE

With the beginning of the current economic crisis, the lowering in value realized by Black Africa's agricultural production assumed catastrophic dimensions. In June 1928, Sierra Leone was selling its palm kernels at £20.15.0 per ton, at £11.3.0 in January 1930, £6.5.0 in December 1930, and £5.5.0 in September 1931. The rate of devaluation has so far continued unchecked. By mid-April 1932, palm nuts were already being sold for £3.15.0 per ton. A peasant in Sierra Leone now receives six times less for a ton of palm nuts than he did in 1928, and palm nuts constitute 75% of the country's total exports.

### West Africa — Prices for Peasant Produce Collapse

In 1920 a Gold Coast peasant received £80.5.0 for one ton of cocoa. In 1930 he received £50, in 1931 £23.10.0, and a mere £18 in 1933. Let us remember that cocoa accounts for 80% of the Gold Coast's total exports, and that the material well-being of the peasantry depends exclusively upon the price of cocoa. The other export crops of British West Africa's indigenous peasant economy are in the same position.

Thus with each successive year black peasants are receiving less and less for their farm produce. But the peasant has to live, buy food, and pay the ever-increasing taxes. The peasant therefore responds to price reductions by increasing, as far as he can, production of commodity crops, and tries to offset the devaluation of output by increasing the quantity of output. This increases stocks still further, which puts pressure on the market and drives prices inexorably downwards. Any increase in volume of output means a worsening of the producer's position. Such is the dialectic of capitalist production: the more a producer produces, the worse his position becomes. In terms of quantity, agricultural exports from British West Africa have fallen only slightly, and have even risen in the case of some crops. For instance, exports of palm oil from Nigeria fell from 135,000 tons in 1930 to 116,000 tons in 1932, a fall of only 14%. During these three years exports of palm nuts *rose* by 15%, groundnuts by 30%, and cocoa by 36%. Between 1928 and 1931 Gold Coast exports of cocoa rose by 7%. In Sierra Leone exports of palm nuts fell by only 10% between 1929 and 1931. But at the same time exports of all these products, in terms of value, declined systematically. The value of Nigerian exports of palm oil fell by 57% between 1928 and 1931, palm nuts by 61%, and cocoa by 53%. Between 1929 and 1931 the value of palm oil exports fell by 70% in the Gold Coast, 74% in Sierra Leone, and so on.

The crisis is resulting in mass impoverishment and ruin of the peasantry. There is now no question of any improved methods or renewal of equipment for agriculture. Agriculture is undergoing a process of accelerated degradation. Imperialism has subjugated the economies of these countries, dragged them into the orbit of the international division of labour, turned them into monoculture producers, and now proves incompetent to guarantee them any sort of bearable existence.

The peasantry of the colonies are trying to escape from the situation which has developed and free themselves from export production by switching to produce for personal consumption, and a natural closed economy. However, these attempts founder on the need to obtain money to pay taxes, for which purpose the peasant is obliged to grow export crops despite falling prices. Moreover, the lower the price, the more he must produce.

The world economic crisis has made it impossible for the natives to fulfil their 'dual function' even if they wish to do so. They must fulfil it, however, even at the price of starvation. Immense potential forces for the struggle against the rule of imperialism are contained in this contradiction.

Such is the development of the world economic crisis in British West Africa. The crisis has had an equal, if not greater impact on the peasantry in other parts of Black Africa where small peasant farming predominates.

In a number of regions of the Belgian Congo the peasants, by order of the government, sow nothing but cotton. The 65% to 70% fall in cotton prices has utterly ruined the peasantry and condemned them to starvation. In the Lake Leopold II region, the population gather palm nuts and sell them to the trading stations. In recent years, the majority of trading stations have closed down due to market difficulties and a series of company bankruptcies, making it impossible for the peasant to sell his palm nuts locally. But the government demands that the taxes be paid. This forces the population to take their produce to the town of Kasai, several hundred kilometres to the south. One journey with his produce takes an African months, and at current prices he has to sell an even greater quantity of palm nuts in order to pay the taxes.

In an interview with a reporter of the newspaper *Libre Belgique*, de Balzac, a former Belgian Cabinet Secretary produced the following facts:

'In 1928 the natives paid B.Fr.36 in taxes, by today they are asked to pay B.Fr.67. In 1928 a negro had to supply 38 kg of cocoa or 128 kg of palm nuts to pay his taxes. Today as a result of the low prices for such produce and increases in taxation, a negro has to supply 128 kg of cocoa or 1,700 kg (almost two tonnes) of palm nuts.'[1]

It would be wrong to suppose, however, that the crisis has had an identical impact upon both small peasant farming and on large plantations and farms. The owners of large agricultural enterprises have financial reserves which the peasants lacks; they have credit, the peasant does not.

As far as possible they transfer the burden of the crisis to the shoulders of the peasants employed on their farms and plantations. Whereas the peasant farms to support himself, and cannot farm on a reduced scale without worsening his position, capitalists farm for profit. Finally, the big plantation owners take advantage of the financial assistance offered by their own colonial governments, whilst the peasants receive no assistance whatever, or rather, they pay for the assistance given to the plantation owners by the government. Consequently, the impact of the crisis upon large-scale farming and plantations is somewhat different from that upon small peasant farming.

## South Africa — Crisis Hurts Big Farmers Less than Peasantry

Let us consider the Union of South Africa, where the bulk of agricultural output comes from large farms. With the beginning of the crisis, prices for maize, wool and hides — the basic agricultural export items — began to fall rapidly. At the beginning of 1931, the *Cape Times*[2] had written:

'In 1924 the Union of South Africa exported 174 million pounds of wool at an average price of 1/9 per pound, earning £15,700,000. In 1930 the Union of South Africa exported 275 million pounds of wool — i.e. exports rose by 100 million pounds in six years. But the price fell to an average of 7½d. Thus despite the growth in exports the farmers made only £8,500,000.'

Much the same applies to hides. The same newspaper wrote:

'In 1924 the Union of South Africa exported 31 million treated and 37 million untreated hides valued at £3,159,000. In 1930 the Union of South Africa exported 33 million treated and 44 million untreated hides, but the sum that this fetched fell to £2,014,000.'

Prices continued to plummet during 1931-32. On the London market the price of South African wool fell from 20d per kg in 1929-30 to 9d in 1931-32. By the beginning of 1932, maize was being sold in London 68% cheaper than in 1928-29. The total export value of wool fell by 66% from £15,000,000 in 1928 to £5,000,000 in 1931. The export value of maize shrank by 84% from £3,000,000 in 1928 to £550,000 in 1931. The export value of hides fell from £4,500,000 in 1928 to £1,000,000 in 1931. This catastrophic devaluation of exports had a varying effect, however, on the different strata of the European farming community and the African peasantry.

The South African Government has taken a number of steps to soften the blow of the crisis upon the white farming community. The government has reduced railway tariffs by 3%, paying for this aid partially at the expense of the railway workers, and covering the railway's deficit from its own budget, i.e., from taxes levied on the peasantry. At the beginning of 1931 the government released £5,000,000 from the treasury to be issued as loans to the farmers. The government subsidizes maize and wool exports to the extent of 25% of the value of exports. The subsidies were introduced to cover the difference in exchange rates between British and South African sterling when Britain abandoned the Gold Standard whilst the Union of South Africa retained it. Although the exchange rates have now equalized, the government continues to pay these subsidies.

Naturally, not all farmers took advantage of this assistance. Considerable sums have accumulated in the pockets of the trading companies and large landowners, and continue to do so. A further portion has been cornered by large plantation owners. The small white farmers cannot avail themselves of this assistance, and, lacking the strength to fend off the blows of the crisis unaided, are ruined, sell their farms for a nominal price, and make their way to the towns. The ruin of the small farmer can be measured by the continual yearly increase in the selling off of land, and the fall in land prices. In 1927-28 the average price of one morgen (2.117 acres) of land was £2.10.0. In 1930-31 it fell to £1.12.0, falling again in 1931-32 to £1.8.0.

Large farmers enjoying governmental support have greater opportunities to resist the crisis. They respond to falling prices by reducing output and building up stocks. This goes hand in hand with the reduction of exports in quantitative terms.

The large farmers are transferring the burden of the crisis to the shoulders of their serfs — the black peasants employed on their farms. In 1932, as we have already noted, a new law on tenant workers was passed, extending the annual period of unpaid labour to 180 days, reducing the wages paid to tenant and seasonal workers, and replacing money wages by wages in kind, etc.

The black peasantry is suffering both as labour on European farms and as a seller of maize, animal skins and other produce. The catastrophic devaluation of agricultural produce is bringing about the peasants' final ruin.

During the last year, the peasantry in the reserves have been literally starving. To this one must add that last year the harvest failed in a number of areas of the Union of South Africa, because of drought. Famine among the peasantry assumed such threatening proportions that the government was obliged to supply them with maize, using this action as a means of pinning down the black slaves still further. The mine owners' newspaper, *The Star*,[3] wrote:

> 'In Zululand the natives have been suffering a real famine. The Ministry has been obliged to supply them with maize at a cost of £300,000. Pledges have been taken from the natives to repay the cost of the maize when their situation improves. In Kulumai* in the Orange Free State, the natives are starving because operations have been halted at the manganese workings.'[4]

These meagre government hand-outs satisfy no one, of course. The peasantry make for the towns in search of work, but the towns are already overflowing with unemployed workers and it is impossible to find any work there. The peasant is forced to return to the reserves and suffer the tortures of hunger.

## IMPACT OF THE WORLD CRISIS ON THE MINING SECTOR

The black peasantry is suffering not only from the agrarian crisis and the reduced prices obtainable for its produce, but also from the crisis in the mining industry. With the exception of gold, every sector of the mining industry is curtailing its operations, due to the impossibility of disposing of output and the fall in prices.

Diamond prices have fallen from $107 per carat in 1928, to $85 in 1930, to $45 in 1932 (a fall of 58%). On the American market the price per pound of copper has fallen from 18 cents in 1929 to 5 cents in 1932 (a fall of 73%). A ton of tin fetched £313 in 1918, £228 in 1928, and £115 in 1931.

Combined with marketing difficulties, the fall in prices has caused a drop in the value of the mining industry's exports and a reduction of output. In Nigeria, the extraction of tin has been reduced by 56%, from 12,183 tons in 1929 to 4,087 in 1932. During 1932 alone, the monthly extraction of tin was cut from 588 tons in January to 241 tons in December. Exports of tin from Nigeria have fallen from £2,000,000 in 1929 to £882,000 in 1932. South African diamond exports have fallen by 80% from £10,732,000 in 1926 to £1,955,000 in 1932. By 1931 the volume of diamonds extracted was only 50% of what it had been in 1928. In April 1932 two of the largest diamond mining companies, producing 75% of total diamond output, closed their mines, and according to reports in the local press in January 1933, they are not expected to be reopened in the near future.

During the first two years of the crisis alone (1930 and 1931) the South African output of copper fell by 41%, tin by 79%, silver by 39%, iron ore by 51% and asbestos by 50%. Exports of copper from the Belgian Congo fell from 146,000 tons in 1930 to 59,000 tons in 1932. One American copper mining company in the Belgian Congo has closed down altogether. Geomines,[5] the largest tin-mining company in the Belgian Congo, has also ceased operations for the present. In 1932 the export of diamonds from the Belgian Congo completely ceased.

### The African Masses Impoverished

What impact has this had on the African population? First of all, one must note a significant reduction in the labour force. In 1929, 38,000 workers were employed in the Nigerian mining industry, but only 22,000 remained by the end of 1932. Of the 16,000 people employed in the

Northern Rhodesian mining industry in 1929, only 8,000 remained by the beginning of 1933. According to the International Labour Office's figures, there were 160,000 hired African labourers working in Kenya in 1930, of whom only 120,000 remained by the beginning of 1932. The reduction in the number of workers in the Union of South Africa has been even greater.

Before the crisis, work in the mining industry provided a supplementary source of income for a section of the black population, which helped them in some ways to extract themselves from debt and avoid going to prison. But they have now lost even this opportunity at precisely the time when, as a result of the devaluation of their produce, they are in particular need of such supplementary income.

This supplementary source of income has shrunk even for those who have remained in the industry. The imperialists are attacking the workers' standard of living to an even greater degree in the colonies than at home. Wages are being reduced everywhere. According to I.L.O. figures, the wages of Kenyan contract workers have been cut by 60% during the last two years. The Nigerian mining companies report that they have managed to reduce the cost of a ton of tin from £113 in 1929 to £79 in 1932, i.e., by 30% in three years. In the Gold Coast gold mining industry, the extraction cost per ton of ore has been reduced from 23/- in 1930 to 19/- in 1932.

The companies do not say how they have managed to achieve this, but it is clear to us that every bit of this cost reduction has been purchased by the health and lives of hundreds and thousands of black miners. One should not forget that in mining, and especially in high-technology industry (particularly in the Union of South Africa) there already exists a black proletariat, for whom wages are the sole source of income. They have already broken their ties with peasant farming and cannot return to the reserves, since there is no land for them there. But since they are paid higher wages than contract workers, wherever possible the imperialist reduces the size of this category of workers first. The black proletariat is simply being thrown on to the streets, where they constitute the basic cadres of the army of the unemployed.

## Rise in Unemployment

We have no figures on the scale of unemployment in Black Africa. No records of unemployment whatsoever are kept in any of the colonies of Black Africa. Nor could any record give a complete picture of the state of unemployment, because of the constant migration of peasants from the villages to the towns in search of work, and of the urban unemployed to their own plots in the villages (which is still possible since the majority have not yet broken their ties with the land).

However, we can clarify the unemployment picture without figures. Mass ruin and starvation are becoming increasingly widespread and acute among the peasantry due to the impossibility of obtaining any suitable price for peasant produce. Peasants are leaving the villages *en masse* to seek work in the towns, the mines and in transport. There they are met by the rising wave of unemployment; workers are being sacked here, there and everywhere. One West African paper writes that the slogan of the day is 'Sackings, sackings and more sackings'. The same paper writes: 'The number of mechanics, skilled workers, clerks, book-keepers, typists and unskilled workers out of work is growing at a phenomenal rate.' A Gold Coast newspaper reports that: 'A considerable proportion of those who used to live on wages has already long been without any means of support, and so far one cannot see when this will end.'

In the Union of South Africa the total number out of work is put at 500,000. There is no social insurance and no assistance is given by the government. In over-populated African areas around the large towns, these victims of imperialist rule drag out an existence of perpetual hunger.

Last year large urban centres, such as Cape Town, Johannesburg and others, passed a law forbidding Africans to enter the city limits without special permission. But perpetual need forces the black peasants to seek better fortune in the towns, and no laws can halt the waves of unemployed. The head of the Johannesburg City Council's Department of Non-European Affairs admits that, despite strict control over blacks coming in to Johannesburg, they daily arrive in the city in their thousands, driven on by the crisis and hunger. 'And although',he says, 'these people walk the pavement all day in search of work, they do not find it and finish up begging for bread on the streets'. The newspaper *Umteteli wa Bantu* remarks that: 'The city authorities of Durban are doing everything they can to ease the position of unemployed blacks — free food is being issued to 70 natives. Nevertheless one often sees these unemployed lying on the ground, weakened to the point that they can no longer move.'[6]

European workers as well as Africans are affected by unemployment in the Union of South Africa. By the middle of 1932, over 15,000 European workers were already registered as unemployed. White workers receive a certain amount of assistance from various semi-official charitable organizations. However, this assistance is far from adequate. There are only five or six places in the whole country where white workers are given these wretched meals. During the second half of 1931 a Rand Assistance Board[7] spent £400 on assistance to 860 families, i.e. £5 per family over six months. According to the bourgeois press, one-quarter of the European population of Durban — 24,880 men and their families — is living on charity.

Unemployed blacks are not even given this assistance. The question of unemployment has more than once been raised for parliamentary debate, but things have got no further than a number of outrageous schemes like organizing agricultural colonies for the unemployed under the slogan 'Back to the land', organizing semi-military camps for the unemployed, and replacing black workers in industry by whites. The unemployed go on starving. Unemployment goes on growing.

## The Colonial Governments' Response

In other parts of Black Africa, such as British West Africa, colonial governments simply do not recognize the problem of unemployment. In one of his speeches, the Governor of the Gold Coast said that his government's central problem was to cover the budget deficit. He has rejected proposals to effect economies by lowering the salaries of white officials, reducing the pensions of retired white officials and lowering the rate of interest on the state debt. He has his own way out of the crisis: the introduction of a new tax which will merely transfer the burden of the crisis on to the shoulders of black workers. This speech deserves quoting:

> 'There is a suggestion to reduce the salaries and various privileges of European officials. This is impossible. The conditions of service are the same in all the colonies, and to impair them here would lead to our best people leaving us.
>
> Another suggestion is to lower the interest rate on the state debt. This is also impossible. The people who lent the Government the money to build the railway and the port of Takoradi did so in the hope that they would receive a certain sum of interest over so many years, and we cannot break our promise.
>
> The third suggestion is to reduce the number of government officials by abolishing the Departments of Land and Forests as separate bodies. We cannot do this, since we must protect the interests of lease holders and concessionaries, and apart from that we are hoping for an expansion of our mining industry in the near future.
>
> I am forced to point out that since the time of my arrival it has not been once suggested *that the Africans must help themselves.* What's to be done! First of all help the people to understand the situation. You may say that they are uneducated, and must be taught. But you *are* educated. So go and explain what I have told you to the people. Tell them that everyone who lives in this country is responsible for its prosperity. I have said several times already that if the people understand they will pay the new tax.'

This is the only way out of the crisis which the Governor of the Gold Coast has found. Instead of help to a starving people, he suggests new taxes. A further attack on the workers, further enslavement of millions of black slaves and the strengthening of oppression is the only way out of the crisis which the imperialists recognize.

But the workers of Black Africa, together with the workers of the world, led and aided by the world proletariat, are seeking and will find another way out of the crisis, which will simultaneously be a final escape from the chains of imperialism. In the following chapters we shall show how black workers are fighting for this alternative, revolutionary way out of the crisis.

Here we may note the further fact that, in its turn, the crisis in Black Africa, caused by the world economic crisis of capitalism, is influencing and intensifying the world crisis.

The present economic crisis is one of over-production. There are no markets for what is produced. But the impact of the crisis in the colonies, particularly in Black Africa, is narrowing the world market still further. Whereas previously, the black peasantry, enslaved and crushed by debts, was never a good customer, its purchasing power has now been reduced even further. The fall in imports to Black Africa is an index of this continuing impoverishment of the masses.

TABLE 4.1

IMPORTS OF INDIVIDUAL COUNTRIES OF BLACK AFRICA

|  | *1929* | | *1932* | |
| --- | --- | --- | --- | --- |
| Belgian Congo | B.Fr. | 1,943,493,000 | B.Fr. | 464,631,932 |
| Union of S. Africa | £ | 83,455,454 | £ | 32,738,036 |
| Nigeria | £ | 16,663,525 | | * |
| Sierra Leone | £ | 2,054,507 | | * |
| French West Africa | Fr. | 1,532,476,000 | Fr. | 707,000,000 |
| Northern Rhodesia | £ | 3,669,648 | £ | 1,959,555 |
| Gold Coast | £ | 12,200,000 | | * |

* No data

The situation is similar in other African countries. The African market for metropolitan industrial goods has thus shrunk by almost half as a result of the conomic crisis. This means a narrowing of the market and a deepening of the crisis, which will lead to future attacks by the imperialists on the workers of Black Africa.

# NOTES

1. *Drapeau Rouge*, 9 January 1932, presumably quoting from *Libre Belgique. Drapeau Rouge* was the newspaper of the Belgian Communist Party.
2. The original read *Cane Times*, obviously a misprint.
3. *The Star* is owned by the Argus Group, whose other newspapers include the *Cape Argus* (Cape Town), *The Diamond Fields Advertiser* (Kimberley), *The Pretoria News, The Natal Daily News* (Durban), *The Sunday Tribune* and *The Sunday Post* (Durban). While Nzula, Potekhin and Zusmanovich are correct in describing *The Star* as a mine owner's newspaper, in addition to mining capital there has recently been an admixture of large, 'English-speaking' industrial

capital in the group.

4.  *The Star* 15 March 1932.

5.  GEOMINES — Compagnie Geologique et Miniere des Ingenieurs et Industriels Belges.

6.  This quotation from *Umteteli wa Bantu* is rather difficult to interpet. Clearly the Durban authorities were not exactly bountiful in their generosity. Are we to take it that the newspaper's reporter is being sarcastic? Or, are Nzula, Potekhin and Zusamanovich pointing to the hypocrisy of this newspaper, known for its conservatism?

7.  The official name for this body is uncertain.

# 5.

# PEASANT MOVEMENTS AND UPRISINGS IN THE COLONIES

The imperialists control Africa by methods of 'fire and the sword', they confiscate the peasants' land, burden them with unbearable taxation, keep them in a condition of slavery and impose forced labour upon them. Naturally, a peasantry doomed to ruin and starvation by imperialist rule has no alternative but to rebel against this oppression.

## DETERMINANTS OF THE PEASANT MOVEMENT

The present peasant movement in Africa differs sharply from that of earlier periods. One should realize that 50 years ago Black Africa, with the exception of a few areas in the west and south, was outside the orbit of capitalist influence. The African population lived in tribal communities, led by chiefs selected from their elders.

The seizure of the colonies by the imperialists during the past 50 years caused a change in the way of life of these tribes. Entire tribal communities were destroyed in the space of two to three decades, ancient traditions and superstitions were deprived of their foundations. The impoverishment of the masses led to confrontations and serious uprisings. By now millions of peasants have been utterly ruined, due, in particular, to the economic crisis. This situation has naturally given rise to extreme discontent among the masses.

The form and character of peasant movements in different African colonies are determined by the extent of capitalist development and penetration of capital: thus for instance in South Africa, an economically developed African colony, the peasant movement is at a different level than in East Africa and, most important, is to a certain extent influenced by the revolutionary workers movement. Nevertheless, despite the presence of definite proletarian cadres, the clergy, chiefs and assorted charlatans are trying to take over leadership of the peasant movement, thus giving it a religious, superstitious character. This gives the imperialists an opportunity to conceal the fundamental reasons for the discontent and anger of the black peasantry, by attributing barbaric intentions to the peasant movement. Clothing themselves in the interests of the 'civilized world' in order to mollify domestic public opinion, they despatch punitive expeditions to restore order and white 'civilization' in areas affected by an uprising.

What drives the peasants to struggle against imperialism? The determining factor behind the various forms of agrarian movement is the expropriation of peasant land by the imperialists. This gives the movement an aggressive anti-imperialist character.

On the other hand, the unbearable burden of taxation and other types of exploitation of the peasants by the imperialists and their lackeys make worse the intolerable position of the peasant masses. The common theme of all peasant complaints is 'more land, less taxes'. This is not just a demand of isolated groups, but of the entire toiling peasantry and of all Black Africa.

## THE PEASANT MOVEMENT IN PARTICULAR COUNTRIES

### South Africa

During the last few years there have been a large number of outbreaks of peasant warfare. The already intolerable position of the black peasantry herded on to the reserves has been particularly aggravated by the crisis. Of the indigenous peasant population 75% holds only 7% of the land, land which is, moreover, unsuitable for farming. The various taxes, which the peasants are totally unable to pay, force them to leave the land to work under contract in mines and other enterprises, and on farms and plantations.

The fate of the majority of peasants thus depends on the sale of their labour to capitalists and landowners. This previously provided the sole means to try to survive and pay the unbearable taxes. In the circumstances of the world economic crisis the situation has changed sharply. The crisis cut off all roads to finding work. Hundreds of thousands were left unemployed in the towns. But the peasantry, which had always depended upon seasonal work, was reduced to utter poverty and starvation. The government brought in draconian laws to drive away peasants who had come to the towns in search of work. The position of the peasants has, moreover, deteriorated still further due to the permanent drought which began in 1930. It is hardly surprising that the peasantry is ravaged by plague and all kinds of epidemics.

The organ of the South African Chamber of Mines and the Native Labour Recruiting Corporation, *Umteteli wa Bantu*, complains that:

'Unfortunately, closures and limited output in the gemstone industry have caused great difficulties for natives who previously lived by working in the mines, and this has led to a high rate of sickness among workers.'

In Zululand the incidence of sickness has greatly risen as a result of the drought. All these disasters are aggravated to extremes by famine. The same paper reports mass epidemics of malaria from which thousands of blacks dragging out a starvation existence, have died. In one region more than 5,000 people died of malaria in the space of a few weeks.

This suffering among the peasantry has led to a large-scale peasant movement embracing a number of different regions. The settlers, however, have many methods of quelling uprisings. In addition to punitive military expeditions and bloody reprisals, the imperialists resort to bribing chiefs to foment inter-tribal wars. In this way the imperialists attempt to undermine the liberation struggle of the oppressed and to hide the true picture of the situation in the colonies.

The peasants, hungry and dying from starvation, owe their survival entirely to their livestock. No assistance whatsoever is given to them. On the contrary, the government continues to levy the most burdensome taxes.

The Communist Party has advanced slogans demanding the abolition of all taxes on the peasants, including taxes on huts and livestock, and has called on the peasantry to make mass protests against these taxes. The Party has put forward in its demands the question of aid to the starving peasants of the reserves from food stocks held in government, missionary and commercial warehouses. The election of committees from peasants and agricultural workers has also been demanded. These slogans have won great popularity. Peasant committees have been organized, and have promoted mass agitation among the peasants. The Communist Party has explained to the peasants the role of the chiefs and missionaries, who are the agents of British imperialism.

The South African Government has passed a whole series of repressive laws to crush this mass peasant movement, in particular the 'Revised Natal Native Code'. An interpretation of the substance of this law has been given by the newspaper, *Umsebenzi*[1] It symbolizes slavery, subjugation and the lash. According to this law, the Governor General is given unlimited power over all Africans, and the right to outlaw and disperse all revolutionary peasant organizations. The law gives the right to:

1   Crush African anti-government agitation by the arrest of peasants considered 'dangerous to public peace and quiet', to imprison without trial for three months and to detain any African agitator in prison for an unlimited period.
2   Divide, subdivide existing tribes or create new ones (the old policy of pacifying warlike tribes by offering certain privileges to individual tribes in order to channel mass discontent into counter-revolutionary and intertribal wars).
3   Prohibit the reading by peasants of any literature which, in the opinion of the 'supreme chief' may cause unrest among them.'

But these draconian measures have not restrained the peasant movement in South Africa. In the province of Natal, and in other native reserves the movement for the non-payment of taxes has recently been growing. Not only is the peasantry refusing to pay taxes, but it has recently taken part in attacks on administrators who tour the villages collecting them.

The Communist Party leads the work of the peasant committees, organizes landless labourers on the plantations and farms, and at the same time is recruiting the support of industrial workers for the peasants' struggle.

## Rhodesia

In this country land is the most acute question for the black masses forced to live in the reserves and black urban quarters where the mine owners and farmers recruit workers.

Within the Rhodesian peasant movement there exists a religious one, known as the Watch Tower Movement.[2] It has become widespread within the country and extends beyond its borders. These organizations, which are closely interlinked, operate in Uganda, East Africa, the Belgian Congo and Central Africa.

The Watch Tower Movement arose from the breakaway of individual sects from the white missionary churches. This movement, however, also has a clearly anti-imperialist character. For example, the leader of the movement in Nyasaland has claimed that a vision appeared to him announcing the end of white rule. An uprising to drive out the British imperialists was raised, resulting in the killing of white plantation employees. The revolt was a small one, and was put down with great cruelty.

According to a *Sunday Times* report of the 22nd May 1933, the Watch Tower Movement is spreading rapidly throughout Rhodesia, particularly in the Lusaka area. The political police have started a campaign of white terror to crush the movement, and have conducted mass arrests.

In November 1932, a campaign of resistance to imperialist policy developed, in connection with an increase in the burden of taxation. This movement assumed large proportions and there were mass peasant refusals to pay taxes. In order to decapitate the movement, the government arrested all its leaders. This action angered the masses still further, and 1,500 people stormed the prison in an attempt to free the imprisoned leaders.

## Kenya

The peasant movement here is developing on a large scale. We quote Johnson Kenyatta,[3] one of its leaders.

> 'All the land in Kenya has belonged to the natives from time immemorial. In spite of this the British Government claims that all the land in Kenya must be under its direct control in order to distribute it at its own discretion, giving preference, of course, to the whites.'

On arrival in Kenya, the British Government declared it a protectorate (later a colony) and the peasants' right of property over the land was ignored. The government took upon itself the role of a controlling organ.

The white settlers were offered land concessions, and, to enable them to work this land, all the blacks were driven from it thus depriving them of land which they had worked for hundreds of years. In addition, they were taxed. The result of all this was that the peasant was forced to go and work for the white colonists in order to earn the money to pay the government's taxes. The white settlers paid the Africans exceedingly little — 12/- per month, at a time when the annual poll tax was 12/-, and tax on huts, likewise, 12/-. This situation caused an outrage in Kenya, and led to the formation of the East African Association, whose task was to fight British imperialism and the measures it was taking for oppressing the black population. In 1920, the government increased the taxes on every African from 12/- to 16/-. The white colonists simultaneously reduced wages.

Meanwhile, quite apart from tax increases and the reduction of wages, forced labour was introduced for girls. This again caused an outrage in the country and provided fertile ground for the outbreak of a rebellion which forced the government to abolish this measure and reduce poll tax and tax on huts to 12/-.

## West Africa

In West Africa the conditions of oppression and exploitation of the black peasantry are essentially the same, but in this region they have assumed somewhat different forms.

One should point out that the policy of British imperialism in West Africa is often described by the national reformists as 'progressive and more enlightened' than its policies in Eastern and Southern Africa. This policy has its essence in the retention of peasant landowning. Here there was no necessity to expropriate the peasants' land, since British imperialism could achieve its aims by other methods. Landlessness and ruin among the peasants of West Africa is taking its own course. The basic forms of exploitation are low local market prices and high rates of interest which peasants have to pay on bank loans. The government and the numerous chiefs have also imposed forced labour and high taxes.

The British imperialist, Lord Lugard, describes the commerical exploitation of West Africans as follows: the traders have reduced prices paid to the native peasants to an excessively low level, subsequently claiming that these minimal prices should remain stable. For example, palm oil is sold at £47.0.0 in Europe, whilst the native peasants receive only £5 to £6 for the same product.[4] This robbery is brazenly justified by the imperialists. Sir Ormsby-Gore says:[5]

> 'Indeed, whilst high prices can stimulate the expansion of production, it may seem strange that low prices can likewise stimulate native production. The native peasant, having acquired certain needs, and a certain standard of living, will work harder to satisfy his customary needs if he has to produce more in order to obtain the same amount of money.'

In December 1930, the Government of Nigeria, being afraid to introduce an additional tax on men, proposed the introduction of a tax on women. Approximately 30,000 women organized spontaneously and marched on the capital of Nigeria, where they attacked the Governor's house and the banks. The troops were called out and fired on this womens' demonstration, resulting in hundreds killed and many wounded. Naturally, this increased the people's anger at the role of British imperialism.[6]

In 1931 an uprising broke out in Sierra Lenone in which 50 soldiers also took part. The government was only able to crush this revolt with the arrival of substantial military reinforcements. Strict colonial censorship has released no more detailed information about this revolt, and the local petty bourgeois press tried to explain it away in terms of purely economic causes.

## The Belgian Congo

Let us turn to the uprising in the Belgian Congo. The intolerable conditions under which the black masses in Africa, and in the Belgian Congo in particular, live have driven them to fight against the colonialists. Numerous bankruptcies, reduction of output in a whole series of enterprises in the Belgian Congo, and a general slowdown in the pace of industrial and commercial life are consequences of the raging world capitalist crisis. One of the root causes of the uprising is the economic crisis and capitalist contradictions which have affected both industry and the government's budget, despite increased exploitation of the workers.

In 1931 the budget deficit was 181,000,000 francs. In order to alleviate the crisis, the government increased taxation at the very beginning of the industrial and agricultural year, whilst prices for rural produce had fallen by 50% and more. Naturally, the vast majority of Africans were in no position to pay the taxes. The brutal methods used by territorial agents to extract taxes were consequently intensified.

*Le Soir*, a Belgian bourgeois paper, writes that the Africans living in the north in Lukenie (the area involved in the uprising) cannot find any further markets for the sale of their produce (the trading stations having been closed) and suggests that the government 'exercise control over output and stimulate its growth'. Thus at a time when it is impossible to sell agricultural products, the black workers and peasants of the Belgian Congo, in the opinion of the article's author, are in need of a 'stimulus' to increase their output still further, i.e., to work even more, simply to be able to pay the exorbitantly increased taxes.

Such are the real intentions of the capitalists and government agents in the Congo. The black population of the Belgian Congo responded to these plans with an uprising, preferring death in battle to starvation.

This is not the first time that the exploited and oppressed blacks have resorted to rebellion. Ever since the 'pacification' of the Belgian Congo over 50 years ago, the discontent of the African masses has grown constantly. In response to exploitation and oppression from the colonialists, the Africans have killed territorial agents, stoned missionaries, and so on. The killing of two territorial agents in Kikwit was an act of desperation on the part of the black proletariat and peasantry. This act forced even the social fascist, Mr Van de Veldt,* to submit a proposal to parliament on the creation of a commission of enquiry. This 'enquiry' was so brilliantly carried out that a second uprising soon broke out.

There are also thousands of men and women from Guinea and the French Congo working in the enterprises of the colonists. In most regions minerals are also mined while rubber and fruit etc. are procured. Large reserves of raw materials for a considerable number of enterprises, require labour to extract them. The imperialists have taken every measure to force the blacks to work. The black supervisors used by the exploiters use violence and deceit in order to force the people to work, virtually unpaid, at gathering raw rubber.

The uprising which began last year was, as the colonial powers hypocritically reported, 'an extremely conservative movement with religious overtones' in which the 'cult of Satan' allegedly played a major role. This gave Belgian imperialism an opportunity to 'defend' European culture from the 'highly conservative natives'. At a minimum estimate, several thousand people were killed during this 'cultural rescue campaign'.

The uprising broke out in the Congo in the Kipanga region of Kasai Province, i.e. in the south-central part of the Belgian Congo bordering on Portuguese Angola, and in the most strongly industrialized region, the Lower Congo. The ports of Boma and Matadi and the industrial towns of Leopoldville and Kinshasa are located in the Lower Congo. Beginning in Kikwit region, the uprising spread throughout the region and into other areas. According to official reports, the numbers involved in the rebellion reached 15,000 i.e. about 10% of the region's male population took part, of which 4,000 rebels were armed with antiquated firearms.

In 1928 a 'mutiny' in northern Ruanda was drowned in blood and smothered by a savage orgy of pogroms. Troops and the gendarmerie burnt down over a thousand peasant huts.

The Belgian colonists' past fully matches their present. The Belgian Congo was conquered by fire and blood. During the uprising of 1920-22 the armed forces of Belgian imperialism razed tens of villages, in the Bas-Congo region, to the ground to subdue the rebels.

As a result of the nightmarish conditions of life, the black masses, driven to desperation by the actions of the colonists and their agents, have united and taken up arms to fight for their liberation. Armed with spears, arrows and slings, they have resisted the punitive expeditions of Belgian imperialism.

The direct cause of the uprising of the black working masses was, as already pointed out, the increase in taxation and the reduction in wages,

particularly at the Kasai Company's enterprises. This company was one of
the first to lower its wages, although they were only 4d to 5d[7] per week
before being reduced. Wages were reduced on the grounds that prices for
the produce of the plantations had also fallen. The government, however,
simultaneously demanded payment of increased taxes from the blacks in
view of the 'crisis' in the Belgian Congo.

To collect the increased taxes in the villages, Belgian tax agents were
installed, who treated the population brutally. This caused intense unrest,
particularly in the area of Basankusu, where at a number of assemblies, the
blacks decided to refuse to pay the taxes.

Here it is worth quoting the statement of the wife of a murdered tax
agent, Ballot.*

> 'The private company agents treated the blacks badly and exploited
> them. People ought to know this. What goes on there must be
> stopped, otherwise there will be uprisings everywhere. Private
> company agents have taken rights upon themselves which belong
> only to the authorities. Moreover many territorial agents have not
> behaved as they should have done. My husband paid for the others.
> We only arrived in Kandola* 15 days ago.

Such was the statement of the murdered Ballot's wife, made on her arrival
in Brussels, whilst the Belgian papers attributed the uprising to the religious
sentiments of 'fascist tribes'.

An emergency military detachment was sent to the village of Lindenzele*,
where it was met by a crowd of Africans singing war songs. The soldiers
promptly killed 12 of them. The news of this reprisal spread quickly
throughout the area, causing massive resentment.

Soon the unrest spread to the neighbouring area of Kandale*, where on
the 8th of July a Belgian tax agent was killed by the inhabitants of the
village of Kilombas*. Meanwhile large Belgian forces attacked Lindenzele,
where they killed 20 blacks. Inhabitants of Lindenzele, while defending
it, wounded two soldiers. In its retreat from the village, the detachment
set fire to the forest. The whole area was in the hands of the African rebels
for several days. All the Europeans, traders and missionaries, fled to the
provincial centre of Kvando-Kikwit. For three weeks the area of Kandale
was completely isolated.

Substantial reinforcement with machine-guns were despatched from
Leopoldville. Belgian troops began reprisals. According to official figures
30 blacks were killed in Bangi* on the 2nd of July. On July 4th, 60 more
(over 100 according to unofficial sources) were killed in the village of
Kitlomba,* which came under machine gun fire. From then on the whole
Kandale region was subjected to systematic looting: African villages were
burnt down, crops destroyed, and animals and poultry rounded up by the
soldiers. The black rebels, pursued like wild animals, defended themselves
energetically, but the Belgian colonists constantly sent new reinforcements.

The official reports of the Belgian colonial authorities show that the
uprising in the Belgian Congo was crushed with the aid of armed force.

However, the revolutionary movement continues to grow with new strength. In the words of *Le Drapeau Rouge*, the Belgian communist newspaper, unrest is still spreading, and has now engulfed the entire part of Kasai Province bordering on Kwango.

In the bourgeois newspaper, *Le Soir*, an official communication from Leopoldville from the Kasai provincial administration appeared, dated 1st August 1932. The communication stated that 'in the southern regions of Kwango Province, where a strong detachment of troops is in action, the situation remains unchanged'.

Huge military forces were brought to the borders of the rebellious regions for two purposes: firstly, to prevent new regions joining the uprising and, secondly, not to allow anyone to retreat from the rebellious Kwango region. The colonialists' plan was to imprison the rebels within a small area, cut them off from other regions, carry out mass slaughter and thus put an end to the 'mutiny'.

It is obviously impossible to reconstruct a full picture of the uprising, but some of the rebels' actions are indicative. They are alleged to have attacked vulnerable police posts and to have driven the police from the area involved in the uprisings; several corpses remained after the fight with the police. The government officials also had to flee. European merchants were attacked and two of them were killed. The warehouses and offices of the Kasai Company were burnt down. African officials employed by the Belgians were killed. Banknotes and workers' identification papers were burnt in the streets.

Whereas official reports claim that this is being done at the command of 'witch-doctors' who have proclaimed the 'Kingdom of Satan', in reality it all testifies to a genuine rebellion against the rule of the Belgian colonists. The actions are in themselves typical, as are their religious overtones, which are particularly typical of this area, which is inhabited by 'Kimbanguists'.[8] The 'Kingdom of Satan' does indeed play a large part in their beliefs; however, they are not proclaiming its coming but are calling for its destruction, since the 'Kingdom of Satan' means the rule of white colonists in the Belgian Congo.

The Belgian Government has repeatedly stated that the uprising in Kwango is over. The military reinforcements from Kasai and Leopoldville have been ordered to return to barracks. The central points of Kikwit, however, have remained under occupation. In the Upper Kwilu region troops have continued to carry on their 'military patrols', arresting any suspicious persons. Military operations have been concentrated nearer to the Portuguese border.

As for Middle Kwango and Luchwadi, the colonists seem to have achieved victory here. The population of these areas, bled white by slaughter, devastated by an epidemic of dysentery and exhausted by a hard life in unhealthy forests, has returned to its original villages, now burnt and plundered by Belgian troops. Meanwhile long columns of prisoners, roped together by the neck, dragged themselves through the region to await the arrival from Leopoldville of Jungers, the Governor General, who was instructed to conduct a government inquiry.

And so in one region the uprising has ended, crushed by Government troops. But elsewhere the population is preparing for a new struggle.

One may observe attempts to conceal the scale of the uprising in Equatorial Province. If one is to believe government bulletins, the uprising was of 'purely local significance'. Thus, in the government's opinion, the reasons for mobilizing troops to be sent to new regions were quite trivial.

The attitude of Belgian metropolitan bourgeois circles to these bloody events is highly typical. To a senator's question in parliament, asking what was going on in the Belgian Congo, and if it would not be better for the government to adopt a more moderate policy of repression towards the rebels of Kwango and Kikwit, the Colonial Minister replied: 'Sometimes this is necessary in order to avoid something worse.' This statement drew no protest whatsoever from senators of all complexions, including the social democrats, who received this minister-cum-executioner with something bordering upon delight.

The words 'sometimes this is necessary', however, meant that the government had decided to drown in blood a black uprising itself caused by systematic plunder, ruthless exploitation and murder. They also meant that, throughout the time taken by the imperialist's troops to restore (imperialist) order, the blood of the black masses would continue to flow, and hundreds and thousands would flee to the forests risking death from predatory beasts, hunger or fever to escape the bullets of the white colonists.

The words 'sometimes this is necessary', uttered calmly in parliament by the Colonial Minister before an assembly of like-minded listeners, whose interests coincide with those of colonial banditry in Black Africa, represent in reality simply the 'rule of blood and iron'.

Only the Belgian Communist Party openly spoke in defence of its black Congolese comrades. The Belgian proletariat has reacted quite quickly to events; an impressive show of solidarity took place. A delegation elected by workers at a meeting on 1st August went to the ministry. The chairman of the delegation, J. Jaquemotte*, handed the Secretary-General (the Minister was not present) a resolution unanimously adopted by the workers at the meeting. We give below the text of the resolution.

> 'Having assembled in Brussels on 1st August to demonstrate their protest against imperialism and war, and having acquainted themselves with the true reasons for the uprising in the Congo, and also with the slaughter and devastation accompanying the crushing of this movement, the workers express their total solidarity with the black rebels.
> We demand:
> immediate withdrawal of the imperialist military from the region involved in the uprising;
> an amnesty for all blacks thrown into jail or exiled for their actions against imperialism;

freedom of assembly and press for our brother workers in the Congo.'

The resolution was given to the press, and the elected delegation was instructed to hand it to the Colonial Minister.

Special leaflets were issued explaining the events in the Congo. A number of demonstrations and meetings were held. The demonstration at Seraing (near Liege) where a number of impassioned speeches were made, was particularly well conducted.

Comrade Jaquemotte, the Communist parliamentary deputy, spoke in parliament on behalf of the revolutionary proletariat, demanding an end to the slaughter in the Congo. This speech had its effect. The bourgeois and particularly the social democratic press, which from the outset had organized a conspiracy of silence on the events, was forced to speak out after Jaquemotte's speech. Information, admittedly understated, on the scale and nature of uprisings, the numbers killed, etc., began to appear in the press. The official newspapers reported the killing of 116 blacks, stating in a footnote that according to official figures the number of people killed amounted to only 86. However, the figure of 116 killed is a long way short of reality. *Le Soir*, for instance, printed a report on a military victory describing one massacre around a certain barn where over 100 blacks perished. The foul gang of lying and slandering Belgian colonialists has no wish to give a correct account of the events in the Belgian Congo.

In recent years the history of this part of Black Africa has been one of bitter struggle by the African masses in the villages and towns against the colonialists.

The Belgian bourgeoisie is in no position to destroy the revolutionary movement. The place of each tortured rebel will be taken up by tens and hundreds. Many black workers know about the Soviet Union. They know that in the Soviet Union the working class is the owner of the means of production, that the working class has overthrown the capitalists and landowners and that every person, even the most backward, has made great achievements in cultural growth and economic development.

The Belgian colonialists are trying to keep the colonies' black working population on a tight rein. But the sea of slander and lies will not deceive the African masses. They know what the imperialist predators are from bitter experience. They have personally suffered from all the horrors of capitalist 'civilization' and feel the growing oppression of decaying capitalism which, before its inevitable end, is attempting to tighten still further the noose around the neck of the oppressed people of the Belgian Congo in order to postpone its downfall by means of increased exploitation. This uprising is only the beginning of a burgeoning growth in the revolutionary movement in the Belgian Congo. The 1932 uprising in the Belgian Congo and Central Africa is typical of all colonies.

## Togoland

In January 1933 an uprising broke out in the French West African colony of Togoland. In order to better understand the reasons for this uprising one must recall, if only briefly, the history of how France received a mandate over Togoland.

On the basis of the Agreements of 30th August 1914 and 4th May 1916, the first partition between Britain and France of the German colonies of Togoland and the Cameroons, which had been conquered by British and French troops, was carried out. According to the 1914 Agreement, the administration of Togoland was entrusted to the government of the Gold Coast. An insignificant part of the country went to France. Since the ports and most of the railways fell into British hands, France insisted upon a second partition of Togoland.

The final partition of these colonies took place in 1919. France received a large part of Togoland and its ports. Despite the fact that these colonies had actually already been divided up, the mandates for them were only officially recognized by the Council of the League of Nations in 1922. Article D of the League of Nations states that France is to receive unlimited powers in the spheres of administration, legislation and jurisdiction in the countries over which she has a mandate. She can establish on her territory fiscal, excise and administrative bodies. She has the right to organize public services, establish a tax system, and create a local police force.

German imperialism naturally considers that its interests have been damaged by the annexation of Togoland's territory. This is also confirmed by the statements of the present fascist government of Germany. Exploiting the discontent among the broad masses of the population generated by the economic crisis, and the appalling weight of taxation under which the Africans are groaning, the *Bund der Deutsche Togoländer*[9] is running an active campaign for the restitution of Germany's former colonies. In an open letter to the Governor of Togoland, one inhabitant bitterly complains that, under French administration, blacks are barred from holding a number of posts, that Africans 'are wandering the streets without work' and that the multifarious levies and taxes are completing the ruin of a population already crushed by the capitalist crisis.

France, disturbed by these pro-German manifestations, has in turn responded with an open letter from a French resident describing the 'cruelty' of the German regime in Togoland and the 'benefits' of French civilization. To us, the meaning of this polemic between the imperialists is obvious. Under cover of these letters signed by blacks, the French and German capitalists are competing for markets for exports and raw materials. Whether German 'civilization' is higher or lower than that of France is an academic question since, in their attack on the Africans, both play the role of executioner. But it is clearly evident from all this that the black people are suffocating under the weight of taxes with which they are being burdened by the French Government.

The uprising which broke out in Lome, the capital of Togoland, on 25th January 1933, is proof that the people's cup of dissatisfaction with taxes and exploitation is running over. An exceedingly brief telegram published on 27th January 1933 in the London *Times*, reports the outbreak of a serious mutiny in Lome in protest against a tax increase. *The Gold Coast Spectator* for 28th January 1933 adds:

'The population has announced that it is overburdened with taxes and that the position of the French Government is regarded by all as despotism and a lack of feeling for the natives. A crowd threw stones at government offices, looted shops and insulted Europeans. An emergency detachment of 800 men has been sent from Dahomey, but the situation has become so acute that in the meantime the Governor has been forced to officially announce that the taxation increase will not be implemented.'

The reprisals carried out on the blacks by the troops sent to the place of the mutiny, were so brutal that the *Bund der Deutsche Togoländer*, availing itself of a welcome opportunity, addressed the following telegram to the League of Nations:

'As a consequence of excessive taxation of the natives and improper treatment of the population, a serious uprising has broken out in Lome. Fifteen defenceless people (women and children) have been shot, and troops have been called up from Dakar to strengthen reprisals against the natives. The rights of the native population are being infringed. The situation is critical. We appeal for mercy.'

The League of Nations, of course, did not answer this telegram and took no steps to restrain this reign of terror. Meanwhile the military occupation was growing stronger each day, and acts of repression against the African population were intensifying.

On 18th February, a second telegram was sent to the League of Nations, saying that the taxes on the black population were out of all proportion to their means, and were in essence equivalent to slavery. In addition to the detachment of 800 men, new troops had arrived from the Ivory Coast.

'Lome is surrounded, the population is terrorized, soldiers of the occupation forces are insulting and raping women in full view of their husbands, houses are being looted, draconian measures have been introduced. 500 natives have been arrested and thrown into jail, where many of them have died. Send a commission to investigate the situation.'

A letter in the *Gold Coast Spectator* for 18th January 1933, entitled 'The French in Togoland', frankly states that the position of Africans under French occupation has become intolerable and that:

'the natives have been forced to leave their homeland for the Gold Coast in order to escape French oppression . . . The natives are obliged to pay taxes, a large part of these taxes being paid by workers for those who are unemployed. (There are no funds for assistance to the unemployed.)'

If anyone refuses, or is unable to pay the taxes, he is thrown into prison and sentenced to forced labour. 'The inhabitants of Togoland were patient and gentle people, but their patience could not last indefinitely.'

Several inhabitants of Togoland have complained about the occupation forces sent to Lome. The uprising was quelled in the most ruthless manner, and four months later the reign of 'order and civilization' had been restored.

Such is the picture of horrors committed by the imperialists in the cowed and blood-stained colonies of Black Africa.

## NOTES

1.  *Umsebenzi* (meaning 'The Worker' in Xhosa) was a South African Communist Party newspaper started in 1930 by Eddie Roux. In his autobiography he provides details of the foundation of the newspaper. Roux, E. and W., *Rebel Pity*, (Harmondsworth, 1972), pp.97 *et seq.*

2.  For a comprehensive account of the Watch Tower Movement during this period, a recent thesis may be consulted: Cross, S.W., *The Watch Tower Movement in South Central Africa, 1908-1945*, D.Ph. thesis, (Oxford, 1973).

3.  Johnson Kenyatta is of course none other than President Jomo Kenyatta of Kenya. He was at that time closely associated with the international communist movement (see Introduction to this book).

4.  The authors do not state the quantity. Presumably this is the price per ton.

5.  Ormsby-Gore was the British Colonial Secretary during the 1920s.

6.  This account seems a little confused. The event referred to was probably the Aba riots of 1929. Aba was not, of course, the capital of Nigeria.

7.  The original states 25 to 30 kopecks.

8.  The literature on this messianic movement started by Simon Kimbangu, a Congolese carpenter, who promised to deliver the Congolese from the hands of Belgian imperialism, is now quite extensive. See, *inter alia*, Balandier, G., "Messianismes et nationalismes en Afrique noire", *Cahiers Internationaux de Sociologie*, 14, (1953) pp.41-55 and Chome, J., *La passion de Simon Kimbangu* (Brussels, 1959).

9.  The Association for a German Togoland.

# 6.

# THE TRADE UNION MOVEMENT IN BLACK AFRICA

Black workers in Africa are one of the most downtrodden and exploited sections of the international working class, since they are the object of both capitalist and pre-capitalist forms of exploitation in the form of one-sided agreements, contract labour and other types of disguised slavery.

The oppressed position of the black worker is made still worse by a whole series of racial restrictions. Blacks are forbidden to live in areas inhabited by whites, to visit public places in the company of whites or walk the streets after certain hours. A special pass system has been established regulating their right of movement not only within the country, but also within the limits of any one town. The system has legal sanctions for imprisoning black workers in special camps (compounds) under special guard and which are frequently surrounded by barbed wire. Special poll and health taxes, levied only on blacks, have been introduced. Thus an entire system has been created which racially isolates the blacks and is known as the 'policy of social discrimination.'

In several countries where black workers work alongside whites, they are disqualified from performing a whole series of jobs which are open only to whites. As a rule, black workers are given heavier work and are, in addition, paid lower wages by comparison with other workers. White chauvinism and pogroms, organized and supported by the bourgeoisie, are contributing to a further deterioration in the already appalling living conditions of the black proletariat. 'The agents of the landowners and capitalists are trying to divide the workers' ranks and increasing racial conflict in order to disarm the workers and strengthen capitalism.' (Lenin).

## RISING REVOLUTIONARY CONSCIOUSNESS AMONGST THE BLACK MASSES

Despite the policy of terror and ruthless oppression carried out by the ruling white minorities against black workers, the revolutionary movement of the black masses in Africa is growing. The struggle in the colonies is being carried on under enormous difficulties, due to the lack of skilled leadership and isolation from the more advanced and experienced proletariat of Europe. The conditions under which the black masses live are such, however, as to drive them into a desperate struggle against the imperialists. The black working masses are hence beginning to take a more prominent place in the common front of the international movement. The task of the African revolutionary trade union movement is to co-ordinate all the workers' isolated outbursts and uprisings with the mainstream of the international revolutionary struggle and to provide the embryonic movement of the black proletariat and peasantry with firm leadership.

In Black Africa, in the Union of South Africa and in the East African colonies in particular, classical methods of imperialist oppression are practised which lead to an inevitable impoverishment and extinction of the African population. The system of compounds, the seizure of the peasantry's best land, the monstrous taxation of plots, huts, livestock and agricultural produce, the absence of political rights and the existence of forced labour are the methods by which the colonialists oppress the working population of the colonies.

## The Duty of Class Conscious White Workers

It is hardly surprising that a bitter hatred is inexorably growing among the blacks towards the capitalist system which binds them hand and foot, and that there is growing suspicion of national reformism which acts as the agent of the imperialist masters, whom it assists in keeping the black masses in chains. Those conscious white workers who adopt the revolutionary platform must strengthen their work amongst the Africans in all the countries of Black Africa, proving by deeds that their struggle is an integral part of the international workers' movement, and of the oppressed masses of the colonial and semi-colonial countries against the common enemy, imperialism.

The sixth Comintern Congress resolution on the Negro Question states that we must involve 'white workers in the struggle for Nego demands'. One should remember that the black masses will be more widely drawn into the revolutionary struggle if the conscious element among white workers proves, by its actions, that it is struggling alongside the blacks against racial persecution and inequality in all its forms. The sixth Congress also stated that in order to eradicate the bourgeois ideology of racial 'supremacy', the struggle, both in words and deeds, must above all be directed against chauvinism among the workers of oppressor countries, and also against the bourgeois tendency towards separatism, evident among downtrodden nationalities and resulting from racial oppression.[1] The propaganda of international class solidarity is an indispensable prerequisite for unity of the working class in this struggle.

In South Africa, a country belonging to British imperialism, where the workers' movement and revolutionary struggle are at a higher level of development than in the other Black African countries, the struggle between the blacks and their oppressors is growing daily in its intensity. Black workers and their class-conscious white comrades have already had to form, more than once, a united front for struggle and action against the entrepreneurs and the government.

Nevertheless, lack of unity among the trade union movement in this country has an extremely debilitating effect upon the struggle. There is a whole series of rival trade unions in South Africa. There are unions which do not admit blacks in their ranks. There is the so-called Industrial and Commercial Workers Union (I.C.U.), a reformist organization which has split into a number of groups under the leadership of Ballinger and the local reformists, Kadalie and Champion.[2] There also exists the revolutionary African Federation of Trade Unions, which has joined the Comintern. This organization enjoys enormous sympathy among black workers owing to its militant and revolutionary programme carried out under the leadership of the South African Communist Party.

The Party and revolutionary trade unions have held mass demonstrations by black as well as white workers. The demonstrations of the 1st May and 1st August, and the day of struggle against unemployment, were particularly successful. One should also mention the large protest demonstrations against the government's attempts to levy an additional tax on the blacks and also against the draft revisions to the law on 'criminal assembly'.

In the Gambia, the British colonial authorities in Bathurst deprived black workers of the right to unite in trade unions, after pressure from businessmen. Shortly after the workers had formed their own trade union, the Chamber of Commerce voiced its opposition to it, and petitioned the authorities to take repressive measures. The 'Workers Government' of Ramsey MacDonald promptly responded by declaring the union illegal. Here is a shining example of the touching unanimity between the social fascists of His Majesty's Government and the British colonists and colonial capitalists.

In Sierra Leone, the Transport Workers Union which previously numbered over 1,000 members has now only 600, despite its long period of existence. This trade union lacks adequate experience of revolutionary struggle, has no concrete programme of action, and is constantly terrorized by British imperialism.

In Nigeria, the African Workers Union (A.W.U.) has existed for over two years.[3] This Union has made it its aim to struggle to develop the national liberation movement of the working masses and to defend their interests. The A.W.U. in Lagos and its two provincial branches now have several hundred members. The British Government has taken a succession of measures against the activities of the A.W.U. It is necessary to obtain a police permit to hold meetings. A police representative who monitors the A.W.U.'s activities is always present at meetings.

There are two national reformist organizations in Nigeria: one of them, under the title of the West African National Congress, covers the whole of British West Africa, the other being the Nigerian Democratic Party.

The former is exclusively composed of representatives of the African bourgeoisie, intelligentsia and peasantry. It was organized in 1920 with the aim of uniting national organizations, particularly peasant ones. It initially enjoyed a certain amount of sympathy among the working class and peasantry, but its reformist policy and practices, and its neglect of the interests of the broad masses, alienated them. The Nigerian Democratic Party is an organization of the bourgeoisie, intelligentsia, chiefs and a substantial number of white-collar workers. Thus the development of the trade union movement in West Africa is only just beginning. Most trade unions have no experience, no programme of action, do not as yet know how to lead the working class, and are constantly terrorized by the authorities. It is natural that at present there is only a very small number of trade unions involving an insignificant section of the working class. There are a number of occupational organizations in the Gold Coast — the drivers' union , the builders' union, the postal workers' union, the fishermens' union, the locomotive drivers' union — but all of these are isolated organizations, having no connections with any international trade union centre.

The protest movement and the black workers' struggle are in need of unification and leadership. Lack of unity and co-ordination between each separate action of the black workers prevents them from gaining the satisfaction of even a fraction of their demands from the imperialist slave-masters. The imperialists exploit the toiling blacks not only as cheap labour, but also as a rich source of cannon fodder in wars of plunder and the fight against the revolutionary movement.

The pre-war and post-war development of capitalism in Black Africa has led to the formation of black proletarian cadres. Due to the world economic crisis, the pressure of exploitation upon black workers has increased still further. As previously pointed out, the agrarian crisis has caused large-scale unemployment, poverty and hunger among millions of peasants, tenants and share croppers.

In the search for an escape from the economic crisis, again the colonial imperialists are transferring their burden to the shoulders of black workers. In order to carry out this policy of super-imperialist exploitation, the capitalists and their governments are raising existing levels of taxation, as we have seen in West and Equatorial Africa, and are simultaneously resorting to new methods of financial oppression (e.g. taxation of women in Southern Nigeria and South Africa). The colonial governments and foreign commerical, shipping and agricultural companies are dismissing black workers on a mass scale, and cutting down all types of public work. This is, in turn, leading to a deepening of the crisis, undermining the purchasing power of the masses and pouring new detachments into the growing army of unemployed dismissed from the factories, mills, mines, transport system and plantations.

## WHITE REFORMISTS — AGENTS OF IMPERIALISM

With the deepening of the crisis, the role of those agents of imperialism, the white reformists, is becoming increasingly clear. They are all attempting to restrain the developing struggle of the black masses. They openly betray the struggle of the working masses by intensifying their policy of chauvinism and setting black and white workers against each other. In their aim to split the fighting front of the working class, the social fascists act under the slogan of 'No work for blacks where there are whites unemployed'. A similar policy is being carried out in European countries, for instance in Britain, where the leaders of the National Union of Seamen have appealed to white seamen in British ports to organize attacks among African and other coloured seamen in order to drive them away from British ships.

## BLACK REFORMISTS — THE COLLABORATORS

The indigenous African national reformists walk side by side with these white agents of imperialism in the fight against the black workers.

In spite of this, however, the workers and toiling masses are meeting their oppressors with firm rebuffs. Black workers in all countries are fighting the burden of taxation, the reduction of wages and the attack on the workers' standard of living. The revolutionary movement among the blacks is developing with increasing speed (e.g. Dingaan's Day, the burning of passes, the 1st of May and 1st of August demonstrations, uprisings in the colonies of Central Africa, Sierra Leone and Togoland, and demonstrations, under revolutionary slogans, in a series of countries).

Let us now turn to the major trade union association of Black Africa. The greatest number of workers are organized in the trade unions of South Africa. A dominion belonging to British imperialism, South Africa is the most economically developed part of Black Africa.

## SOUTH AFRICA'S TRADE UNION MOVEMENT

The trade union movement in South Africa bears the clear imprint of all those features typical of Africa. In this country, trade unions are divided into white unions and black unions. The policy of social discrimination towards the black population has led to a deep rift in the ranks of the working class there.

The white workers' trade union movement is the oldest working class movement in South Africa, and in Africa as a whole. The white workers who emigrated from Great Britain brought with them the traditions of British trade unionism (*tred-yunionizm*).[4] On arrival in Africa, they

121

merely established branches of British trade unions. These were mainly workshop unions, uniting the most privileged of the working aristocracy. The first branches of British unions in Africa appeared during the 1890s. At present about 100,000 white workers (40% of all white workers) are organized within reformist unions. All of them are either direct members of the South African Trade Union Congress (which includes 31 unions from practically every branch of industry) or are indirectly affiliated through the Cape Federation of Labour Unions. All the occupational associations of Cape Town are members of this Federation — the transport workers, electricians, building workers, clothing workers and so on. Here both white and black workers are united within the same unions.

About 10,000 railway workers (10% of all railway workers) are organized in a union which is not affiliated to any central body. In the Cape Province, the Union of Shop Workers (mainly organizing blacks on the Reef) also includes so-called 'Coloured' workers, and is entirely reformist oriented. The Cape Town dockers join African organizations — the Federation of Industrial Workers and Commercial Employees (founded in 1919). In the building industry, which employs about 10,500 white workers and 14,000 Africans, the white workers are members of eight different unions, whilst the African workers have remained unorganized. There are 30,734 workers in the furniture, clothing and leather industries, including 14,961 whites, of whom 4,300 are unionized. A total of 52,000 are employed in engineering, of whom 27,000 are whites. Of these 4,000 white workers are organized in eight workshop unions. About 200 black workers are members of the metal workers' union. Of 20,000 white miners, only 5,000 (25%) are members of one of the several unions, the most influential one being the reformist South African Mineworkers' Union.

At present there are four main central trade union bodies in the Union of South Africa:

the South African Trades and Labour Council (S.A.T.L.C.) (reformist); the Cape Federation of Labour Unions (reformist); the Industrial and Commercial Workers Union (I.C.U.) (national reformist); and the African Federation of Trade Unions (revolutionary, and a member of the Profintern). There are, in addition, the so-called independent unions, which do not belong to any central body. Of these, the main one is the union of railwaymen.

Let us examine each trade union group separately.

## The South African Trades and Labour Council (S.A.T.L.C.)

This organization came into being in October 1930 at the united conference of the South African Trade Union Congress. The aim of creating this organization was to unite the trade union movement in South Africa into a single concentrated central trade union body. However this aim was not achieved.

At this Conference an executive committee was elected which included representatives of all the organizations taking part in the Conference. The Conference also took the decision to set up local committees, subordinate to the central executive committee, in each of the union's industrial centres. It was this very decision which was the basic reason for the breakaway and departure of some of the unions. The Cape Federation of Labour Unions, for instance, an organization with an extremely large membership, refused to implement the decision. The reason for this was that the head of the Cape Federation of Labour Unions, who had been an initiator of the Conference, was not elected to the leadership of the executive committee of S.A.T.L.C. For this reason, the aim — the 'amalgamation of the trade union movement' — was given second priority. Personal interests came to the fore. In order to dress up their refusals to amalgamate as considerations of principle, an accusation of chauvinism was made against S.A.T.L.C., since there was 'no access to S.A.T.L.C. for coloured and native workers'. Thus the Cape Federation of Labour Unions did not join the new organization, and remained independent.

The S.A.T.L.C. then organized local committees in the six major industrial centres, and managed to include in its ranks all the minor, previously independent unions. The policy of this organization is wholly reformist.

## The Cape Federation of Labour Unions

Having broken away from the S.A.T.L.C. this union conducts its business in the same spirit of reformism as the latter body. The Cape Federation unites white and coloured workers. All its activities and policies are purely reformist. It unites white and coloured workers, not because it has overcome the residues of chauvinism, but because the coloured workers are the main and basic force in all industries in the Cape Province. The reformist essence of the Cape Federation of Labour Unions has been particularly borne out, in recent years, by repeated cases of betrayal of the economic struggle and actions of the working class. This was exposed with particular clarity by the tram and omnibus workers' strike in December 1932, which was defeated because of the Federation's betrayal.

## Reactionary Roles of Reformist Trade Unions

The reformist trade unions in South Africa are the most reliable agents the government has in implementing laws against the workers, and are the defenders of the policies of 'civilized labour' and the 'colour bar'. As ardent devotees of parliamentary struggle, the reformists are presently taking up the matter of creating a 'trade union political party', which would have representatives in parliament (*The Star*, 15th March 1932). Now, especially, given the critical growth in unemployment, the reformist organizations, instead of leading the workers' struggle, are betraying their interests by channelling all their actions into arbitration and agreements with the capitalists. For example, the reformists have recently been backing the campaign for wage cuts on the grounds that the entrepreneurs are in no position to 'avail themselves of workers' services at the present high level of wages'.

We quote below a typical example of the S.A.T.L.C.'s activities. The annual report of its Executive Committee states:

> 'The organization received a circular from the International Trade Union Committee of Negro Workers in Hamburg, reporting the impending execution in April 1932 of eight young Negro workers in Scottsboro. The Executive Committee supported this protest, and sent a delegation to the American Consul in Johannesburg to protest against the execution. The Consul forwarded this protest to the Governor of Alabama in the United States, together with a request to initiate a new legal investigation of this matter. The letter was returned by the Governor. The American Consul very pointedly told the delegation that before protesting against the treatment of negroes in the United States, the Council of Trade Unions' delegation ought to protest against their treatment in the Union of South Africa.'

What is the reformists' policy on the question of workers in South Africa, bearing in mind the presence of Africans and other so-called 'coloured' workers? In this respect they lag behind the wildest medieval prejudices of feudal landowners. The poison of reformist ideology has been painstakingly inculcated in the workers. This is evident from the fact that, to this day, all reformist trade unions have categorically refused to admit Africans to their ranks. On the contrary, the leadership of the S.A.T.L.C. has spared no efforts to assist the imperialists in dividing the ranks of the working class, supporting and theoretically justifying the 'colour bar' and the policy of 'civilized labour', and setting the most backward and chauvinism-infected section of the white workers upon the blacks, accusing the latter of being the cause of all the white workers' deprivations.

In juxtaposing their own interests to those of black workers, as beings of 'a lower order', the white trade unions have never attempted to involve the black workers in a united front or nationwide struggle against the capitalists. Looking upon Africans only as competitors in the labour market, these unions have fought against black workers and their recruitment into industry.

In 1911, under pressure from white reformist unions, Parliament passed a law reserving certain categories of work for white workers. Only unskilled, dirty and heavy work was offered to blacks.

The 1914-18 War somewhat weakened Britain's pressure upon South Africa, as a result of which some secondary branches of industry came into being. The shortage of white workers, caused by military mobilization, compelled the capitalists to take on black workers and give them skilled as well as unskilled work. Once given the opportunity, the black workers rapidly began to acquire skills and perform work done by whites although, as before, their wages remained several times lower than those of white workers. This radically changed the relationship between white and black workers. Whereas this had formally been one of whip-bearing overseer to slave, they now became workers on a more or less equal footing. As a result of this, so-called 'coloureds' and Indians were given access to reformist unions such as the Cape Federation of Labour Unions, although for Africans there remained as before 'no admittance'.

The bureaucrats of the reformist miners' union, the most reactionary and influential trade union in South Africa, were frightened by the blacks' invasion of industry and the possibility of some whites being replaced by Africans. They forced the Chamber of Mines to sign an agreement accepting a ratio of 1:10 between whites and blacks in the mining industry, i.e. for each white worker there were to be no more then ten blacks. However the Chamber of Mines did not fulfil the agreement, and told the miners' union that, in future, it would fix the ratio of white and black workers according to its own interests. This meant the immediate dismissal of 5,000 white workers. A 25% cut in the wages of white workers was also announced.

The white miners' discontent was expressed in a strike which, in January 1922, then became an armed uprising in which over 20,000 miners took part. One of the strikers' basic demands was the restriction of black workers' access to the mining industry. Clearly, one cannot involve black and white miners in a united front and a joint struggle against the capitalists with prejudices of this nature.[5]

For a summary of reformist trade union bureaucracy's attitude to black workers, the following statements on this question are extremely interesting.[6]

> 'The greatest disaster which could befall the workers of the Union of South Africa is the organization of non-European workers.'
> 'The organization of black workers and a rise in their standard of living would represent a grave threat to the welfare of white women and children.'
> 'The Kaffir (black) is a being of a lower order and should always remain a slave.'
> 'The negro can only be controlled with the aid of the whip, and Afrikaners would sooner destroy their own trade union, rather than do anything together with the negroes.'

All this shows the sort of animal hatred with which the white trade union bureaucracy looked upon black workers. In the war years this hatred was similarly to be seen at every step in the activity of white reformist trade unions. Black workers have more than once declared strikes of solidarity with white workers. But on every occasion these black workers' strikes were betrayed by the white reformist unions.

In recent times, and especially during the years of the world economic crisis, the influence upon the workers of reformist poison, spread about by the chiefs, has weakened owing to the activity of the Communist Party and the revolutionary trade unions. The capitalists' attack on the working class, including its European part, the mass sackings of white workers (especially in transport), unemployment, systematic wage cuts and the reformists' policy of 'peaceful co-operation' with the masters, preaching the need for the workers to carry the weight of crisis 'equally with the capitalists' — all clearly show white workers the consequences of dividing the working class according to skin colour. The reformists' chauvinist exhortations are gradually carrying less weight and the white workers have a growing inclination to unite with blacks in a joint class struggle. This is forcing the reformists to manoeuvre with still greater effort and skill, especially in the economic struggle.

## The Industrial and Commercial Workers' Union

The black proletariat's trade union movement came into being in 1919, beginning with the organization of the Industrial and Commercial Workers Union, which became a member of the Amsterdam International. In 1926, this organization was the largest in the Union of South Africa, uniting about 60,000 African workers. It had no specific tasks. It was a semi-trade union, semi-political organization, built on individual membership on an area basis. It organized all workers irrespective of occupation or job. In 1926, the blatant desertion of Kadalie, the union's leader, to the camp of reformism, and the activities of the British T.U.C. adviser, Ballinger, led to the disintegration of this union into a number of small groups.

At present, three independent groups of this former union exist (those of Kadalie, Ballinger and Champion) numbering barely two or three thousand followers. Other breakaway groups continued to grow and, together with the revolutionary trade unions organized by the South African Communist Party, have united to form the South African Federation of Trade Unions.

## The Occupation Structure of South African Workers

Let us turn, for a moment, to the position of the working class by occupation, particularly the question of the miners, whose struggle is of great political significance in South Africa. Mining is one of the fundamental sectors of the South African economy. It contributes 28% of the country's total production output, and 70% of its exports. 360,192 workers, or 52% of the total industrial proletariat are employed in the mining industry of whom 311,582 are blacks, and approximately only 10% are whites.

The miners are a highly heterogeneous body of workers in terms of composition. About 10% of white workers are predominantly skilled workers, senior workers and supervisors. The blacks are exclusively un- skilled workers, who have been driven to the mines by force from all parts of Africa. The composition of black miners is shown in Table 6.1.

TABLE 6.1

GEOGRAPHICAL ORIGINS OF BLACK MINE WORKERS

| Place of Origin | Number |
|---|---|
| Transkei | 85,000 |
| Portuguese East Africa | 80,000 |
| Basutoland | 25,000 |
| Natal | 12,000 |
| Transvaal | 10,000 |
| Swaziland | 500 |

The bulk of miners are contract workers; only roughly 1,000 to 2,000 blacks can be considered permanent workers. Due to this heterogeneity of composition, their position differs both in terms of wages and working conditions.

A white worker receives ten times as much as a black worker. The average wage of a white worker in the mining industry is £253 per annum, and that of a black £27 to £31. But even wages among black miners are not identical throughout the industry. In gold mines, for instance, a black worker's monthly wage rate ranges between £1.13.0 and £2.4.0. Under- ground workers are paid 2/- to 3/- and surface workers 1/- to 1/8d. One must also bear in mind the fact that all, or nearly all, black miners are employed under contracts, which involve various deductions from wages: travelling expenses, pass fees and the compulsory purchase of goods in company shops. Wages, moreover, are only paid every 45 days, and then only in part, the rest being paid upon final expiry of the contract.

The living conditions and food of black workers are so disgusting that there is nothing with which they can be compared. Black miners, as pre- viously stated, live in 'compounds'. These camps are surrounded by barbed wire or stone walls, with police constantly on duty at the gates. The barracks where the black miners live are cramped and dirty. 50 to 100 men sleep on planks. There are no beds. Sanitary conditions are appalling. A camp inhabited by 9,000 to 10,000 men has no more than 10 toilets, the only extra facilities being buckets in the living quarters. Baths are extremely infrequent, and even then washing is only allowed with dirty mine water. The food is vile, the usual dish being soup, the so-called *makha*, made from spoilt maize flour. Social insurance, labour legislation and labour protection are non-existent. A worker is not paid during sickness. No payment is made in the event of injury. If a worker on piece-work fails to meet his quota, he is paid nothing.

To this description one should add the legal position under the colonial regime in which the black miner finds himself. He has no right to leave the camp at will. Permission to leave the camp is given only on public holidays, and then only by a special pass indicating where the worker is going and until what time. Blacks are put in the camp prison for the slightest misdemeanour or insubordination. It is not surprising that, despite the severe punishments, black miners desert the mines in tens of thousands.

Agricultural workers make up the largest section of the proletariat; approximately 600,000 landless labourers, if one counts day and seasonal workers, work on the farms and plantations. [The regional distribution of agricultural workers in South Africa is as follows:] Cape Province, 229,769; Natal, 128,639; Transvaal 122,922 and the Orange Free State, 158,845. The composition of the agricultural work force is also diverse: 23% European, 2% Indian, 11% so-called 'Coloured' and 64% African. Here, too, Europeans are in a privileged position; they work mainly as farm managers, agronomists, veterinary surgeons, mechanics, supervisors etc. The average wage of a white worker is £9 per month. Indians work exclusively on the sugar plantations of Natal, their average wage being £3 per month. The majority of Coloured workers are employed on tobacco plantations. Average wages are £4.10.0 per month for adults and 1/6d per month for youths.

The bulk of black workers are employed on farms. Their position is that of landless labourer and tenant worker. The majority of blacks work and live as tenant workers, working either unpaid or for extremely low wages in return for the right to use the land. The position of black workers becomes clear if one takes into account the recent law requiring every black living on a farmer's land to work 180 days per year for him, the time for this work being determined by the farmer. The farmer may refuse a black leave of absence to earn money. No one can hire him for work if he has no pass certifying that he has been released by his previous employer. When land is sold by a farmer, the black labourer automatically passes to the new owner together with the land. He can be punished by whipping or imprisonment etc. for failing to obey the owner. Such a position makes the black agricultural worker essentially a slave.

There is as yet no trade union movement among agricultural workers. The Communist Party and the trade unions have only recently begun to work on the organization of agricultural workers.

In 1930 about 100,000 workers were employed on the railways of South Africa: 58,000 whites and 42,000 blacks. There were 81,608 full-time manual and clerical workers, the rest being employed in construction and temporary work. As a rule the skilled workers are exclusively white, and blacks perform temporary and unskilled work.

The position of the railway men is no different from that of other workers. Wages also vary widely. The 'colour bar' and the 'policy of civilized labour' are particularly rigidly observed on the railways. The average annual wage of a white worker is £100, whereas that of a black worker barely reaches £25. In 1931 the wages of railway workers were cut by 25% but the government was not content with this. As the *Cape Times* reported on 15th January 1932, the Ministry of Railways has raised the question of a further cut of 5% to 20% in the wages of manual and clerical workers.

Of the total number of railway workers, about 10,000, i.e. 10%, are organized in railway trade unions. The Union of Railwaymen does not belong to any central organization, but it is clearly reformist in its activities. It unites exclusively white workers — blacks are not admitted to the union. The main body of black railway workers is completely unorganized.

Over 50,000 people are employed in the clothing industry, 53% of them being white. In some provinces — the Cape Province for instance — the majority of clothing workers are Africans. Workers for certain jobs — pressers, for example — are recruited exclusively among Africans. The wages of white men go up to 120/- per week, those of women and girls up to 70/-, and those of Africans up to only 35/- to 40/- per week. This situation is now changing since as a result of the crisis, the wages of all workers are being steadily reduced. At present about 30% of clothing workers are unemployed. Nearly all factories are working a short week. The length of the working day is up to 11 hours. A further wage reduction of 10/- to 15/- per week has been proposed. The policy of replacing skilled workers by young girls is being stepped up.

Clothing workers have a number of trade unions. In Cape Town white and black clothing workers have their own separate unions. The white clothing workers' union is a member of the reactionary Cape Federation of Labour Unions. The black union has joined the African Federation of Trade Unions. In Johannesburg there is a white clothing workers' union, uniting 2,300 workers, which has joined the South African Council of Trade Unions. The Union of Native Clothing Workers unites about 1,000 workers, and has joined the African Federation. The revolutionary movement has recently been growing among clothing workers, due to the deepening of the crisis.

At one time 28,000 people were employed in the South African construction industry: 10,000 whites and 18,000 blacks. As in other sectors of industry, white workers held a dominant position as foremen, contractors, supervisors and in other posts. All skilled work was, in general, in the hands of the whites. Africans did only unskilled work. Wages and working conditions in this industry are in no respect different from those in other branches of industry. The only difference is that construction workers are subject to dual exploitation by private construction companies and labour recruiters.

Among construction workers, only whites are organized in unions.

There are eight construction trade unions in the main industrial centres, uniting 2,000 construction workers. All these unions are reformist. African construction workers are completely unorganized.

The crisis has hit the construction industry especially hard. Unemployment among construction workers is growing rapidly. About 50% of them are at present unemployed. In Durban alone there are over 1,000 unemployed construction workers, and the rest are working a short week at reduced wages.

In addition to these categories of workers, a part of the South African workforce is employed in secondary sectors of production, about 125,000 being employed in processing industries, according to 1928 figures. The approximate composition of these workers is given in Table 6.2.

TABLE 6.2

WORKERS IN SOUTH AFRICAN MANUFACTURING INDUSTRY

| | |
|---|---|
| Engineering | 52,000 |
| Chemicals | 14,500 |
| Brickworks | 9,815 |
| Furniture making | 8,912 |
| Electrical manufacturers | 8,700 |
| Printing | 8,162 |
| Flour Mills | 5,500 |
| Footwear industry | 5,383 |
| Bakeries | 4,460 |
| Tobacco factories | 3,245 |
| Oil production | 1,495 |
| Leather | 1,459 |
| Breweries | 1,402 |
| Cement | 400 |

# The African Federation of Trade Unions — South Africa's Only Revolutionary Trade Union

A revolutionary trade union organization which has joined the Profintern was the African Federation of Trade Unions, created from the former (South African) Federation of Non-European Trade Unions. The latter was a narrow organization, uniting black and white workers in Johannesburg. From the moment of its foundation, the Non-European Federation limited its practical activities to fixing wage rates and concluding agreements and contracts. This narrow activity undermined the union's militant character and the mood of the black workers. It ultimately became a purely reformist trade union organization.

The new organization arose as a result of opportunistic leadership in the Communist Party, which was removed at the end of 1931. Along with this liquidation of the right, opportunist leadership in the Communist Party, the Non-European Federation of Trade Unions was reorganized to form the African Federation of Trade Unions (A.F.T.U.) — the national organization of the working class.[7]

The A.F.T.U. now acts as the revolutionary leader of the South African workers. Adopting a clear, class-based and uncompromising position on reformism, and providing independent leadership in economic struggles, it is creating a strong class organization. The African Federation has also played a leading part in organizing the unemployed. On the basis of the instructions of the Comintern to the South African Communist Party regarding the tasks of communists in the trade union movement, and the Profintern's instructions and assistance, the African Federation has made a radical alteration in its activities.

By the end of 1932, the African Federation of Trade Unions united about 4,000 African, so-called 'coloured' and white workers employed in light industry. The work of the African Federation of Trade Unions was mainly based upon the unions of clothing workers, furniture makers, bakers and laundry workers. So far, the Federation has been influential only in the secondary sectors of industry. Only recently has the Federation established its first links with workers in heavy industry — the miners, metal workers and construction workers.

## Problems Faced by the A.F.T.U.

In 1932, the Federation underwent a crisis in the shape of a decline in the strength of the ranks of the revolutionary trade union movement, due to loss of membership. This was caused by a rift between the growing revolutionary orientation of the working masses and the Federation's lack of organized political activity.

The severe economic crisis which was shaking South Africa, the unparalleled impoverishment and hunger of the masses and the headlong offensive of capital, had driven the masses towards struggle. The Federation, however, was not in a position to take command of the movement. The reformists' domination of the Federation's membership and leadership of individual unions, and the former opportunistic Communist Party leadership, prevented the Federation's practical implementation of the Profintern's revolutionary line. The Federation constantly adopted the line of least resistance, limiting its activities to light industry, whereas the need was to direct its main effort at the basic sectors of industry, particularly at the miners and agricultural workers.

The working conditions of the miners are, as we have already pointed out, exceedingly severe. Their links with the outside world are highly restricted or totally non-existent (e.g. in the diamond mines). It is impossible to distribute revolutionary literature legally and it is extremely difficult for revolutionary trade union workers to visit the compounds.

The composition of the work force is highly varied. The African Federation did not know how to overcome these difficulties.

The Federation was also unable to make use of the full arsenal of the methods of class struggle, and plunged from one extreme to the other, either continuing its activities of providing legal aid to union members, or calling general strikes on any pretext without adequate preparation. The Federation was unable to implement the Profintern's decisions on the tactics of the united front. Criticism and exposure of reformist trade union bureaucrats, through concrete examples of their treacherous activities, likewise failed to become a major element in the daily work of the Federation. The Federation would sometimes substitute agreements with a union's reformist top leadership for the tactics of the united front from below (as in the clothing workers' strike of 1930).

The Federation was slow to adapt the methods and forms of its work to the heightened level of activity and growth of class consciousness of the working class. This was the reason for a certain backwardness and disorder in the ranks of the revolutionary trade union movement at the beginning of 1932.

What is the situation at present? To begin with, it is essential to note that, despite a profound deepening of the crisis which has been accompanied by a sharpening of all class contradictions in South Africa, the struggle by means of strikes during the first half of 1933 was insignificant. On the other hand we have further growth in unemployment and the numbers of the hungry. An important feature of the present situation is the joint struggle of black and white workers for the immediate payment of benefits. The hunger marches and mass demonstrations of the unemployed, particularly in the Johannesburg region, were characteristic of the marked revolutionary nature of the unemployed, which they manifested in their fights with the police and armed soldiers.

The peasant movement is similarly growing in strength as is evident from the number of confrontations resulting from hunger and the confiscation of livestock in Natal, and the recent battles in which blacks and bankrupt farmers have fought together. A sizeable group of blacks and farmers came to Springbok, broke into shops and threatened armed action if they were not paid benefits. These actions on the part of the unemployed and peasantry, led by the revolutionary movement, show that it is extending its influence, and is gaining a growing control over the broad masses.

The union of seamen and port workers in Durban, the union of fishermen in Port Nolloth and the revolutionary opposition of the Cape Town Union of Tram and Omnibus Drivers are now joining the African Federation of Trade Unions. There are also sections of the African Federation (such as the agricultural workers' section and others), several industrial branch groups and tens of individual members who are not members of sections or groups, but who pay membership fees directly to the Federation.

In April 1933 the Federation had 655 members, and if one includes five agricultural groups numbering 166 members, the total membership of the Federation amounts to 821. There are, in addition, links with the seamen in East London, and with the tobacco and clothing workers' unions in Cape Town. Links with the seamen's union in Lüderitz Bay have also been established.

One must point out that the Federation has recruited an insignificant number of workers by comparison with its opportunities. Its ideological influence is substantially greater than its growth in numerical terms.

Let us examine the situation in individual sectors of industry. We begin with marine transport workers, of which there are two categories: 1) stevedores, quayside workers, crane operators and coal loaders; and 2) sea-going and coastal sailors. There are a total of 2,000 port workers in Cape Town, and a similar number in Durban. There are no more than 600 fishermen and sailors.

The crisis in the shipping industry has led to massive unemployment and the introduction of short time for all workers. Port workers, for instance, are employed on average for two days per week. The pressure of work has been pushed to the limits due to the reduced number of workers. Workers also suffer indirect wage cuts through the three-quarter-day system, which operates as follows: workers turn up for work at 7.20 a.m., but are not allowed to start before 9 or 10 o'clock. Although obliged to perform a full day's work, they are only paid for three-quarters of a day.

Four further committees have recently been formed in Cape Town, despite the fact that there is no union (but only groups), uniting a total of 56 members. The Federation also has several groups on coastal vessels.

The basic work carried out among Cape Town seamen consists of holding meetings at the dock gates, explanatory work, oral agitation and the distribution of regularly published bulletins. In addition, demands on the entrepreneurs have been worked out jointly with non-organized workers, and a series of mass and group meetings arranged in pursuance of these demands.

In Durban, as we have already pointed out, there is a seamen's union with 227 members. The activity of the Federation has met with considerable response among the workers due to the development of its work on the docks, and the raising of demands for discussion and approval by workers' general meetings. In January 1933, two highly successful sit-down strikes were held. Two dock workers', and also seamen's and fishermen's conferences were held. Meetings are regularly arranged at the Durban International Seamen's Club in which foreign and local seamen take part, and where literature in various languages is distributed. In one month alone eight meetings were held on ocean-going steamers, in which several hundred men took part.

The organization of a national seamen's trade union is an immediate task. This union must bring together all sections and groups in the various provinces of South Africa and expand further recruitment. A national conference to determine the basic structure of this organization is to be held shortly.

Organization of the miners so far remains the weakest element of revolutionary trade union activity. The position of black miners is one of semi-slavery. Rising at three in the morning to go down the mine, they work till 4.30 p.m. The system of compounds and constant terror means that trade union activity among miners can be conducted only on a strictly illegal basis. Literature is distributed among miners, groups are arranged to discuss the workers' direct daily needs, and group preparation and educational work etc., is carried out. As a result of the work of these groups, a delegation was recently elected and sent to the mine management to protest against a scheme for the repatriation of miners who have worked for more than nine months. (Black miners are sent away from the mining regions upon expiry of their contracts.) The groups at the mines are still very weak. They are not doing enough to strengthen their organizational work.

The main difficulties of work among miners are the illegal nature of the work, the semi-proletarian composition of the miners, the fact that miners are not permanent workers and the lack of properly trained cadres.

Organization of agricultural workers has recently gained significantly in strength. By February 1933, there were already several hundred members organized in a whole series of groups belonging to the League of Agricultural Workers. By May, the number of workers had almost trebled. A programme of action for work among agricultural workers has been drawn up. Three local conferences have been held to discuss the programme and its most urgent tasks.

Although the Federation previously consisted mainly of unions from secondary branches of industry, its organized influence in these branches has now declined. The one exception is the tram and omnibus workers of Cape Town, where a great deal of work was done during the most recent strike. Prior to the strike, the Federation distributed leaflets among the workers urging them to step up the fight against wage cuts and sackings. The Federation took an active part in the strike, helping to organize strike committees and maintaining a ruthless struggle with the reformist leadership of the Tram Workers' Union.

When the strike ended, the Federation called a mass meeting to expose the leaders of the reformist union who had betrayed the strike. As a result, some of the workers joined the Federation. The reformists attempted to obtain the dismissal and exclusion of workers who had joined the Federation. Thanks, however, to the active work of the Federation, which exposes the treacherous manoeuvres of the reformists, they failed to exclude them from the union's ranks. On the other hand, certain comrades showed a tendency to leave the ranks of this reformist union on the grounds that it is a reformist organization collaborating with the entrepreneurs. But the necessity of working within reformist unions was successfully proved by the explanatory political work of groups favourable to the African Federation of Trade Unions.

The Federation has very few members in other secondary branches of industry such as clothing, tobacco and laundries. Appropriate work is nonetheless carried out in these branches of industry. Mass meetings are held at factory gates and leaflets are distributed.

It should be noted that the Federation has so far achieved only modest success since comrades have not yet correctly learnt how to approach the workers and bring them into the organization. For example, after a series of meetings, workers from the Johannesburg food industry asked senior comrades from the Federation for the organization's address in order to make contact with them, as they were ready to join the fight against the entrepreneurs, wage cuts and the extension of the working day. The Federation's comrades did not take advantage of this approach from the workers to strengthen links with them. Meanwhile, a strike in which the Federation has been unable to take an active part, has taken place in factories of the food industry.

There is also a lack of sufficiently vigorous work among laundry workers, where the Federation has a certain amount of influence and considerable opportunities for the organization of a union.

Despite the massive scale of unemployment, the work done among the unemployed by supporters of the revolutionary trade union movement is still unsatisfactory. Both unemployed blacks and whites live in conditions of unparalleled deprivation. Some unemployed whites are still receiving miserly benefits, but unemployed blacks receive no assistance from anyone. According to official figures there are as many as half a million fully and partially unemployed. Unemployment has recently led to a large number of spontaneous conflicts. One characteristic feature of these actions is a growing militant alliance between unemployed blacks and whites.

In recent months six hunger marches have taken place, mainly in the Johannesburg region. On 15th April, 200 blacks also took part in a hunger march. Unemployed blacks fought with police for two hours with sticks and stones, and were dispersed only after the arrival of large police reinforcements armed with machine guns. Eight policemen were wounded and fifteen black workers arrested as a result of this clash.

In the recent period there has been a marked growth of the unemployed in the membership of organizations. In February a total number of 1,613 unemployed people were organized in committees as follows: in Johannesburg, there were 2 committees with 250 members; in Durban, 1 committee with 22 members; while in Cape Town, there were 6 committees with 1,341 members.

A major difficulty for the leadership of the movement of the unemployed is the high turnover of unemployed blacks, especially in

Johannesburg, where by law they are given a period of only six days to find work. When this period expires, Africans who have failed to find work are obliged to leave the town.

Moreover, despite increasingly frequent instances of united action between unemployed whites and blacks, the question of co-operation between them continues to encounter considerable difficulties. There still exist separate councils for unemployed whites and blacks. The sole connecting link between these councils is a general committee made up of unemployed whites and blacks, the work of which is very weak. It should be noted that both the Federation and the Party have failed to make the necessary effort to weld both groups firmly together in order to broaden the movement of the unemployed.

The continuing growth of unemployment, and the growing strength of the decisive actions of unemployed blacks under revolutionary leadership, provide ample opportunities for the broader development of this movement. In order to achieve this one must struggle resolutely in one's own ranks, against the view that 'it is useless to organize unemployed whites, since they are steeped in white chauvinism'.

The workers' open resentment at wage cuts and the deterioration of their position forces the reformist trade union bureaucrats to intensify their demagogy, and they are increasingly prone to disguise their treacherous role with 'left' phraseology. This can be seen best in such demagogic demands as the introduction of the 36 hour working week without reductions in wages, the repeal of the laws on arbitration and 'seditious' assembly, and the calling of a special conference aimed allegedly at fighting unemployment.

The national reformists are making immense efforts to counteract the work of revolutionary trade unions. This is evident from attempts to revive the Industrial and Commercial Workers Union and set up workers' clubs in order to wrest black workers from 'the hands of hostile organizations'. The Federation's position regarding national-reformist and reformist organizations remains so far unsatisfactory, their role in the workers' movement being underestimated. They are frequently dismissed in general statements to the effect that national-reformist organizations are in any case incapable of achieving anything, that they have no further purpose and that to have relations with them is a pointless waste of time. Such a mistaken view contradicts the line of the Comintern and Profintern on this question. The need for systematic work within reformist and national-reformist organizations must be explained to all politically conscious workers.

The African National Congress (A.N.C.) has recently been extending its activities among black workers, calling regular meetings and launching the most savage attacks on the revolutionary movement. In their speeches, the leaders of the A.N.C. call for the commencement of the eradication of radicals and communists. However, there has been no proper rebuttal

of these attacks by the Federation. This 'left' sectarian line is expressed
in an inability to understand workers who are influenced by the reformists
and national reformists, an inability to organize united front action, and
to ruthlessly expose the treacherous role of the reformists.

Conferences to establish a united front have recently been held at
which questions concerning the fight against unemployment and wage cuts
have been discussed. The main task proposed was that of ensuring the
possibility of systematic and concentrated organizational work, pene-
trating enterprises and reformist unions and creating within them a base
through which the influence of the African Federation can be strengthened.
People elected from groups of black and white workers took part in this
conference. Decisions were made to stage a series of hunger marches, and
to assist in the creation of committees of the unemployed.

The fundamental weakness of the work of the conference was the very
small-scale and sporadic nature of work at enterprises and in individual
branches of industry.

## WEST AFRICAN TRADE UNIONS

### Sierra Leone

All the workers in Sierra Leone are Africans. The Europeans are
employed in commerce (banking, shipping and trade) or as government
officials. There are a certain number of small Syrian traders in Freetown,
and other Syrian merchants engaged in the export of kola nuts. There are
no large African landowners. Some chiefs in the protectorate, however,
own big farms which are worked with peasant labour.

European competition apart, the African bourgeoisie has lately been
ousted from its field of activity by the Syrian bourgeoisie. This is giving
rise to a strong nationalist movement. The African bourgeoisie is trying to
use the working masses as a weapon in their fight against European and
Syrian capitalists. The agitation carried out by the African bourgeoisie
against the foreigners has caused a great deal of unrest and numerous
demonstrations.

Rail and road transport is owned by the State; shipping is under the
monopoly ownership of British finance capital. The administrative posts
in these two branches of industry are in the hands of Europeans, as are the
technical jobs (engineers, specialists, etc).

The vast majority of railway workers are recruited from the colonies.
Sailors and other marine transport workers are recruited from the Kru
tribe in neighbouring Liberia. Skilled workers are paid an average of 2/- to
3/- per day, whilst unskilled workers are paid between 10 and 24 cents.
Women and children are generally paid less than men. The average length
of a working day is 10 to 12 hours. Skilled workers, especially on the

railways and other public services, work for 10 hours per day, but the working day of unskilled workers is not limited in length. The government uses forced labour for road building and other public works within the protectorate.

The vast majority of workers in Sierra Leone are unorganized. The Railwaymen's Union, which was once a mass organization, now has about 600 members and is the only existing workers organization. In July 1930 it sent representatives to the International Negro Conference (Revolutionary).[8] Since then the Hamburg Committee has maintained close contacts with the Union, which is trying to extend the industrial base of its activities and gain new members. This Union also conducted organized work among other groups of the proletariat in an effort to create a central revolutionary trade union body in Sierra Leone.

## The Gambia

The overall political situation in the Gambia reflects the struggle of the working masses who, especially recently, bear the entire burden of the taxation which supports the colonizers.

A shipbuilders' union was created in the Gambia more than 40 years ago. This is a semi-trade union, semi-political organization. The shipbuilders' union began the organization of the Gambian Workers Union on a national scale. In 1929, over 500 shipbuilders and seamen went on strike due to pressure from company owners, wage cuts, and increases in colonial taxation. The Gambian Workers Union took command of this struggle. As a result of the struggle, the Union succeeded in recruiting seamen, carpenters, bricklayers and building and engineering workers. The Union's membership rose to 1,000.

The official organ of the company owners demanded that Government liquidate the Gambian Workers Union. Thus in its earliest days the Union had to develop the struggle for the workers' elementary right to form trade unions. In the Gambia an eight hour working day is laid down by law, but is not implemented in practice. The Union has adopted the task of fighting for social insurance against sickness and unemployment.

The Gambian Workers Union is organized as follows. The organization in each branch of industry constitutes a section of the Union and elects its own committee providing leadership to subordinate organizations. Section committees elect their own representatives to the Union's Executive Committee.[9]

## The Gold Coast

In the Gold Coast the trade union movement has been in existence for about 20 years. Up to the present time, the trade unions have not joined any central international body. The International Trade Union Committee of Negro Workers has recently established links with various Gold Coast unions.

Miners represent the most important section of the working class. There are a total of 16 to 18,000 miners. In 1930-31, 7,302 workers were employed in gold mines, of which 7,121 (97.5%) were Africans and 181 were Europeans. No recent figures exist for the number of workers in the manganese industry. There were 4,000 men employed in the industry in 1925. The largest diamond mining company employs 1,750 Africans and 80 European workers.

Mining has always experienced a major shortage of labour. Blacks do not want to work in the mines because of the hard working conditions, low wages and appalling treatment by overseers. But as shown above, the Gold Coast labour market is highly dependent upon prices for peasant produce, primarily cocoa prices, and this forces the Africans to work in the mines. As in South Africa, mining companies practise extensive labour recruitment. There is a network of agents who travel the country making work contracts with blacks. Chiefs and local officials are obliged to render all possible assistance to these recruiting officers. If an African leaves work before the expiry of his term of contract, it is treated as a criminal offence under the law of 1921.

These measures notwithstanding, the Gold Coast is unable to satisfy the total demand for labour. Only 20% of the mining industry's labour is provided by blacks from the Gold Coast itself; the remaining 80% are imported from other colonies. The mining companies once developed a scheme for importing workers from China and Western India, but, for a number of reasons, the scheme was not carried out. In 1921, an agreement was signed with the Nigerian Government, under which the latter undertook the annual supply of a specified number of workers; however, the agreement was annulled after three or four years. At present the mining companies recruit workers in Liberia, Southern Nigeria, the Ivory Coast and, in particular, Upper Volta, through their own agencies.

In his report for 1927-28 the Governor General of the Gold Coast wrote:

'Throughout the Gold Coast one may find large numbers of illiterate workers who come from French territory in search of work. These and natives from the northern territory, who have come to the south in search of work, constitute the bulk of unskilled workers. Part of the workers is made up of natives from French territories evading military service. The position of this section of workers is particularly hard, since they have no farms here, and are unable to return home.'

The living and working conditions of the miners are no less severe than in other African colonies. Miners live in special barracks resembling the South African compounds, but differing in that these are open-type barracks. A miner's working day is between 10 and 12 hours long. Wages vary from 20 to 35 cents, depending on the nature of the work, and are

lower even than those of South African miners. There are company shops
in mining settlements where the miners purchase all their necessities at
'company' prices. One indication of the severity of the living and working
conditions is the high mortality rate: the average mortality rate among
miners during the recent years was 75.27 men per thousand.

The miners have no trade union organizations. As far as one may judge
from the press, the last miners' strike occurred in 1930 at the Ariston
Company's mines, when the company decided to introduce quarterly
payments of wages in place of the existing monthly system. The miners
declared a strike. Meetings were held in the surrounding villages where
miners lived. The company's European employees formed armed detachments and dispersed them. In one village they opened fire on a meeting
without warning, killing five Africans and wounding ten. When news of
these bloody reprisals reached the neighbouring villages, several hundred
men and youths armed themselves with sticks and knives, came to the
mines and drove away the European guards. The strike lasted several days.
Its outcome is not known.[10]

The economic crisis has had varying effects upon individual branches
of the mining industry. Gold mining has been on the increase throughout
the crisis years, and in 1931 production reached a post-war record. This
increase, however, has not prevented the mining company from mounting
an attack on the miners' standard of living. This attack has been made
possible because of the enormous over-supply of labour. By means of a
series of rationalization measures, carried out at the expense of the
working class, they have managed to reduce the cost of extracting one ton
of gold ore from 23/- in 1930 to 19/- in 1932.

Exports of manganese have fallen steadily, and by 1930-31 were already
only 59% of exports in 1929-30. In 1931 there was a further fall in exports.
The manganese companies, incidentally, have put the blame for the fall in
exports on 'dumping' by the Soviet Union. For the miners, the crisis has
brought a significant reduction in the number of workers, and reductions
in wages. A report on the mining industry for 1931-32 states that (1) there
is a large surplus of labour on the market, (2) the extraction of manganese
has fallen due to Russian competition, and the number of workers employed has been substantially reduced, and (3) 11,839 blacks and 232 Europeans were employed in all branches of the mining industry.

If one subtracts from this the 7,500 working in the pits, there remain
only 4,000 workers in the diamond and manganese industries, whereas in
1925 the manganese industry alone employed 4,000 workers. According
to our estimates the workforce has been cut by 5,000 to 7,000. On the
one hand there is an influx of workers, and on the other, cuts in the labour
force. As a result, the company owners are making substantial cuts in
wages.

The railway network of the Gold Coast consists of two main lines —
Sekondi-Kumasi and Accra-Kumasi — and two branch lines Tarkwa-Prestea

and Oda-Kade. The total length of track is 500 km. In 1928-29 the railways employed 181 European and 667 African clerical and station workers, 678 in the workshops, 304 foremen and 4,281 labourers — a total of 6,111 men.

The crisis made the position of the railways considerably worse. The railways' main freight items are cocoa and the products of the mining industry. The volume of freight has fallen substantially and there has been an accompanying drop in railway income. In recent years the railways have operated at a permanent loss. In its report for 1931-32, the railway management stated that the railways' income had fallen from £1,183,035 in 1930-31 to £761,396 in the current year, or by 35.64%. In the same report the management stated that it had reduced expenses on all services from £525,860 to £437,812. During one year, according to the management, 40 Europeans and 92 Africans were dismissed, and at existing levels of freight volume, further staff reductions were essential. The management is thus putting the burden of the crisis on the workers' shoulders and the situation is made worse by the fact that the railwaymen of this part of Africa have no trade union organizations.

The Gold Coast has nine ports. Exports go mainly through the ports of Winneba and Accra, and imports through Accra and Takoradi. The fall in the Gold Coast's foreign trade turnover has meant a reduction in the freight volume handled by the ports. In 1930-31 the main port of Takoradi had a deficit of £30,702, rising to £43,645 in 1931-32. In his financial report the Governor of the Gold Coast states that employment in the port of Takoradi has had to be considerably reduced, although he does not state the number of those dismissed. Although the port workers have their own union, we have no information about it.

The extreme commodity orientation of African farming (a cocoa monoculture), and the underdevelopment of the railway network, create a considerable demand for road transport. The latter plays a very large part in the economic life of the Gold Coast. There are over 6,000 km of roads suitable for motor traffic, and about 7,000 motor vehicles. A large proportion of vehicles belong to the government, a further number to commercial companies, and a small number are owned by African drivers.

The drivers have their own rather old organization — the Gold Coast Driver and Mechanics Union. This Union was organized in 1915 in response to a government attempt to lower wages. At present it has about 7,000 members, of which 1,000 are from Accra, where the board of the Union meets. There are 21 local departments in Ashanti, Togoland and the northern provinces. The Union is not a member of any international trade union association.

The position of the drivers has now considerably deteriorated: a large number are unemployed due to a reduction in the transport of cocoa.

In January 1928, the Gold Coast Carpenters Union was organized in Accra, with departments in a number of towns. The work and wages of building workers are controlled by the government. A carpenter's working day lasts from 6 a.m. until 4 p.m. with a one-hour lunch break. In the climatic conditions of the Gold Coast, 9 to 10 hours in the open air has an extremely harmful effect upon workers' health. Sickness and mortality rates are very high. There is, of course, no insurance. Wages range from 2/6 to 6/- per day. A foreman is paid 6/- per day. Apprentices receive 1/6 per day in their first year of work, 2/- in their second, and 3/- in their third.

There is a fishermen's trade union in the Gold Coast, but we have no information on either the union or on the working conditions of the fishermen.

There is practically no processing industry at all in the Gold Coast, with the exception of a few enterprises of a semi cottage-industry type for the extraction of oil from palm nuts. The largest of these enterprises, the Bakaner Palm Oil Mill*, with a maximum monthly capacity of 2,000 tons, is at present closed. There are also vehicle repair workshops and a small amount of cottage-industry in the towns.

It is quite impossible to assess the number of unemployed in the Gold Coast, as they are not registered in this country. Moreover the majority of workers have not severed their ties with the countryside; workers return to their own villages when unemployed. However, there is a significant amount of unemployment in the towns. The national-reformist press speaks unanimously of a large growth in urban unemployment and mass hunger in the countryside.

In their address to the Governor General in 1932, the citizens of Accra wrote:

> 'Changing conditions resulting from the world trade depression and the fall in prices for our produce have seriously affected not only Government finances, but have brought us to such poverty that a considerable number of His Majesty's subjects have difficulty in avoiding hunger, which was once unknown in the Gold Coast colonies. An important feature of the present situation is the daily growth in the number of unemployed among our people. The problem of our young people, who are unable to find work on finishing school, and thus swell the already large ranks of the unemployed, is becoming increasingly acute.'

One article on unemployment, which appeared in a national-reformist newspaper, states that urban artisans such as tailors, shoemakers and others are in a particularly serious position. Despite the absence of precise information on unemployment, one may still conclude from the available data of the reformist press, that the world economic crisis has affected the working class and peasantry with greater effect and devastation than in other colonies, due to the monocultural nature of indigenous peasant farming, and the dependence of the country's economy upon cocoa prices.

## AFRICA'S SAILORS AND DOCKERS

In examining the trade union movement in Black Africa, one must deal at some length with one of the most important strata of the black proletariat — the seamen.

Black seamen and dockworkers on ships and in the ports of the principal capitalist countries, and also in the main ports of Black Africa constitute not only a significant part of the black proletariat, but also a substantial part of the proletariat working in transport.

Not only are black seamen and dockworkers in the metropoles treated like workers from colonial and semi-colonial countries, but the nature of their working conditions is worse than slavery. Their wages, particularly on liners of the British shipping company, Elder Dempster, are £5 to £7 per month, i.e. 25% lower than those of white seamen. Their food and living conditions are inferior. In many cases they have to prepare their own food out of working hours, for which they do not receive overtime. Their work-load is constantly increasing, and in many cases five black seamen now do the same amount of work as was previously done by ten white seamen.

On the coast of Africa, particularly the West Coast, seamen from the Kru tribe earn only 2/- for a 12 to 14 hour working day. The only food that they receive is rice and dried fish. Of these 20,000 Kru sailors, about 50% are unemployed. They receive no assistance whatsoever. They live under continual threat of arrest and expulsion, especially in European ports. In many cases they do not have the right to organize: on Elder Dempster liners they are refused employment or sacked if they belong to a trade union. They are in an unequal position as regards recruitment since they are not hired through labour exchanges, as are white seamen. In addition they are robbed by African elders who are given extensive powers in the area of recruitment, and usually demand a part of a seamen's wages for their services.

In order to attack the seamen's general standard of living more successfully, the ship-owners split the ranks of white, so-called 'coloured' and African workers through the policy of white chauvinism, inciting racial hatred and racial disturbances. They also support tribal and other disagreements, setting different tribes and groups of blacks against each other.

The bourgeoisie finds reliable agents for its exploitation of seamen in the form of reformist trade unions. The reformist British National Union of Seamen is savagely persecuting the Seamen's Revolutionary International, because the latter is organizing a joint struggle and creating a united front of white and black workers against the company owners. The reformist Union of Seamen accuses the Seamen's International of attempting to replace white by black seamen. In Britain the reformist trade union leaders are trying to stir up national enmity between black and white seamen in Cardiff.

In other countries, the reformists are similarly running a slanderous propaganda campaign alleging that black seamen are to blame for unemployment among white seamen. The French section of the International Federation of Transport Workers (reformist) is openly demanding the dismissal of black seamen from French vessels. Reformist leadership is also conducting a policy of propagating imperialistic chauvinism among white and coloured seamen.

Not only do the imperialists spend large sums on training African troops in order to prepare for military intervention against the U.S.S.R.,but they also train seamen intensively in transport for the movement of troops, particularly from Dakar and North African ports.

Despite the bourgeoisie's campaign of terror and the splitting tactics of the reformists, black seamen and port workers are showing a readiness to fight (witness the strike in Durban and the creation of a dockers' union resulting from a Dingaan's Day demonstration in South Africa). At the same time black seamen, particularly in European ports such as Liverpool, Cardiff and Hamburg, are joining the ranks of the seamen's revolutionary movement. Despite the searches for literature on ships in Freetown, despite the threat of fines should literature be found, and despite the fact that, in some cases, seamen have been arrested on suspicion of keeping literature and acting as 'ship's delegates', black seamen are struggling courageously for revolutionary unity.

The guiding principle of the organization of black seamen is on one ship or in one ship's group, namely a group of the national section under whose flag a ship sails. In other words, black seamen from colonies where there are no revolutionary national trade unions are organized in groups of those nations under whose flag they sail (for example the movement of minority seamen on British ships, or the French Union of Seamen on French ships).

The basic demands of black seamen are as follows: (1) equal pay with white workers for equal labour, (2) an increase in wages, (3) a seven-hour working day during time spent in port, (4) one free day in port for every Sunday spent at sea, (5) social insurance to be paid by the ship owner, (6) unemployment benefit and free food, clothing and accommodation during periods of unemployment, (7) double pay for overtime, (8) equalization of the procedure for hire and registration at labour exchanges, (9) the right to organize meetings, fight against arrests, expulsions and cases of persecution in foreign ports, full rights to go on shore in foreign ports and to struggle against reactionary legislation affecting seamen, and (10) freedom to organize revolutionary trade unions.

## FIRST WORLD CONFERENCE OF BLACK WORKERS

In order to unite and involve the broad masses of the black proletariat in trade unions on a class struggle basis, and to establish links with the black workers of the world, it was decided to set up the International Trade Union Committee of Negro Workers, which was instructed to convene an international conference.

The first international conference of black workers in the history of the workers' movement met in Hamburg on 7th July 1929. The conference was called by the Trade Union Committee and Preparatory Committee of Negro Workers, elected at the second congress of the League Against Imperialism in Frankfurt. This committee, convened at the initiative of black workers, devised a plan for convening the international conference and prepared a draft programme of struggle.

Acknowledging that leadership of the revolutionary section of the national movement to liberate blacks from the imperialist yoke in the various countries of the world, is the historic task of the international proletariat, and in the first instance of black workers themselves, the Preparatory Committee issued a proclamation to all workers of colonial and independent countries where the multi-million strong mass of black workers live. The Preparatory Committee also resolved that the conference should make the creation of a permanent central organization, which would unite black workers throughout the world, its first priority.

It was only possible in this book to give an exhaustive analysis of the conditions of the struggle of each individual colony and semi-colony through the study of these colonies and the discussion of their actual situation with the delegation from each country in question. The delegates' reports were to give a clear picture of the disposition of forces in order to enable the conference to plan the further development of the anti-imperialistic liberation struggle of the black peoples.

The programme worked out by the Preparatory Committee laid down the movement's goals and tasks with perfect clarity. It clarified the role of black workers in the black liberation movement; the significance of the slogan of self-determination and the attitude of the black movement to class struggle; the need to expose the petty bourgeois intelligentsia and the black national bourgeoisie and the necessity for trade union and political organization and united leadership of the national liberation struggle.

At the conference itself there was no place for hesitations and the capitulationist policy of 'a united front from above', which typifies the policy of black reformists in the United States. The conference was also free from the spirit of narrow sectarianism. The final programme pointed out and exposed weak aspects of their work in extremely concrete terms, and pointed the conference towards internationalism. The central point of the programme was, of course, the shifting of the centre of gravity of work to Africa.

Seventeen delegates attended the conference, representing ten different countries. In terms of social origin, workers predominated at the conference. The Report of the International Committee of Negro Workers (a body affiliated to the Profintern), and its discussion, clearly brought out the class nature of the black masses' struggle against imperialist rule. The role of black workers was characterized in the speeches of delegates as the driving force of the black liberation movement. At the same time note was taken of the movement's immaturity, its unbalanced development, and the fundamental need for internationalization of the struggle.

Discussion of economic struggle and the tasks of black workers was exceedingly lively. A picture was revealed of the insupportable burden which has been placed upon the colonial peoples as a result of the world economic crisis. All the problems connected with the fall in world market prices for colonial goods and its influence on colonial exports, the purchasing power of colonial peoples, imperialism's policy of developing colonial production only by the continued extraction of raw materials, and the consequent impoverishment and degradation of the colonial peoples were clearly revealed at the conference. The inevitability of imperialist wars was examined in the reports that were presented and debates were held on the danger of war and its implications for the black working masses. The delegates' reports exposed imperialism's methods and policies in the colonies. The role of the African chiefs and the national reformists was also exposed. A horrifying picture of poverty, ruin, ignorance and physical devastation was drawn in detail by the black African delegates. The conference was infused with a militant spirit of struggle against imperialist rule.

The newly-elected Committee was instructed to extend (its) influence and maintain contact with the workers' organizations of Black Africa, the West Indies and other countries, and to take the steps necessary to ensure the organizational strengthening of the conference's work. For this reason, the Hamburg Conference was a landmark in the history of the oppressed masses' struggle for liberation.

The International Trade Union Committee of Negro Workers has taken a series of measures to establish and maintain contact with workers' organizations in South and West Africa. The Committee has given help in organizational work among blacks in the European ports of Marseilles, London, Liverpool and Rotterdam. Work among black seamen in Hamburg has developed vigorously. The Trade Union Committee has conducted a campaign on the case of the Scottsboro prisoners and others.

An immense amount of work has been done to popularize the resolutions of the Hamburg Conference and the Fifth Profintern Congress in the sphere of work among black workers. These resolutions were reprinted in the black newspaper, *The Negro Worker*, and special pamphlets were published. The following pamphlets have also been published: *Anti-Soviet Intervention; What is the Hamburg Committee and its Tasks?; Child Labour in the Colonies; American Imperialism Enslaves Liberia*, and a number of others. Special attention has also been given to the U.S.S.R. Five Year Plan, and to the way in which the nationalities question has been solved in the U.S.S.R. and the cultural level of national minorities raised. A series of proclamations have been issued in connection with the war in the Far East, and regarding black soldiers in the French army, black seamen, etc.

In France publication of a black newspaper, *La Cri du Negre* has begun. It has proved possible to establish links with the countries of Equatorial and Central Africa with the aid of this paper.

During its brief period of existence, the International Trade Union Committee of Negro Workers has drawn a number of groups to its side and has made contacts with a whole series of organizations in Black Africa. The Committee has succeeded in involving a large number of new comrades in its work, mainly from among workers, and in establishing links with individual workers' organizations, especially with organizations of agricultural workers in those colonies with which there had previously been no links whatsoever.

The *Negro Worker* has become a popular mass newspaper for black workers, examining their day-to-day struggle and summarizing the experiences of that struggle. The paper is distributed in all colonies of Black Africa, America, the West Indies and other countries.

## NOTES

1. The inclusion of this passage and interpretation of the Sixth Congress is of great interest in view of the South African Communist Party's adoption of the Black Republic slogan proposed at the 1928 Comintern Congress (see Introduction).

2. The British Independent Labour Party and Walter Citrine, the British T.U.C. leader, arranged for William Ballinger, a Glasgow-born member of the Motherwell Trades Council, to go to South Africa to advise the I.C.U., then a large but slowly disintegrating general union uncertainly led by Clements Kadalie and the I.C.U. secretary in Natal, A.W.G. Champion. Kadalie found, in his words, that he had a dictator on his hands, not an advisor. The tensions between the leaders of the I.C.U. were a contributory cause to the decline of this initially highly successful union. Throughout this book, Nzula and his co-authors consistently downgrade and attack the I.C.U., but the virulence of their attack is an indication of how important the union was to working class aspirations at the time. For further information, see Simons, H.J. and R.E., *Class and Colour in South Africa, 1850-1950*, (Harmondsworth, 1969), Chapter 15; Kadalie, C., *My Life and the I.C.U.*, (London, 1970); and Johns, S.W.,'Trade Union, Political Pressure Group or Mass Movement? The Industrial and Commercial Workers Union of Africa', in Rotberg, R.I., and Mazrui, A.A. (eds), *Protest and Power in Black Africa*, (New York, 1970), pp. 695-754.

3.  Some details of the origin and character of this organization, which advocated mass technical education and the promotion of indigenous industries, in addition to defending the rights of wage earners, can be found in Hughes, A. and Cohen, R., 'An Emerging Nigerian Proletariat', in Gutkind, P.C.W., Cohen, R. and Copans, J. (eds), *African Labor History*, (Beverly Hills and London, 1978). For information comparing Nigeria to the Gold Coast, see Cohen, R., 'The Making of a West African Working Class' in Shaw, T. and Heard, K., (eds), *Africa: The Politics of Dependence*, (London, 1978).

4.  'Tred-yunionizm' is here clearly used in its derogatory sense and denotes 'economism', i.e. trade union activity directed towards the attainment of exclusively economic goals.

5.  For a recent reassessment of this critical event in South African labour history see Davies, R., 'The Rand Revolt of 1922', in Gutkind, P.C.W., Cohen, R. and Copans, J. (eds), *op. cit.*

6.  The authors do not make clear which leader of the white unions made these statements. From the context, it is possible that it is a leader of a white mine workers union.

7.  This version of events does less than justice to the Non-European Federation of Trade Unions. According to the Simons, when the Industrial and Commercial Workers Union split into warring factions, African workers looked to the communists for leadership. At a well-attended conference in March 1928, the Non-European Federation was formed under communist control. The Non-European Federation was the first body to lead a joint strike of black and white clothing workers in Germiston and also set up an inter-racial committee of laundry workers in Johannesburg. See Simons, H.J. and R.E., *op. cit.*, p.400. What Nzula (certainly the author of this passage) was probably objecting to, was the domination of the Federation by the old-time white communists.

8.  This refers to the first International Conference of Negro Workers, held in Hamburg in July 1930. The Sierra Leone delegate, 'E.A. Richards', was in fact I.T.A. Wallace-Johnson, a radical Sierra Leone journalist, who at one time acted on behalf of the Comintern at several places along the West Coast of Africa. For a man usually so voluble, his speech to the Conference was terse and uninformative, suggesting that his credentials to represent the union were poor. See *Report of the Proceedings and Decisions of the First International Conference of Negro Workers*, (Hamburg, 1930), p.20 (copy in Editor's possession).

9.  For a scholarly discussion of the history of Gambian trade unionism, see Allen, C.H., 'African Trade Unionism in Microcosm: The Gambian Labour Movement, 1939-1967' in Allen, C.H. and Johnson R.W., (eds), *African Perspectives*, (London, 1970).

10. See *Report of the Gold Coast Enquiry into the Wounding of Eight*

# 7

*Africans at Prestea on 15th September 1930* (Accra Go
Printer, 1930).

# THE ECONOMIC STRUGGLE OF THE WORKING CLASS IN BLACK AFRICA

The characteristic features of the current economic struggles in Black Africa are the capitalists' attack on the working class (primarily the African proletariat), the transfer of the weight of the crisis to the shoulders of the colonial working masses, a systematic reduction of wages, the unprecedented scale of unemployment throughout the colonies, especially in South Africa, the growth of the workers' movement, and the growth of class solidarity and the level of revolutionary activity.

Strikes, workers' struggles, mass demonstrations and meetings, accompanied by a fierce struggle with the power of the state, have now become an everyday phenomenon in the colonies, particularly in South Africa.

We shall provide a brief survey of individual strikes in order to give an outline of the economic struggle. To begin with, we shall consider the strikes and workers' struggles which occurred in South Africa during the first six months of 1933. Despite cuts in wages and a worsening of working conditions, the trade union bureaucrats have systematically restrained the workers from protests and strikes.

## STRIKES AND WORKERS' STRUGGLES IN SOUTH AFRICA

During recent months small-scale fishermen's strikes have occurred at Lüderitz Bay, which ended in victory for the workers. Among the tobacco workers of Cape Town, opposition to a new system of rationalization has grown rapidly, culminating in a strike. Due to organized action, the workers' demands were satisfied and the sweated labour system, which the rationalization involved, was withdrawn. The food and clothing workers have also held a series of strikes. The diamond workers elected a strike committee and held mass meetings in preparation for a strike. Powerful political forces were set against the workers and the legal clause forbidding strikes in the Industrial Conciliation Act was enforced. Thirteen strikers and the entire strike committee were arrested.

The African Federation took no active part in any of the above strikes and gave the workers no real help, although its influence in these sectors of industry is quite considerable. This is basically due to the current weakness of the work of Africa's revolutionary trade union organizations and their

lack of knowledge as to how to establish themselves at enterprises and develop closer contacts with the workers.

Among one section of comrades leading the revolutionary trade union movement there still exists the view that small-scale strikes and limited conflicts are of no great importance, and that the working class needs only widespread strikes on an industrial sector or nationwide scale. The result of this neglect of limited conflicts has been that, even in those reformist unions where the revolutionary trade union movement has had a certain amount of influence, this influence has declined in strength. Such are the results of ignoring the everyday needs of the workers of any enterprise or sector of industry.

A large number of strikes were recorded in 1932. In Durban there was a dockers strike. On 2nd April 1932, 1,000 port workers went on strike. Work in the port was halted, and only 300 day-labourers, usually employed during labour shortages, and ten Europeans continued working. 'For the first time in the history of the Port of Durban, white workers pushed barrows for 6/- a day' wrote *The Star*.

The strike was caused by a lengthening of the working day from eight to ten hours, with a simultaneous reduction in wages from 2/6 to 2/-. Some workers who had initially continued to work joined the strike following pressure from the strikers. The management hired a further 700 day-labourers to carry out the work of the port, paying them 3/6 per day as against the 2/6 paid to the regular workers.

## The Strike in Port Elizabeth

On the 1st April 1932, 240 African workers went on strike. At midday 150 casually recruited Europeans were put to work and unloaded the steamer *Winchester Castle*. Prior to the strike the workers received 4/- for an eight-hour working day, and were paid daily. The strike was caused by the port management's order to change to a ten-hour working day with wages to be paid on a weekly basis. The strike ended in the defeat of the workers.

One should, in passing, take note of a typical instance of the capitalists' manoeuvres in the fight with the workers in this port. Some years ago the port employed mainly Africans. When they went on strike, the management paid off the Africans and engaged other black workers: coloured people, Asians and even some Chinese. Then these black workers went on strike. The management sacked them and took on the same Africans who had previously been fired.

## The Johannesburg Chemical Workers' Strike

At the end of February 1932, a strike broke out at the chemical works of Crystallisers Ltd* in Johannesburg. Initially communists assumed leadership of this strike, which made good progress. However, reformists from the South African Trades and Labour Council (S.A.T.L.C.) managed to persuade the strikers to agree to arbitration, and the strike was broken.

The policy of the reformists stands forth in all its squalor in the events of this strike, if only in the role of Andrews, the General Secretary of the S.A.T.L.C. who attempted to introduce 'a more moderate spirit into the negotiations' and authorized the correspondent of the bourgeois *Star* to report that 'the subscription list for collections to support the strikers has not received the approval of the Council of Trade Unions'. On the other hand it is interesting to note the solidarity of workers from other factories in the struggle against strike breakers.[1]

We quote the substance of *The Star's* reports on the strike (25 to 27th February 1932): A strike was declared at the factory of Crystallisers Ltd (on which date it began is not stated, but it is reported that a workers' demonstration was held in front of the factory building on the 24th).

The reason the strike began was that a former female employee told the management that the workers were stealing materials. The management informed the workers that everyone leaving the factory would be searched. The angry female workers decided to organize their own trade union at the factory to defend themselves against the arbitrary acts of the management. A union was organized, and all the women joined it.

'Whereas all the factory's women workers were previously one happy family [or so the paper wrote], from the moment of the union's creation the women began to voice their dissatisfaction with the management's treatment and working conditions at the factory.' Soon after that, the chairman of the new union was dismissed, allegedly for 'having been three times late for work'. The women then declared a protest strike, forcing the management to reinstate the dismissed worker.

The management, however, resorted to sterner measures, and dismissed 14 women as being 'responsible for agitation threatening to bring the work of the factory to a halt'. The remaining women again immediately declared a solidarity strike, demanding the reinstatement of those dismissed, an increase in wages, and certain other privileges.

The management refused to increase wages on the grounds that the level of wages at the factory was adequate and 'even if somewhat reduced by comparison with the past, such reductions have in any case been implemented at all the country's enterprises'.

On 25th February a joint meeting was held between representatives of the management and the strikers. After five o'clock (while the meeting was still going on) the women who had not joined the strike, having finished work, left the factory under police escort to protect them from the strikers. Having escorted them a considerable distance, the policemen turned back. The strikers and workers from other factories then attacked the strike-breakers, who hid themselves in the nearest houses. This scene ended with the police again coming to the aid of the strike-breakers.

In the evening the crowd outside the factory gates was addressed by representatives of the clothing workers' union, whilst the crowd grew continuously with the arrival of further Africans. A police detachment dispersed the crowd, after which, as the paper says, 'all was quiet'.

'The activity of Communist Party members hindered the peaceful resolution of the strike at the chemical works of Crystallisers Ltd' reports the same newspaper's issue of 26th February. 'On the morning of the 25th the strikers' representatives agreed to arbitration, but 28 women strikers and several unemployed Party members declared their representatives' decision invalid and, on the morning of the 26th, young women again set up pickets at the factory gates.'

Andrews, the secretary of the Trades and Labour Council, Senator Briggs, a representative of the Council and the leader of the Labour Party, and Mr Kalk, a prominent trade unionist, visited the factory in an effort to 'explain' the situation which had arisen to the women. When the strikers turned to the Trades and Labour Council for financial assistance, Mr Andrews refused on the grounds that the leadership of the strike had passed into the hands of the Communists.

In the end the reformist leaders succeeded in persuading the women to accept arbitration. The arbitrator was Mr (Morris) Kentridge, a Labour Party Member of Parliament. The dismissed women were reinstated at the factory, except for one woman who had taken a particularly active part in the strike.

## The Clothing Workers' Strike

The strike in Cape Town was caused by a factory owners' decision (in particular the African Clothing Factory*) to reduce wages by 10 to 15 shillings. The reformist clothing workers' union at once tried to break down the workers' resolve to oppose this attack. It appealed to the workers for class co-operation, arguing that during the present difficult period 'everyone must make sacrifices'.

The Department of Labour considered this union the only body with which it was possible to negotiate. But the African Federation of Trade Unions took charge of the dispute, having organized a united action committee. The Committee made the following demands: a ten minute break for meals, improvement of sanitary conditions, and an end to the coarse treatment of workers by factory owners and managers. Despite the arrest of the leaders, the workers won the strike.

The strike in Johannesburg was also caused by wage cuts. The demand put forward by the workers included an eight-hour working day, and eight days annual holiday on full pay. The strike was broken because of the reformist union's betrayal and an incorrect use of united front tactics. Two months prior to the proposed wage cuts the Johannesburg African clothing workers' union went to the European clothing workers' union with proposals for a united struggle, but, having signed an agreement with them, failed to raise the question of a joint front towards all the owners.

As soon as the strike began, the reformist union began negotiations with the company owners, and at once refused to support the workers' demands. The union then began negotiations with individual company owners on the establishment of local agreements.

The African Federation of Trade Unions again took charge of the strike. It succeeded in exposing the tactics of the traitors and uniting around itself militant elements from the union of white clothing workers, establishing a revolutionary opposition within that union. The reformist leaders' attempt to expel the members of the revolutionary opposition from the union was overturned by a powerful protest from union members, who fully supported the tactics of the African Federation of Trade Unions.

The dockers' strikes, as we shall see, were exclusively defensive in nature, whereas elements of a workers' offensive were already discernable in the strikes of the chemical and clothing workers. The most important strike was that of the chemical workers. In essence it achieved a higher level of class struggle, since in this case the workers were not simply fighting for everyday economic demands, but for the right to organize — they were defending the union which they had created. In this strike the workers demonstrated firm class solidarity. The strikers demanded (and this was one of the fundamental demands) the reinstatement of dismissed female workers, actively fought with the strike-breakers and — what is especially important — in this they were aided by workers from other factories and unemployed workers. This strike, during which pickets were set up and money collected for the strike fund, was the most organized of all.

The militant nature of the chemical workers' strike is mainly explained by the considerable influence of the Communist Party at the factory. A further interesting aspect of the strike is that the reformist union leaders were forced to expose their own treachery. Andrews, the Secretary of the Trades and Labour Council, did everything he could to break the strike. Under his pressure the chemical workers agreed to arbitration, but in the arbitration commission he failed to support the strikers' demands and denied them assistance.

All the strikes of 1932 ended in defeat for the workers. This is to a significant degree the result of weak leadership of the strike movement on the part of the African Federation of Trade Unions and a consequence of the treacherous activities of the reformists. The strikes broke out spontaneously. No preparations were made. There were no strike committees, and the trade unions had no strike fund. Moreover, the strike movement was not linked to the movement of the unemployed. The use of united front tactics was either totally absent or incorrect.

## STRIKES ELSEWHERE IN AFRICA

### Sierra Leone

There was also a whole series of strikes in Sierra Leone, but during the last year there have been only a few rather limited strikes, despite the appalling effect of the world economic crisis. The largest of these was the railway workers' strike. Even policemen took part, declaring their solidarity with the railway workers. The railway workers gained satisfaction of some of their demands due to the leadership of revolutionary-minded workers.

The other railway workers' strike occurred in 1926. Afraid that the police, who were recruited from the same tribe as the railwaymen, would support the strikers, the government used the regular army to put down the strike. The strike was destroyed through savage reprisals. The leaders were arrested, and many workers were sacked. Due to the lack of revolutionary leadership in this case, membership of the railwaymen's union fell by almost half. The workers have now lost everything that they had gained in their desperate struggle with the company owners.

There is now intense unrest among not only the workers but also the peasantry. In February 1932 a peasant uprising broke out in the protectorate in protest against intolerable taxation. There was armed fighting between peasants and soldiers, as a result of which many peasants were killed. It must be noted that the workers responded warmly to peasant appeals for support and helped them a good deal by their participation in the struggle.[2]

### The Gambia

There have also recently been a large number of limited strikes in the Gambia. The largest was in 1930, when the seamen and shipbuilders went on strike. In response to the company owners' decision to cut wages by 50%, the union demanded a 50% increase in wages for all workers, and threatened a general strike. Thanks to good leadership and the firm resolution of the workers, a mass struggle against the company owners' attacks was successfully organized.

The seamen's strike lasted for more than 50 days. During this time workers from other sectors of industry joined the strike and a general strike of Gambian workers began, which lasted for 20 days.

As a result of this strike, it proved possible to make a stand for the workers' minimal demands. Thus in the construction industry, for example, the workers managed to preserve their original wages, as did the shipbuilders and bricklayers. Only the wages of Gambian seamen and engineering workers were still cut by 20%.

Due to the successful outcome of the strike further elements of the workers joined the Gambian Workers Union. The port and agricultural workers organized their own sections under the Gambian Workers Union. By 1930 the Union had been able to unite about 5,000 members, but in doing so it made the mistake of also admitting African peasants to its ranks (50%). The number of workers in the union directly employed in production is about 2,000.

## Mozambique

There has recently been a series of strikes in Portuguese East Africa (Mozambique). In the autumn of 1932 the workers and clerical employees of a private company supplying Mozambique's main port of Lourenco Marques with electricity, went on strike. The trains and water works belong to the same company. The trains came to a halt. But the water works continued to operate, since the strikers were consciously reluctant to bring these workers out and leave the town without water. The town was without electric light for a while, but the government then took over the power station and demanded that the company reach an agreement with the workers and clerical employees. This induced it to make some concessions which, however, were soon rescinded, and the main instigators of the strike were arrested.

On the Delagoa Railway 800 railwaymen went on strike, demanding the reinstatement of two dismissed comrades and the lifting of changes in regulations made by the management which encroached upon the workers' interests: extension of the working day to twelve hours, non-payment of wages during sickness, etc. Making use of the government's protection, the board of the railway company had no hesitation in raising its hand against the legally sanctioned rights won by the workers through years of struggle. The railwaymen's union declared a strike which then spread to the shipyards and the power station.

In order to break the strike, the government resorted to the following methods. The strikers were summoned to appear for active military service within 48 hours. No one turned up, and all of them were declared deserters with all the ensuing consequences. Savage reprisals began. The main instigators of the strike were transported to Portugal. The position of those remaining was extremely serious. Some of those who had escaped from the town hid in the forests. The union was closed down, and indiscriminate searches were made in the workers' quarters. Traffic on the railways was partially maintained by troops and strike-breakers. The strikers repeatedly stopped the trains. The town was guarded by reinforced detachments of mounted and foot police.

## Southern Rhodesia

Turning to Southern Rhodesia, the government there, in order to guard itself against the wide ranging and massive strikes which had swept the whole country in 1932, submitted in April 1933 a draft law on compulsory military service during 'internal or external aggressive actions or internal disorders' to the Legislative Assembly.

## THE REVOLUTIONARY TRADE UNION MOVEMENT AND RISING CLASS CONSCIOUSNESS

The growth of the revolutionary movement is in particular the result of the various mass campaigns held by the Communist Party and the revolutionary trade union movement. There has recently been a significant increase in the number of demonstrations and meetings.

Over the last two years, the revolutionary trade union movement, under the leadership of the Communist Party, has built up an extensive struggle against the pass system in South Africa. This campaign reached its height on Dingaans Day — the 16th of December. A wave of mass demonstrations swept all the country's major centres. There was a particularly powerful demonstration in Durban on this day.

The revolutionary trade union movement has done a great deal of preparation for various campaigns, especially in the main industrial centres. On 1st May 1932 impressive demonstrations were held in which whites participated together with blacks.

It is only in more recent years that we encounter joint demonstrations of black and white workers in the history of the South African working class. The meetings, in which 15,000 Johannesburg workers, 12,000 workers in Cape Town and 3,000 in Pretoria took part, show that the revolutionary trade union movement is beginning to encompass broad masses of the working class. Tens of thousands of people were also involved in the actions of 1932.

In 1932 the Communist Party and the African Federation of Trade Unions put forward a demand for social insurance against unemployment. This slogan also united black and white workers, who demonstrated their readiness to fight. It is characteristic that rank and file members of reformist unions also took part in this movement against the wishes of their leaders.

This is how the Communist newspaper *Umsebenzi* describes the events connected with the discussions of this demand at workers' meetings:

'On the 12th of May a meeting of white workers and unemployed assembled in the building of the Johannesburg Town Hall. Before the meeting had started, crowds of coloured and native workers began to gather at the doors of the Town Hall, but they were not admitted to the building.

At the meeting the agents, Pirow (the Minister of Justice), Andrews, Merkel* and other self-styled 'leaders' of the workers' movement[3] attempted to make fools of the white workers with their characteristic 'left' phrases. But although Andrews had also invited his friends, the police, to the meeting in case of outbursts from revolutionary elements, and although the social fascist leaders[4] had carefully prepared their defence against active and revolutionary-minded white workers, it was quite clear that the majority of white workers present was utterly disgusted and angry at the dictatorial methods of Andrews and his friends.

The police and social fascist elements in the hall tried everything to obstruct the speeches of the revolutionary workers, but the latter prevailed, and the police were forced to leave the hall.

When the meeting ended another meeting of unemployed was held outside the Town Hall, attended by more than 2,500 whites and blacks. The Communist Party's demand for social insurance against unemployment was carried by an overwhelming majority of votes.'

All this testifies to the growth of class consciousness of African workers, their growing desire to unite with their white and black comrades, the escape of workers from the demoralizing influence of the reformists and the growing revolutionary upsurge which opens up broad opportunities for a correct solution to the tasks confronting the revolutionary trade union movement led by the Communist Party.

The turning point which we have traced in the work of the Communist Party and the Federation presents an opportunity for correcting previous mistakes and leading the working class to victory.

## NOTES

1. This attack on W.H. Andrews, one of the white founders of the South African Communist Party, is characteristic of Nzula's strong stand against compromises with reformist unions. Andrews was one of several prominent members of the Communist Party (the others being E.S. Sachs, C.B. Tyler, S.P. Bunting, Fanny Klenerman and B. Weinbren) who were expelled by order of the political bureau in September 1931 for neglecting the red trade unions, and drifting into reformism and social democratic methods of work. See Simons, H.J. and R.E., *Class and Colour in South Africa 1850-1950*, (Harmondsworth, 1969), pp.447-8. One cannot but feel sympathy with Andrews' defence, where he pointed out that the Communist Party had ordered him to work in reformist trade unions. Apparently a person was meant to engage simultaneously in entrist tactics whilst ignoring the democratic wishes of one's fellow trade unionists and officials!

2. For a discussion of early labour protest in Sierra Leone, see Conway, H.E., 'Labour Protest Activity in Sierra Leone' in *Labour History*, 15 (1968), pp. 49-63.

3. The literal translation is unclear here, as it is unlikely that Pirow himself would address any workers' meetings. The sentence should

probably be read as follows: 'At the meeting, the agents *of* Pirow (the Minister of Justice), *namely* Andrews, Merkel and other self-styled 'leaders' . . .'

4.   The epithet 'social fascist' was generally used at the time by Party members to denote those who followed a line exemplified by the British Labour Party. By this was meant working through strong independent trade unions and seeking electoral support via a separate political wing — i.e., a labour party. The expression 'a parliamentary road to socialism' would cover the meaning intended.

# 8.

# THE LIMITS OF NATIONAL REFORMISM

## IMPERIALISM'S CATASTROPHIC IMPACT ON BLACK AFRICA

Let us now summarize imperialist rule in Black Africa. Below we give a picture of the true situation in the colonies:

(1) The mass pauperization, almost to a man, of the black peasantry which constitutes the vast majority of the population. The principal figure of the African village is the landless or almost landless starving peasant, bound to the plantations or the farms of the European landowner, burdened with taxes and exploited by the trading companies.

(2) The extremely widespread and systematic use of slave labour in the mining industry in the form of contracted labour. An unparalleled and utterly unchecked exploitation of black workers devoid of political rights. Mass extermination of human beings in the construction of railways in the Belgian Congo and French Equatorial Africa.

(3) The current economic crisis has increased tenfold the rate of peasant impoverishment and thrown workers previously employed in production on to the street, leaving them totally helpless. Millions of people have been thrown into the clutches of starvation, social alienation and moral degradation.

(4) An appalling growth of poverty, increase in oppression and brutal exploitation of enslaved people at one end of the scale accompanied by the accumulation of wealth at the other. Even in the moment of crisis, the mining and trading companies, the white landowners and slave owners, aided by their imperialist governments, are making profits running into millions through the continued robbery of the workers.

Such is the sum total of the white gentlemen's 'civilizing' activity in Black Africa, confronting the black African working masses with the supreme but immensely difficult choice of accepting continued impoverishment and extinction for the sake of enriching the imperialists, or of following the example of the workers of Russia and China in a ruthless and selfless struggle against imperialism.

The birth of this understanding of the situation and the recognition of the need for revolutionary struggle is attended by great effort and pains.

The imperialists have taken, and continue to take all possible measures to suppress the slightest glimmering of revolutionary consciousness amongst the black masses. Extreme poverty and slave-like working conditions exclude all possibility of raising the cultural level, and the virtually 100% illiteracy, the work of Christian missions, and the fanning of national and tribal hostility together retard and obstruct the growth of revolutionary self-consciousness among black workers.

But the days are already over when imperialism could calmly convert the blood of black workers into dollars and pounds. The October Revolution in Russia, the fifteen-year existence of the U.S.S.R., and the communist movement in China — all these circumstances show clearly where the door to liberation lies. Despite the desperate efforts of the imperialists and the attempts of their lackeys, the social fascists, the black masses of Africa are also learning this lesson. And it is leading them to revolution.

## ROADS TO REVOLUTION IN BLACK AFRICA

What are the roads to revolution in Black Africa?

The teachings of Lenin and the programme of the Comintern and its Congress decisions provide a perfectly clear and precise answer.

The programme of the Communist International basically divides all countries into three groups from the point of view of the conditions of, and roads towards, the victory of the proletariat. To the third group belong:

> 'colonial and semi-colonial countries (China, India, etc.) and independent countries (Argentina, Brazil and others) with some rudimentary, and even sometimes well developed industry which, however, is in most cases inadequate for self-sufficient socialist construction: in short, countries with a preponderance of feudal and medieval relations both in the country's economy, and in its political superstructure, and finally, where industrial, commercial and banking enterprises, the basic means of transport, land latifundia, plantations etc. are concentrated in the hands of foreign imperialist groups.
>
> Of central significance in this case are the struggle against feudalism and pre-capitalist forms of exploitation, and the agrarian revolution systematically carried through by the peasantry on the one hand; and the struggle against imperialism and for national independence, on the other. Here the transition to the dictatorship of the proletariat is, as a rule, attainable only by means of a series of preparatory stages, and as the result of a long period during which the bourgeois-democratic revolution develops into a socialist revolution and successful socialist construction — in most cases, only given the support of countries where the dictatorship of the proletariat is in force.'

One may include the Union of South Africa in this group. This country has a well-developed mining industry, and the major rudiments of processing and light industry which are monopolized by British imperialism. Here we already have substantial working class cadres. But the struggle for land and national independence takes central importance.

This (third) group also includes more backward countries. In these countries,

> 'where there are virtually no hired workers or none at all, where the majority of the population lives under conditions of tribal life and where the vestiges of primeval ancestral forms still survive, where the national bourgeoisie is almost absent, and foreign imperialism acts primarily as a military occupier expropriating the land, the national liberation struggle is of central importance. A national uprising and its subsequent victory can open the road for development towards socialism, avoiding the capitalist stage altogether, if powerful practical assistance is given by countries under proletarian dictatorship.'

## Importance of the Peasantry

We should include all the remaining countries of Black Africa in this group. Here the overwhelming majority of the population are peasants, and even the working class comprises, in substantial part, peasants working under contract.

What are the interests of this peasantry? One cannot of course expect the entire peasantry as such, in the concrete conditions of Black Africa, to be conscious fighters for socialism at this stage of the struggle. At the present stage, the peasantry is not fighting and is no longer capable of any struggle against capitalism. At present it is fighting existing forms of land-owner capitalism, the exploitation of feudalism and serfdom, and for free and unimpeded development of peasant farming.

Black Africa lacks the conditions required for such a development of peasant farming. Imperialists rule erects a series of barriers which retards the development of peasant farming, and ruins and impoverishes the peasantry, whilst simultaneously tying them to the land.

The principle of these barriers is the co-existence of large-scale land-ownership with a landless peasantry. From this everything else follows: the tying of peasants to white landowners, the wholly unlimited exploitation of the peasants by the representatives of commercial and money-lending capital, and so on.

The fundamental issue is land. Without obtaining the land of the white landowners and the free use of this land, there can be no free development of peasant farming. In the struggle for the free development of their farming, the indigenous peasantry must first of all gain possession of the land and eradicate the remnants of feudalism.

## Stages of the Revolution

The first task of the revolution is to take the land from the landowners, eradicate all pre-capitalist, feudal and serf-owning relations and in so doing clear the ground for the free development of peasant farming. This alone will make it possible for the black peasantry to 'raise itself from the mire of semi-serfdom, from the darkness of oppression and bondage and improve its living conditions to the extent possible, given the limitations of a commodity economy'. (Lenin)

The land is held by the white landowners, private companies, banks and the other organizations of finance capital, which represent world imperialism in Black Africa. It is therefore impossible to gain possession of the land without a struggle with imperialism and the liberation of the country from imperialist rule.

In each part of Africa the struggle for land is directly linked with the struggle with imperialism, for national independence and for independent African republics. Victory would ensure the seizure of the white landowners' land and its distribution among the African peasants and (in South Africa) the small white farmers. This would free the peasantry from all pre-capitalist, colonial forms of bondage and exploitation. It would lead to the nationalization of foreign enterprises — railways and banks, establish black equality, cancel all the laws discriminating against blacks (the pass system, 'the colour bar', contract labour, compounds, etc.) and at the same time guarantee the rights of the white working minority.

The basic content of the first stage of the revolution in Black Africa is a struggle for land and a war of national liberation. In this case, therefore, the revolution will in its initial stage be a bourgeois democratic revolution.

As in a number of other colonies, the specific feature of the revolutionary movement in Africa is that, even during its initial democratic stage, the proletariat will be compelled to carry out important socialist measures — nationalization of the mining companies, railways, banks, and so on.

In South Africa the subsequent course of the revolution will proceed through a gradual development of this national agrarian bourgeois-democratic revolution into a socialist revolution, which in terms of economic content will be a process of strengthening socialist elements against local capitalism, of struggle for a socialist path of development for peasant farming, and in political terms one of turning the revolutionary democratic dictatorship of the proletariat and peasantry into a dictatorship of the proletariat.

In all other parts of Black Africa, the anti-imperialist revolution, together with the support of the countries of the dictatorship of the proletariat (i.e. socialist countries) will make possible the non-capitalist path of development for peasant farming.

What are the driving forces of the revolution in Black Africa? How are the various classes grouped in relation to this revolution? We have already

163

shown that, owing to imperialist rule, there is no local indigenous industry in Black Africa, and hence no indigenous black industrial bourgeoisie. This has its impact on the development of the revolutionary movement and on the role of the individual classes in this movement.

The indigenous exploiting classes of Black Africa are the commercial and money-lending bourgeoisie and the tribal chiefs, i.e. those strata of the population which do not share the industrial bourgeoisie's contradictions with imperialism. They are representatives of a pre-capitalist social structure, and consequently have no interest in the free development of capitalism. On the contrary, the free development of capitalism would be an infringement of their interests.

## Africa's Proletariat Must Lead the Struggle

In Black Africa there was, and still is, no class other than the proletariat able to raise the banner of anti-imperialist struggle. There is no other class capable of uniting the isolated and unorganized masses of the African peasantry, giving them leadership and leading them against imperialism in the struggle for land and national independence. Thus here, at the very beginning of the national liberation movement, the proletariat becomes the organizer and leader of the toiling masses. Without the leadership of the working class and hegemony of the proletariat in this movement, a victory over imperialism is inconceivable.

All the necessary conditions for such a proletarian hegemony are already sufficiently present in Black Africa. The black proletariat is a numerically large body, extensively schooled in class struggle. Due to the specific nature of the colonial economy this proletarian body is intimately and directly linked with the peasantry.

The existence of a proletarian dictatorship in one-sixth of the globe, the international revolutionary workers' movement, and the assistance of European Communist Parties, Comintern and Profintern, provides an opportunity for the black proletariat to assume leadership of the anti-imperialist struggle. Ultimately the basic condition which makes possible the hegemony of the proletariat in the coming revolution is the fact that the proletariat of the most developed part of Black Africa — that of the Union of South Africa — possesses an independent revolutionary party — the Communist Party of South Africa.

Only the working class, having once gained hegemony over the national liberation movement in Black Africa, can ensure the success of the struggle. The working class, and the peasantry in alliance with and led by the working class, are the basic driving forces of the revolution in Black Africa.

## AFRICA'S INDIGENOUS EXPLOITING CLASSES AND THE ANTI-IMPERIALIST STRUGGLE

And what is the position of the African exploiting classes — the indigenous commercial bourgeoisie and the tribal chiefs?

### Africa's Commercial Bourgeosie

The African commercial bourgeoisie conducts no independent trade whatsoever with the outside capitalist world. Foreign trade is concentrated in the hands of British, French, American and German trading companies. The local commercial bourgeoisie merely acts as an intermediary between these companies and the population, between the large-scale wholesale trade controlled by whites in the towns and the African masses in the remote parts of the country. They are commercial travellers, agents of the imperialist bourgeoisie, and operating under their control. The African commercial bourgeoisie dutifully and faithfully serves the interests of the imperialist oppressors, adopting an anti-national position. They are true allies of imperialism.

### The Chiefs

As for the tribal chiefs, their strength lies not only in the fact that they are now representatives of the imperial government, but also in the persisting deep-rooted tradition of long-standing respect and submission to the chief as the erstwhile sole seat of power, and in the fact that the distribution of land is in the hands of the chief. In using his power and helping the imperialists to plunder his own land, the chief in various ways (abuse of the collection of taxes and fines, the use of blacks in farming, participation in labour-recruiting, trade, money lending, etc.) takes a major part in sharing out the booty, thereby bringing about primary accumulation of local capital. But in this attempt to accumulate capital the tribal chiefs meet with an imperialist policy which severely limits the opportunities for such accumulation.

A chief's source of accumulation can only be his people, the peasantry. But the peasantry, deprived of land and all rights, and barely able to feed itself, is so crushed by taxes and various extortions levied by the imperialist predators that the chief receives very little. What can a peasant give to the chief if he works unpaid for 180 days a year for a white farmer? How can one collect substantial sums from the peasant by cunning and deception, when the peasant cannot even pay what is demanded of him by the government?

Contradictions arise in a further respect. The whole system by which the African population is deprived of rights is also applied to the chiefs. Like all blacks, they are obliged to carry the necessary pass with them;

like any black, a chief cannot go to a town without special permission from a white official (particularly in South Africa); like any black, he can be arrested, imprisoned and sent to perform forced labour etc. for the same acts. In fact, in legal respects, a chief is just as fettered as any other African. But he is still a chief. He or his father was once absolute ruler of his people, enjoying full state power, and recognized and respected by his people. But now he is forced to submit to every white colonial official, run errands for him, and carry out his orders. He is now forced to plunder his own people in the interests of the imperialists, leaving little or nothing for himself. For carrying out the most unpleasant administrative duties (the extortion of taxes from a ruined peasantry, sending peasants to forced labour etc.) the chief receives totally inadequate remuneration, which bears no comparison whatever with the salary of his official colonial superiors.

All this creates a mood of opposition among the chiefs and sets them against the colonial policy of the imperialists. But in opposing the colonial policy of imperialism, the chiefs must still keep watch on movements. among the mass of the people. Imperialism may have stripped them of their former power and privileges. Imperialism may keep them in the position of servants. But imperialism nevertheless offers them an opportunity, however restricted, to fleece their own people, to grow rich at their expense, and to accumulate capital.

The methods by which this accumulation is at present carried out (labour recruitment, money lending etc.) are possible only under conditions of imperialist rule. The victorious people's revolution, which will destroy imperialist oppression, will also destroy the slavery of the labour recruiting system, give the land to the peasants and open the way for the free development of peasant farming, and thus deprive the chiefs of their former opportunities for self-enrichment. For this reason the chiefs, for whom signs of a popular uprising are more frightening than they are for the African industrial bourgeoisie, have even less thoughts of any struggle against imperialist rule. This narrows the goals of their struggle, reducing them to a desire to grab a bigger share of the peasants' surplus labour, and the aspiration to escape from the position of rightlessness in which they are held by imperialism.

The chiefs can therefore fight for an easing of peasant taxation, additional land for their use, minimal political rights for the black population, and an extension of self-government, which would enable the chiefs to play a more prominent political role. But the whole of this struggle is conceived of within the conditions of imperialist rule. Not a violent struggle, not a revolution, but reform, a peaceful deal with imperialism — that is the motto of this movement which, in the theses of the Fifth Comintern Congress, is given the name of the 'National Reformist Movement'.

We shall demonstrate the essence of national reformism in Black Africa by the concrete facts of the activity of the most prominent national reformist organizations.

## NATIONAL REFORMISM — THE SOUTH AFRICAN EXAMPLE

National reformism's chief and longest established organization in South Africa is the African National Congress, founded in 1912. Its guiding force is the African chiefs, followed by the black intelligentsia: teachers, lawyers, priests and others.

### The Black Intelligentsia and the A.N.C.

The black intelligentsia already represents a fairly important stratum of society. The material and legal position of the intelligentsia, particularly of black teachers, differs in virtually no respect from that of black workers. Like all black workers, the intelligentsia is deprived of political rights and barred from participation in political life. The policy of social discrimination is extended to the intelligentsia, just as it is to the working class. Imperialist rule obstructs the black intelligentsia's access to all branches of public life in every possible way: theatre, art in general, engineering, medicine and so on. This causes the African intelligentsia to recognize the need for a struggle against imperialism for rights, the chance to work, and for further self-development. A substantial majority of the African intelligentsia, however, are descended from the families of chiefs and are closely connected with them. This drives the intelligentsia into alliance with the chiefs, and into their organizations.

The social base of the African National Congress of South Africa consists of the chiefs and the intelligentsia. During its initial years the Congress enjoyed considerable support among the working class and the peasantry. This was a period when the black toilers were first rising to the struggle against imperialism, when there was still no differentiation of anti-imperialist forces into two fronts, those of revolutionary struggle and those of reformism, peaceful deals and agreements with imperialism.

During that period the black worker had already undergone a severe schooling in class struggle, and had tested for himself both revolutionary and reformist methods of struggle.

The creation and activity of a Communist Party and red trade unions have been a powerful factor in the rapid growth of class consciousness among black workers. The boundary between the fronts of revolution and reformism is becoming increasingly well-defined, and at the same time large masses of toiling people, especially workers, are breaking away from national reformist influences and shaking off the illusions of a 'peaceful deal' with imperialism instilled in them by the reformists.

To outline the policy and tactics of the national reformists we shall examine the resolutions of the Conference, called at the instigation of the African National Congress, of all the South African reformist organizations — the so-called 'Non-European Conference' — which was held in

Bloemfontein in January 1931. The Conference discussed and took decisions on a number of fundamental questions of current concern to the blacks. These were:

1) **The Bill on Africans and the Bill on the Coloured People's Rights.**[2] Makabeni and Abdurahman[3], the principal speakers on this question, concentrated the fire of their eloquence wholly on the fact that the government had not invited them to discuss these laws, rather than on their essential content. It was resolved that:

> 'Conference condemns the Bill on Natives and the Bill on Coloured Rights, and urgently requests the Government to convene a round-table conference of, on the one hand, authorized leaders of the Europeans and leaders of the Non-Europeans on the other, in order to discuss political relations between Europeans and Non-Europeans.'

2) **The 'Colour Bar' Law.** The Conference voiced its protest at this law because it:

> 'deprives certain sections of the population of their ancient rights and of earnings commensurate with the abilities given to them by God.'

3) **The 'Civilized Labour' Policy.** The Conference adopted the following resolution:

> 'The policy of civilized labour carried out by the Government is cruel and unjust, since it deprives a large number of Non-Europeans workers of a job, impoverishes them and closes many paths to work, which have since time immemorial been open to them. Moreover it lays a heavy burden upon the whole country in the form of additional taxation to subsidize this policy.'

4) **Wages of Non-European Workers.** It was resolved that;

> 'South Africa will not become a rich country until the purchasing power of Non-European workers is increased. Conference requests the Government to examine the question of establishing a minimum wage for Non-European workers.'

5) **Pass System.** The Conference resolved on this issue, in its most interesting resolution:

> 'In view of the fact that the pass system is seen as a mark of slavery, Conference respectfully but firmly demands that the Government take steps to eradicate this system. If such steps are not taken, a day must be fixed in 1934 when all natives will destroy their passes. This should not be Dingaan's Day.'[4]

6) **Relations between South Africa and the British Empire.** The majority of delegates came out categorically against forcible (i.e. against the will of British imperialism) secession from the Empire.

References to humaneness, injustice and ancient African rights, and tearful and 'respectful' requests to the Government were all that this Conference proved capable of. There is not even a hint of calling the masses to struggle, let alone any attempt to organize and prepare for this struggle.

But even this servile posture adopted by the national reformists fails to satisfy the government of South Africa. Despite all the efforts of the reformists, there is no way in which they can please their white masters. In his attempts to curry favour with British imperialism, one of the leading national reformists, Professor Jabavu, stated whilst in London: 'The natives love their British masters (and curse the Boers), and they are happy to live under the Union Jack. Although the Africans are not rich, they do not go hungry'.

Nevertheless, the imperialists are not pleased with the African National Congress's policy. The leftist prattle of the Congress leaders and its criticism of various government measures are unacceptable to the imperialists. They want direct leadership of the Congress and to channel its activities in the furtherance of their own interests.

In order to bring about a 'unification' of interests, a 'united council'[5] was set up, composed of representatives of Congress and the Europeans. As one might have expected, this council took the national reformist chiefs in hand and made them dance to the imperialists' tune. This was done so blatantly and openly that the true colours of British imperialism could be seen by all rank and file Congress members.

## Rank and File Pressure for Revolution

The lower ranks rain protests down upon the treacherous policy of the Congress executive committee and its leaders. The newspaper *Umteteli wa Bantu*, which offered its pages to the national reformists, is a colourful source of letters from rank and file members directed at the high-handedness of the 'united council'. The author of one of these letters writes:

'The African National Congress is now incapable of leading the masses. The leadership of the Congress is in the hands of the 'united council'. The 'united council' is an anti-native organization. It has adopted the perpetuation of racial subjugation of blacks to whites as its goal. It claims leadership, control and supervision of all African affairs and denies the African peoples the right to independent solution of questions which affect them racially. The impotence of Bantu organizations lies in their European-Bantu leadership.'

The world economic crisis has sharpened all contradictions to an unprecedented degree, and raised the temperature of the political atmosphere to an extraordinary level.

The ruined peasantry is restating all the issues in a new way, and demanding a solution from their chiefs. The ruin of the peasantry has rebounded upon the chiefs, cutting their sources of accumulation and in some places even worsening their material position. The crisis has also had a violent impact upon the African intelligentsia: the allocation of funds for education has been systematically cut year by year, masses of teachers have been thrown on to the streets and wages have been systematically cut.

The newspaper *Umteteli wa Bantu* points out the following facts on this matter:

> 'In 1931 the wages of teachers were cut by 15%. Since July teachers with diplomas have been paid the same rates as teachers without them. At the beginning of 1932, the wages of all native teachers were again cut by 8%. Newly appointed qualified teachers are worse paid than ordinary domestic servants.'

At this moment the African National Congress is faced with the demand for effective resistance to imperialism and for organization of the masses for the struggle for vital and pressing demands. The Congress, however, having handed over leadership to the white henchmen of imperialism in the 'united council', gets away with silence or tearful addresses to the government. This naturally causes dissatisfaction with their leaders among the masses of the Congress, and creates a movement in opposition to them.

In May 1932 a group of members of the Congress executive committee delivered a declaration which, having outlined the serious economic situation of the black masses brought about by the crisis, accuses Seme[6], the President of the Congress, of total inactivity, silence on fundamental issues and the handover of leadership to the Europeans. On 2nd July 1932 an extraordinary meeting of the executive committee members was called at the initiative of this group over the head of the chairman. The meeting issued a declaration to the entire black population, calling upon them to protest against the Bill being debated in parliament on African labour, the government's unwillingness to take measures to combat the malaria epidemic in African villages, etc. The meeting demanded that Seme convene the Congress at once.

This in itself was something of a shift to the left. But this still does not mean that the group of chiefs heading the opposition movement really wants to lead the masses into a struggle. It only shows that the masses which the Congress claim to lead have taken a significant and serious step towards the left, and have temporarily taken with them that section of the chiefs which is afraid of losing its influence over them.

The Congress leaders themselves are forced to admit that the masses have become significantly more left wing in their attitude. One of them, defending Seme in the press, writes that 'the masses are no longer what they used to be. The masses are now more involved with class, rather than racial, interests.'

The masses are breaking away from the influence of the Congress. Within the Congress a struggle is raging. The Congress leadership, along with their European masters from the 'united council', is taking urgent measures to avert even temporary shifts of the Congress towards the left.

Imperialism's task is to fence off the Congress leadership from the movement of the revolutionary masses, to concentrate leadership in the hands of those people most loyal to imperialism, the most vocal opponents of the national liberation movement. To this end, Seme has made proposals for the division of the Congress executive committee into two chambers, upper and lower. The upper chamber is to consist of chiefs who have not been elected by the people, but who have inherited power from fathers who were chiefs; the lower chamber is to be elected by Congress members. Seme wishes to concentrate leadership of the Congress in the hands of the upper chamber, isolating it not only from the ordinary people — 'the plebeians' — but also from the chiefs drawn from these people.

At a time when the sharpening of contradictions is at its most intense, imperialism now fears to trust even those African chiefs which have supported it. The government is beginning to take hurried measures to strengthen this support. Of course, the government and chiefs can strengthen the leadership of the Congress, protect it from the pressure of the masses and ensure that it faithfully serves imperialism, but they cannot halt the swing of the masses towards the 'left' and their escape from the influence of reformist illusions.

## NATIONAL REFORMIST ORGANIZATIONS IN THE GOLD COAST

In West Africa, the largest number of national reformist organizations has been created in the Gold Coast. The National Congress of British West Africa, uniting all the British colonies of West Africa, has its headquarters here. The West African Youth Congress (W.A.Y.C.) was established here in 1932.

The longest standing Gold Coast national reformist organization is the Aborigines Rights Protection Society. The society was formed in 1897 in connection with a mass protest campaign against the land law which the British Government passed for the Gold Coast.

### The National Reformists' Coalition of Classes

The Society consists mainly of chiefs, representatives of provincial councils, African traders and the African intelligentsia. There are no peasants in this organization. They cannot be members of the Society, if only because Society members pay a subscription of £10. Moreover, additional collections are made from Society members to conduct various campaigns. For instance the members of the Society were obliged to contribute between £90 and £350 towards the organization of the forest protest campaign. In 1932 the vice-president, William Brew,[7] was expelled from the Society for his refusal to subscribe to a fund for a delegation sent to England. Naturally no peasant could afford such contributions.

The conditions which determine the national reformist policy of the African exploiting strata and intelligentsia on the Gold Coast are essentially the same as those in other colonies of Black Africa. It is admittedly true that, in this country, the tribal chiefs have the appearance of having greater political rights than in South Africa — they sit, for example, as representatives on provincial councils and the colonial legislative council, and have their own courts. But this does not prevent European officials treating them very little better than in South Africa.

A Gold Coast chief, relates the following facts in a complaint about a European district commissioner:

> 1. I departed for a conference of the Aborigines Rights Protection Society without the commissioner's permission. On learning of this, the commissioner recalled me by telegram and fined me.
> 2. I collected money for a journey to Cape Coast. The commissioner found out and forbade the journey.
> 3. A sanitary official visited my house during my absence, found it dirty, and imposed a fine.
> 4. The sanitary official was passing along the street where I lived, and, catching sight of me, beckoned me with his finger. I took offence at such disrespect and remained where I was. The official then forced me to sweep the street.'

Another chief complains that 'my position is now such that I am a chief in name only. This is not what I was before, but this is what the government has made me'.

The chiefs' lack of political rights, the restrictions upon their opportunities to become wealthy and other limitations drive them into opposition to imperialist rule. But the same factors as in other colonies turn this opposition into a revolt on bended knees.

Here the African intelligentsia is likewise devoid of political rights, is virtually deprived of any opportunity for higher education, and is unable to find work. It is, however, closely linked to the chiefs. Moreover, the upbringing received by them in missionary and government schools makes them slaves of imperialism and instils in them the poison of reformism.

To outline the mood of the intelligentsia we quote extracts from a conversation of a West African reformist, I.T.A. Wallace-Johnson[8].

> 'During a talk on the development of the fishing industry with one of the so-called educated Africans, the person to whom I was talking told me: "surely you do not expect a man of my qualifications, wearing a collar and tie, to be interested in fishing? That's a job for those who haven't been to school." I shall quote another example of a talk with a certain negro, whom I had reckoned better informed on the position of the working class. He said: "these matters do not interest me — they concern farm workers, technicians, farmers, fishermen, and so on. I am an accountant, not a worker. If I ever join a workers' union, I shall do so purely out of feelings of humanity'."

It is members of the intelligentsia and chiefs of this type that make up the Aborigines Rights Protection Society. Its programme and tactics can be judged by an article written by one of its leaders and published in *The Independent Gold Coast Observer*, 1st October 1932. He writes that the main aim of the Society is 'to defend the rights of Gold Coast people'. The basic law for which the people are fighting is that of equal and effective popular representation in the country's legislative organs.

## Reformists Are Not Concerned with Imperialist Exploitation of the People

The reformists are not concerned with the exploitation of the people by the imperialists. It is their own lack of rights which concerns them. They want to share government over their own people with imperialism, and take a larger part in plundering them. To do this they appeal to the people, aiming to gain this opportunity through the hands of the toilers.

A struggle has recently been raging in the Society between the chiefs and the intelligentsia. The intelligentsia has suffered more than the chiefs from the crisis. Moreover, whereas the chiefs sit on provincial councils and pass judgement in the courts, the intelligentsia lacks these rights. At present the intelligentsia sees the reason for its disastrous position in the failure of the chiefs in council to defend their own people (by whom it primarily means itself).

The intelligentsia is trying to bring about direct government by the imperialists, rather than by the chiefs. It opposes the election of chiefs to the legislative assembly, and their investiture with judicial functions. The main argument put forward in support of these demands is the illiteracy of the chiefs. The introduction of 'direct government' along French West African Lines, and the withdrawal of the chiefs' judicial functions would bring the intelligentsia into a newly-established administrative and judicial apparatus, and give work to a substantial number of currently unemployed members of the intelligentsia.

A struggle is now being fought out within the Society itself between the two groups as to which is to be the direct weapon in the hands of the imperialists, the chiefs or the intelligentsia, and which is to oppress and suppress directly the toilers of the Gold Coast. This is not a struggle against imperialism, but a struggle for a bigger slice of that part of the booty that the imperialists leave to the indigenous exploiting strata and the intelligentsia.

The Society has more than once stated that it has never planned a struggle against the colonial government — i.e. British imperialism. On the contrary, it has taken, and will continue to take, all possible measures 'to help to ease the work of the government' — i.e. to aid British imperialism's enslavement of the Gold Coast toilers. The Society asks that its opposition on certain questions should not be seen as evidence of ill intentions against imperialism. In entering into opposition, it desires the 'correct' solution of the issues in question.

The Society compares itself in this respect with the British parliamentary opposition. Not a struggle against imperialism, but help in the enslavement of the toiling masses; not a struggle against imperialist looting, but a struggle for a larger part of the spoils — such is the platform of this organization.

The Society nevertheless still has considerable influence among the masses. It has now been running a protest campaign for two years against the Governor General's proposed poll tax, holding extensive meetings, adopting resolutions and sending delegations to the British King. By so doing it is making political capital in the form of authority among the masses, in order to use them for the achievement of its own ends (which far from coincide with the interests of the masses) and in order to betray them if they attempt to rise against imperialist rule.

## NATIONAL REFORMISM IN KENYA

In East Africa the Kikuyu Central Association represents the main organization of national reformism. From the moment of its rebirth in 1925, following its complete defeat in March 1922, the association has taken an ultra-reformist line, while flirting simultaneously with the revolutionary movement. It has sent delegates to the League Against Imperialism; the Profintern, and the International Trade Union Committee of Black Workers, and at the same time has grovelled for the most minor concessions before the British King, Parliament and Lords.[9]

As proof of the duplicity of the Central Association's policy we quote a small extract from a servile memorandum presented to the British Colonial Minister in February 1932. Paragraph 40 of this memorandum contains the following:

'The Association requests that the articles depriving certain Africans of the freedom of speech, press and assembly be withdrawn from the Law on Native Government. These freedoms are the prime foundations of any democracy, constituting the traditional privileges of all free citizens under the British flag. To deprive Africans of these freedoms is to deprive them of the elementary rights of citizenship, which is the reason for the dissatisfaction of the Kikuyu, who takes an active part in the civil life of the country for the furtherance of the common good.'

The drafting and despatch of such notes and petitions has been the sole activity of the Central Association during the recent period. Not one grovelling request or petition, however, has been satisfied. On the contrary, there has been an incessant stream of vicious laws designed to plunder and expropriate the land of the Kenyans. Such was the case with one East African tribe: In 1932 gold bearing veins were discovered on land occupied by the tribe. Numerous official statements and 'white papers' assured the tribe of their unobstructed ownership of this land. But no sooner had gold been discovered there than the British imperialists immediately found new interpretations of their own statements in order to justify plundering these peasants.

This measure caused major disputes among the imperialists themselves, of whom the most far-sighted predicted the outbreak of disorders resulting from such actions, which would shatter all surviving illusions regarding British democracy — illusions to which the masses had clung with such desperation. The monster of imperialist overlordship had opened its jaws and shown its teeth in such a manner that even a blind man could see them.

The disillusionment and leftward swing of the masses put an end for a while to the composition of notes and petitions by the leaders. They are now flirting once more with the revolutionary movement, writing thunderous articles branding the acts of the imperialists and repenting of their past. The price paid by these arch-conciliators for their sincerity is well known, But despite whatever may have happened in the past, the organization's secretary now says: 'We have had one commission after another appointed to investigate land questions etc., but despite all manner of commission reports and missions, the plundering of African lands and exploitation have not ceased. What Africans need now is the restoration of their confiscated lands, not commissions.' (*Negro Worker*, January 1933.) He also calls upon the working class of Britain and other countries to work hand in hand with them, in order that 'we may overthrow our common enemy — British imperialism'.

A chance has now arisen in Kenya to create a revolutionary opposition groups within the Kikuyu Central Association. These would subsequently act as independent communist worker groups, ready to lead the national liberation movement towards a struggle with British imperialism. The entire history of the Kikuyu Central Association shows that this organization cannot and will not fight for the liberation of the Kenyan masses from the chains of British oppression.

Such is the face of national reformist organizations in Black Africa.

## THE TASK OF REVOLUTIONARY-MINDED WORKERS IN AFRICA

It is the task of communists and revolutionary-minded workers to systematically and daily expose the treacherous activity of these organizations. Leaning upon the ancient tradition of obedience of the masses to the chiefs, and hiding its true face behind 'left-wing' phrases ('Africa for the Africans' — cried the Cape National Congress), national reformism still manages to retain a substantial following among the peasant masses. Only through extensive and systematic exposure can communists wrest these masses from national reformist influence.

'Without this struggle and the liberation of the toiling masses from the influence of the bourgeoisie and national reformism, the

communist movement's prime strategic aim under a bourgeois-
democratic revolution — the *hegemony of the proletariat* — cannot
be achieved. Without the hegemony of the proletariat . . . the
bourgeois-democratic revolution cannot be fully pursued to its end,
let alone a socialist revolution.'
(Sixth Comintern Congress)

## NOTES

1.   This is an interesting anticipation of the success a communist
     revolution was later to have in China.

2.   The legislation probably referred to here is the Native (Urban Areas)
     Act first passed in 1923. An amendment to this act was passed in
     1930 which severely restricted the freedom of movement of Africans
     and extended the application of the pass system.

3.   Quite why Gana Makabeni, a former I.C.U. officer, then a staunch
     member of the Communist Party, is identified here remains uncertain.
     The attack on Dr Abdul Abdurahman, a distinguished medical
     graduate from Glasgow, is more explicable, Abdurahman was a
     leader of the African Political Organization, a highly constitutional
     and sober body.

4.   The reason for including this proviso that pass-burning *not* be held
     on that day, is instructive. The Communist Party, with Albert
     Nzula taking a leading role, had designated Dingaan's Day for their
     own anti-pass demonstration. The Non-European Conference was
     therefore consciously repudiating the leading role of the communists,
     which fact Nzula (who must have written this section) does not
     mention.

5.   This 'united council' is a mysterious body. It may be intended to
     refer to the Joint Councils of Liberal Europeans and Africans which
     were set up at about this time to seek mild and reformist changes in
     the South African system of political control. This our authors agree was
     supporting British imperialism.

6.   Dr Pixley ka I. Seme was president of the African National Congress
     and, even given the standards of the body at the time, a conservative
     leader.

7.   The Brews were a prominent trading family on the West Coast of
     Africa. According to Peter Lloyd, in settlements around the coastal
     forts of Elmira and Cape Coast, certain local families — the Brews,
     the Bannermans, the Casely Hayfords — dominated commercial and
     political life. Often they were partly descended from a European
     trader, hence the English-sounding names. Lloyd, P.L. *Africa in
     Social Change*, (Harmondsworth, 1967), p.130.

8.     Though I.T.A. Wallace-Johnson ultimately did compromise his earlier radical position, it is unexpected to see him referred to as a 'reformist' here. Under the name of E.A. Richards, he had attended the International Conference of Negro Workers in Hamburg, and was certainly regarded as something of a Comintern bogeyman by colonial officials in British West Africa. This quote also does not indicate Wallace-Johnson's reformism, as he is simply reporting on the limited political consciousness of his respondent.

9.     The Kikuyu Central Association was formed in 1928, with Jomo Kenyatta as its secretary. Kenyatta was also on the Provisional Executive Committee of the International Trade Union Committee of Negro Workers, the body which convened the 1930 conference. As with Wallace-Johnson (see note 8 above), it is unexpected that Kenyatta's organization was already being consigned to the category of 'national reformist'. This has a special irony in view of C.L.R. James' claim that Kenyatta was provoked to turn his back on Moscow because of the treatment meted out to Albert Nzula (see Introduction).

# APPENDICES

## APPENDIX A

## PUBLICATIONS (OUTSIDE SOUTH AFRICA) BY ALBERT NZULA

1931    Letter from Durban, January 1931, reporting pass burning and poll tax demonstrations on Dingaan's Day, in *The Negro Worker*, Vol. I, No.2, (February 1931). (Reproduced below, Appendix B)
Nzula, A. 'Native Workers Make Organizational Advances in South Africa', *The Negro Worker*, Vol. I, No. 2, (February 1931). (Reproduced below, Appendix C)
Jackson, T., 'South African Negro Workers and Dingaan's Day', *The Negro Worker*, Vol. I, No.12, (December 1931). (Reproduced below, Appendix D)

1932    Jackson, T., *Country of Diamonds and Slaves*, (Strana Almazor i Rabor), (Moscow, 1932).
Jackson, T., 'Negro Misleaders in South Africa', *The Negro Worker*, Vol. II, No. 4, (April 1932).
Jackson, T., 'South Africa and the Imperialist War', *The Negro Worker*, Vol. II, No. 6, (June 1932). (Reproduced below Appendix E)

1933    Speech of Comrade T. Jackson, delegate from South Africa to the International Labour Defense Conference, *The Negro Worker*, Vol. III, Nos. 2-3, (February-March 1933). (Reproduced below, Appendix F)
Jackson, T., 'The International Labour Defense and the Negro Peoples', *The Negro Worker*, Vol. III, Nos. 2-3, (February 1933). (Reproduced below, Appendix G)
Anon. (but probably A. Nzula), 'South African Imperialists Initiate New Terror Actions Against Natives', *The Negro Worker*, Vol. III, Nos. 2-3, (February-March 1933) (Reproduced below,

Note: The words 'Native' and 'Negro' which had fewer unfavourable connotations in the early 1930s are here reproduced as they appeared in the original English language version of *The Negro Worker*.

Appendix H)
Zusmanovich, A., Potekhin, I., Jackson, T., *The Working Class Movement and Forced Labour in Negro Africa*, (Rabochee Dvizhenie i Prinuditel'ni trud v Negrityanskoi Afrike), (Moscow, 1933). (This volume)

1934    Nzula, A., 'The Fusion Movement in South Africa', *The Negro Worker*, Vol. IV, No. 1, (May 1934). (See Appendix J).

1935    Nzula, A., 'The Struggles of the Negro Toilers in South Africa', *The Negro Worker*, Vol. V, Nos. 2-3, 4, 5, 6, 10, 1935 (Published posthumously in five parts). (Reproduced below, Appendix I).

# APPENDIX B

## LETTER FROM DURBAN — JANUARY 1931

Comrades:

I am writing from Durban, the scene of revolutionary mass conflicts arising out of Dingaan's Day, pass and poll tax burning demonstration. We are concentrating the greatest part of our activities on the organization of the Negro workers of South Africa. We are carrying out many actions. I shall write you again from time to time of what progress is being made. The masses are surging forward to struggle against imperialism and its reformist agents.

With Revolutionary Greetings,

A. Nzula

# APPENDIX C

## NATIVE WORKERS MAKE ORGANIZATIONAL ADVANCES IN SOUTH AFRICA

The consolidation of the achievements of the campaign for the burning of passes on Dingaan's Day is proceeding at a rapid pace. Concentration groups have been and are being set up as rapidly as possible, while the nucleus of a powerful Dockers', Railwaymen's and Transport Union is already functioning.

The police are as active as ever in trying to prevent the activities of the Party, but the masses are not frightened or in any way deterred by the police from following in their hundreds the lead of the Party. The Native reformist leaders, who opposed the pass burning campaign, are being forced by the upsurge of the revolutionary mass movement to adopt left-wing phrases and slogans, while they are at the same time looking out for the first opportunity to betray the movement.

## The Arrested Men

The 33 prisoners arrested on Dingaan's Day on a charge of inciting to violence are as determined as ever. The number 33 reminds one of the 33 Meerut prisoners in India languishing in the gaols of British imperialism since March 1929. Will the fate of the Durban '33' be the same? The inquiry into the death of Comrade Nkosi will without doubt cause a sensation and so will the trial of the '33'. The allegations against the police are of the most serious character.

## Consolidating the Position in Durban

The completeness with which the Durban workers, in spite of reformist opposition and police intimidation, responded to the Party's call for action against the pass laws is a clear indication of the correctness of the Party line and policy.

The situation in Durban (the revolutionary enthusiasm of the masses [and] the rate at which they are flocking into the Communist Party) places a grave responsibility upon our Durban branch. It is necessary that earlier mistakes should be avoided and that the work in Durban should proceed on correct lines. The Durban branch is tackling this task with determination. The old idea of the formation of groups composed of loose and unrelated elements is giving place to the Bolshevik form of organization — concentration groups, factory cells, nuclei.

## Prepare for Police Opposition!

At the same time it is obvious that police action will soon make the carrying out of work very difficult if not impossible. When that time comes (though we shall fight hard against its coming) we shall be ready and prepared for it. Comrade Gana Makabeni is already being intensely persecuted by the police, with a view to his deportation. He has already appeared in the courts on various charges, half a dozen times in the last two weeks.

To prepare for possible deportation of our leaders and to ensure the continuation of our work, classes are being run nightly. The comrades who attend these classes are very enthusiastic and are making rapid progress. Soon they will be ready to take up the leadership; while, with the release of the '33', all of them capable and trained in the earlier struggles in Durban, the work should not suffer from a lack of capable revolutionary leaders.

The question of the organization of agricultural workers and peasant committees is not being neglected. The measure of achievement in this direction can be gauged by the fact that on Dingaan's Day two bags full of passes were brought from Zululand and outlying districts in a mud bespattered motor car for the burning process.

The masses are rapidly moving forward. The spirit of disillusionment and despair, engendered by the tragic failure and opportunism of the I.C.U. under Kadalie's and Champion's leadership, is being overcome. We are entering a new period — a period of mass action and conflicts against tyrannical laws, slave conditions and economic misery.


## APPENDIX D

## SOUTH AFRICAN NEGRO WORKERS AND DINGAAN'S DAY

During the last two years, Dingaan's Day, December 16, has become a day of mass demonstrations of increasing revolutionary intensity on each successive occasion against Dutch and British imperialism by the Negro workers of South Africa. Negro workers in other parts of the world, and the revolutionary proletariat in general, must be interested in learning what significance Dingaan's Day has for the South African Negro toiling masses.

What is Dingaan's Day? We shall answer the question by recounting an incident from the bloody history of imperialist partitioning of Africa. After two centuries of wars and punitive expeditions, by 1836, the Dutch and British imperialists had practically succeeded in subduing all the South African Negro tribes, with the exception of the Zulus who occupied Natal and Zululand, the most fertile of the provinces of South Africa. The Zulus are a fighting race and militarily the strongest of the Negro peoples. The Dutch had suffered several very severe defeats at their hands. Finally, the Dutch combined their forces with the British, and also succeeded in buying over a number of Negro chiefs to assist them. They were armed with the latest weapons of war that Europe could supply at that time. The Zulus had only their assegais and *obildo* (an assegai is a short spear which the Zulus are experts in handling).

On 16th December 1838, the issue as to who was going to retain mastery — the white imperialists or the Zulus — was to be finally settled. The Zulus, in spite of their bravery and reckless daring, were not a match for the guns of the white robbers who had entrenched themselves in 'laagers', formed by their wagons with bags of sand in the spaces between. The Zulus left 5,000 of their men on the field of battle. The river, on the banks of which the battle raged, literally flowed with blood and has been known ever since as the 'Blood River'.

The defeat of the Zulus was followed by a ruthless punitive expedition: the blacks were driven out of Natal into the wild regions of Zululand. Such, in brief, is the history of Dingaan's Day, but this is not all.

The Dutch, who are a 'religious' and bigoted people, committing all their warfare on the Negroes in the name of 'God', had promised this same 'Lord' of theirs, that if 'He' gave them victory over the Zulus, they would always remember it by an annual 'Thanksgiving'. They kept their promise. Every year, since 1838, they have used this 'holiday' to continue to terrorize the Negro masses by brutal assaults upon the workers, and general propaganda about the 'White Man's supremacy' in the African sub-continent. For a time this policy succeeded. Under the misleadership of the missionaries and black lackeys of the imperialists, such as Kadalie and Professor D.G. Jabavu, the Negro toiling masses confined their protest against this jingoism by offering up prayers to the 'Lord' to 'deliver' them from their oppressors. By and by, the more militant elements began to realize the uselessness of prayers and started to organize 'timid' protest meetings.

With the beginning of 1929 and the acceptance by the Communist Party of South Africa of the programme of the Communist International to stop praying and begin to struggle for a South African Black Republic, slogans for mobilizing the Negro toilers against imperialism and for national independence were popularized among the masses. The Communist Party, which is the only party fighting for the freedom of the natives, proclaimed Dingaan's Day an anti-imperialist national liberation day, a day of mass demonstrations and strikes against Dutch and British oppression and tyranny.

For those who know South Africa, it is easy to realize what consternation this decision caused in the camp of the white ruling classes. They mobilized all their reactionary forces, including Negro reformist 'leaders', middle-class doctors, lawyers and teachers, to spread rumours to frighten the masses away from the communists by telling them that they would be massacred. The whole capitalist press, a powerful and mighty force, published the most hair-raising stories of what would happen if the Negro toiling masses dared to go on strike and demonstrate. The right-wing opportunists who were still in the leadership of the Party succumbed to this propaganda, but a determined and energetic campaign overcame these hesitations.

The response of the Negro workers was astounding. Throughout South Africa, on 16th December 1929, thousands of Negro workers came out into the streets in all the chief industrial centres. The white fascist bands organized to break the demonstrations were repulsed. Only at Potchefstroom, a hotbed of reaction, did they dare attack the demonstrators, killing one and wounding four Negro workers. The Negro workers replied to this cowardly shooting in such hot fashion that for the fortnight following this attempt, these 'brave saviours of white civilization' in 'dark, benighted' Africa, were nowhere to be seen at demonstrations.

With the deepening of the economic crisis in South Africa, severe in its effects, especially upon the Negro toiling masses, the demonstrations on Dingaan's Day 1930 were even sharper than in 1929. Five Negro workers, including Comrade Nkosi, were killed by Pirow's armed police thugs at Durban. The South African Negro masses are realizing however, in the face of landlessness, unemployment, misery and starvation, that the only force capable of their emancipation is their organized strength and the fighting solidarity of black and white workers against their common enemy — the imperialist exploiters. They are realizing that the only way out of imperialist bondage and economic misery is the revolutionary way out — a South African Black Republic as a stage towards a Workers' and Peasants' Republic.

## Soviet Movement in China

Since the Japanese invasion of Manchuria and the open surrender policy of the Nanking Government headed by Chiang Kai-shek (the bloody murderer of the Chinese toilers), great mass demonstrations of workers and students are taking place throughout China. Even the non-toiling masses of China are beginning to realize that the Kuomintang, the counter-revolutionary party which controls the Nanking Government, is nothing else but a tool of the imperialists, and they are going over to the side of the Communist Party, which alone carries on an uncompromising fight for the liberation of the Chinese masses from the yoke of imperialism and capitalist exploitation.

Already the Communist Party of China has succeeded in establishing a provisional Central Soviet Government over one-sixth of China, embracing a population of more than 80,000,000 people.

Because of the ever increasing successes of the Chinese Revolution, the success of which means the end of imperialist domination in the East, we see all of the imperialist nations, headed by Japan, carrying on open warfare against the Chinese people in order to overthrow the Soviet Government.

The Negro workers in Africa, America and the West Indies, must see in the Chinese Revolution an inspiration for their own national liberation struggles. They must defend the Chinese Revolution because the Chinese masses are fighting against the same imperialists who have stolen Africa and enslaved the Negro peoples in all parts of the world.

A victory of the Chinese Revolution means a death blow to the Japanese, as well as to the European and American imperialist exploiters, and hastens the emancipation of the Negro peoples.

## New Revolt in India

Despite the betrayal of the Indian revolution by Gandhi, which was most openly revealed at the recent Round Table Conference in London, the Indian masses are once more in open revolt against their British oppressors.

Great mass movements have broken out among the peasants in Bengal, Kashmir and the United Provinces, where they are refusing to pay taxes and to obey the orders of the British officials. The Indian capitalists and landlords control the National Congress, a party which is betraying the Indian workers and peasants just as how the Kuomintang, headed by Chiang Kai-shek, betrayed the Chinese workers in 1927. These rich Indians are afraid that if the revolution develops in India, the masses will confiscate their property together with that of the British imperialists; so the Congress leaders, headed by Mahatma Gandhi and Nehru, a lawyer who like Garvey is fond of making radical speeches, have been going around the country advising the workers and the peasants in the villages not to fight but to adopt passive resistance while they are being shot down.

The British Government is taking advantage of the treachery of the so-called Indian leaders and is enacting the most brutal ordinances. Under these laws wholesale arrests, house searches and raids are being carried out by the police and military officials. The terror in India is so great that the students are provoked to commit outrages against these tsar-like officials, which gives the Britishers an excuse to carry on their reign of terror.

The Indian workers are deprived of every elementary right of freedom. Although they hardly receive more than 10 cents a day wages, they are not permitted to organize into militant class unions. Thirty-three trade union leaders have been arrested and thrown into jail because they attempted to organize the workers. They have been allowed to remain in Meeruth jail for three years without a trial, to the everlasting shame of MacDonald and the British 'socialists' and reformist trade union leaders who are supporting British imperialism in India.

It is the task of all oppressed peoples, whether they be Chinese, Indians or Negroes, to recognize their common class interest and unite together against their common enemy — imperialism.


## APPENDIX E

## SOUTH AFRICA AND THE IMPERIALIST WAR

The Anglo-Boer imperialist rulers of South Africa had gained a certain cheap 'notoriety' through their opposition to the creation of black armies in Africa, especially does it show this opposition towards the black army of French imperialism, while glossing over the existence of the King's African Rifles in East Africa and the West African Frontier Force, two native armies of British imperialism which African children in the schools are taught to admire and feel proud of.

The reason for this policy and attitude of the South African slave holders is quite understandable. A black army in South Africa would cause the bourgeoisie sleepless nights. They can only feel a certain amount of 'security' while the natives are completely unarmed and defenceless. But this is only one side of the question. The other side is that this policy lulls the vigilance of the revolutionaries in the struggle against imperialist war. South African natives have participated in every recent war of the imperialists in one way or another. This participation was especially significant during the War of 1914-1918.

It is an incident in this connection that has impelled me to write this article for the benefit of the readers of the *Negro Worker* because it exposes the despicable role of the African lackeys, better known as 'good boy' reformists in South Africa, in the service of British imperialism. The incident I have in mind is the foundering of the 'Mendi' (a British steamer) in the English Channel on 21st February 1917, with 800 African workers bound for the battle fields of France, an incident 'immortalized in song' by middle-class Negro composers in South Africa, and around which the imperialists, with the aid of their black agents, especially the parsons, have spread a halo of mystic glamour, taking good care in hiding the ugly reality of African workers and peasants dying in the cause of their bloody capitalist enslavers.

For fifteen years the imperialists forgot all about the widows and dependents of the men who went down in the 'Mendi'. But on February 21st this year, they staged a huge memorial service in the 'Bantu Sports Ground' in Johannesburg, attended by the 'respectable' citizens of the city, from the white Mayor and Bishops down to the native parsons and underpaid teachers, who brought native boy scouts and girl guides and all the reformist misleaders whom they could mobilize for the occasion. It is interesting to give quotations from the speeches of the white citizens, which were very 'nice' indeed, and then to ask the question: why is it that these arrogant people, whose usual references to the native people of South Africa are of the most insulting, humiliating and revolting nature, thought fit to make such 'nice' speeches on this occasion? When we keep in mind the fact that heavy war clouds are hovering over the East and West, that war has already started in the East in China and Manchuria, we will understand why these jingoists made such speeches on February 21st.

For example, the Mayor of Johannesburg said: 'It was not an adventure for those natives to go to Europe. They went to South West Africa [now Namibia (Ed.)] and endured the extreme heat and thirst of the desert, and they went to East Africa and ran the risks of malaria and other diseases. Perhaps white people forget, as the years go by, that natives died for the Empire in the Great War.'

White people (read white imperialists) forget, but the experience will be valuable for the Negro workers who don't need to go to France or for that matter China, for their greatest enemies are the very South African capitalists whose spokesman was the Mayor. How did these people meet their death?

Dr Lewis E. Hertslet, the medical officer in charge of the Africans on the 'Mendi' at the time of the incident, says [in] his hypocritical tribute: 'Never will I forget the courage and bravery shown by that band of African manhood in the face of death. The men were calm and composed. Each man got his life-belt, they all went on deck with an orderliness which might have surprised orderly seamen. The weather was extremely cold. The lifeboats were small and could not take all those who could reach them.'

'The lifeboats were small and the weather was extremely cold' — 615 Africans perished, drowned like rats for the 'greater glory' of the British Slave Empire and capitalist civilization, or is it — 'syphilization'! Thousands of other Africans perished from cold and exposure in the labour battalions in France, hundreds in the Cape Coloured Corps in the blazing heat of the desert in Palestine. Yet nothing is ever said about them, much less done for their dependents.

Finally, let me quote from the message of Mayor T.E. Leifeldt, D.S.O., a highly placed official of the South Africa Defence Force, whose first duty, by the way, is suppression of native revolts. 'Exclusive of those who served in Europe, some 40,000 natives served in South West and East Africa. They were unarmed and very often found themselves under the fire of the enemy. Many lost their lives in German East Africa in 1917, when the whole force had to make its way through many miles of mud and water to Kilwa and the sea coast. Where pluck and daring were called for, it was never lacking in these men.'

This chief recruiting agent of the Chamber of Mines concludes: 'While the loss of these men is today brought to tearful memory, we are proud of them. They perished doing their duty, serving King and Country.' What hypocrisy!

The imperialists know their job and their 'good boys'. For would you believe, the native lickspittles who were present, instead of denouncing the cynical speeches of these white exploiters, were moved to tears. Smarting under a sense of humiliation at the daily insults hurled at them and their race in South Africa, they would sell their small souls to hear such 'nice' speeches from their masters. But for the toiling masses, whose fathers, sons and brothers perished in Europe, West and East Africa, and who were deceived by these same imperialists that they were engaged in a war for 'democracy', and 'to end all wars', such sloppy sentimentalism has no meaning.

The *Negro Worker* has pointed out time and again that the imperialists intend to make even greater use of the Negro workers and peasants as cannon fodder in the coming World War; that all this sudden concern for the 'Mendi' victims after fifteen years of silence is merely part of the campaign to again mobilize the masses against the imperialist war of intervention, for the defence of the U.S.S.R., and to intensify the struggle against the South African and British Government of hunger and oppression, against the whole catalogue of slave laws under which the native toiling masses suffer, against the treachery and cowardice of the national reformists and 'good boys', for national liberation and social emancipation is the task of all sincere revolutionists in Africa.

Down with Imperialist War!
Defend the U.S.S.R. and the Chinese Soviets!
Long live the Federation of Independent South African
Native Republics.


# APPENDIX F

## SPEECH OF COMRADE T. JACKSON, DELEGATE FROM SOUTH AFRICA

Comrades, allow me on behalf of the toiling masses of South Africa to bring hearty greetings to the International Labour Defense Congress.

Comrades, we formed the I.L.D. in South Africa in 1931. Before that time there had been some defence groups in Cape Town and Johannesburg, but these were mainly groups of foreign workers from Poland, Latvia, Lithuania and such countries. They were mainly concerned with sending aid to the revolutionary fighters in their native countries, but did not participate very much in the struggles of the native masses in South Africa. But in 1931, we decided to form a section of the I.L.D. in South Africa which would pay more attention to the terror situation in South Africa itself.

This was a period of sharp struggle in South Africa. And we were able to mobilize great masses of the Negro toilers in the fight against the terror, especially against the pass system. We were able in the course of six months, February to July 1931, to organize 500 individual members into the I.L.D., as well as to secure the affiliation of the revolutionary trade unions and a number of reformist unions in South Africa.

We were able to be of much assistance to the victims of the capitalist terror. On 16th December 1930 we had a big campaign against the pass laws, when great numbers of the natives came out on the streets and took part in the mass burning of these hated passes. The capitalist government replied with a ferocious reign of terror. There were hundreds of arrests, hundreds of deportations and several workers were killed. The I.L.D. not only gave legal aid to the arrested comrades, but was also able to give material support to the dependents of those in prison.

We were also able to give support to the victims in strikes and in this way we drew many of them into the work of our section. Another action of the I.L.D. was in defence of the struggle of the toiling masses in South West Africa, the former German colony, which is now a part of the Union of South Africa. Because of the agrarian crisis and unemployment, the peasantry revolted against the payment of taxes, and the Government of South Africa sent aeroplanes, tanks and machine guns and destroyed whole villages because of their inability and refusal to pay the taxes. Our I.L.D. section was able to organize not only the Negro workers but white workers as well in defence of the people of South West Africa.

We have also participated in international campaigns and organized demonstrations in defence of the Indian revolutionist, Haghat Singh, in support of the Meerut prisoners and to a great extent in the Scottsboro campaigns.

But while we have registered some successes in our I.L.D. work, this Congress should also be told of our weaknesses. Ours is the only functioning section of the I.L.D. in Black Africa and we should have established contacts with East, West and Central Africa which was clearly our duty, to give them the advantages of our experiences and to help them to establish organizations of I.L.D. in these countries. We have not done nearly what has been called for nor what has been in our power to work among the peasantry. We have not maintained a sufficiently independent existence and have not sufficiently given aid to all sections of the toiling masses in their struggles against oppression and exploitation.

I should state here that we have, with the able assistance of the International Trade Union Committee of Negro Workers, greatly assisted in the formation of the section of the I.L.D. in Madagascar, a colony of French imperialism, which has been active in the struggle of the workers in Madagascar, carrying out mass campaigns for the release of political prisoners, etc.

Comrades, the crisis in Africa is very severe. Whole masses are destitute and seeking a way out of the position in which imperialism has driven them. Because of this we have a wonderful opportunity in Africa which we must take full advantage of. And because of this, the imperialists are trying to stem the tide of revolt of the Negro workers in South Africa with a monstrous reign of terror. Comrades, we have spoken of imperialist terror here in this Congress. We know the imperialists are only able to maintain their position in the colonies by the exercise of violent and brutal terror — terror which is intended to drive fear into the masses. This is what we have to face in Africa: a terror that tries to make the people go in fear every moment of their existence.

In this situation the I.L.D. has proven an inspiration, a great light that will show the Negro masses that they are not alone in their struggles; that they have allies in various parts of the world; that they can be confident of receiving the support of the workers of Europe and America.

We must increase our mass work in South Africa and, in this respect, I too must emphasize what Comrade Padmore said: that the Comrades in the metropolitan countries — in England, in France and the United States — can do a great deal in the way of assistance to the struggling toilers in Africa. They have greater experience and greater possibilities. They also have the elementary rights of moving from one country to another. The Negroes in Africa are denied this right because the passes tie them down. These passes keep the Negro workers in Africa isolated. It is far easier to get from Africa to Europe than from one part of Africa to another in Africa itself.

Today we see a big delegation of Negroes in this Congress, largely through the instrumentality of the International Trade Union Committee of Negro Workers. The comrades here in this Congress must establish contact with the toiling masses in Africa. You must help us develop our initiative. You must help us build a powerful I.L.D. movement in Africa — an organization that will be able to give full support to all the victims of the struggle against imperialist oppression, an organization that will organize and lead the struggle against the terror, and that will do its part in the emancipation of all the toilers from the yoke of imperialism.

Long live the International Labour Defense Congress!
Long live the solidarity of the toilers of all countries!

(Applause)

# APPENDIX G

## THE INTERNATIONAL LABOUR DEFENSE AND THE NEGRO PEOPLES

Among the hundreds of delegates from all parts of the globe who attended the First World Congress of the International Labour Defense (I.L.D.), the Negro delegation was quite conspicuous, both by its size and geographical distribution. Trinidad and British Guiana in the West Indies and South America, the United States and the Union of South Africa, Nigeria, Kenya and Liberia with a proletariat just awakening and making the first approach towards the international revolutionary movement, were directly represented, while Madagascar and Senegal were only prevented from sending delegates by the action of the French Government which arrested hundreds of our comrades in Madagascar and made it impossible for them to send a representative.

The social composition of the delegation is also interesting because it is symptomatic of the state of the organizations of the Negro toiling masses in the colonies. The intellectuals who formerly predominated in the leadership of the movement are giving place to proletarian leadership, so that in the I.L.D. delegation we find them evenly matched, fifty-fifty. There is, of course, still a great disparity in the development of the movement of the Negro toiling masses in the various countries — the movement in the West Indies and South America being much more advanced than in Negro Africa outside of South Africa which has a well developed and advanced proletariat.

The participation of representatives of the Negro toiling masses in the I.L.D. World Congress is not accidental, but is the result of inevitable historical development. The I.L.D., with its programme of struggle against the terror and offensive of the imperialists whose system is tottering under the shattering blows of an acute and universal crisis, has a natural appeal to those sections of the toiling masses, the oppressed nationalities in the colonial and semi-colonial countries, and particularly the Negro toilers, those victims of the most savage and ruthless forms of terror by the imperialists, who are seeking a way out of their present predicament.

## Negroes in Revolt

This offensive of the imperialists is calling forth a great movement of resistance and revolt in the black colonies — strikes of the dockers and other sections of the working population of Trinidad and British Guiana, the mobilization of unemployed and slogans: 'No work, no rent, we want bread', peasant revolts in Nigeria and Sierra Leone, while in Belgian Congo the oppressed Negroes wage a struggle for liberation with the cry of: 'Land, or death to every white man'. (This slogan grows out of the monstrous oppression, relentless terror and land robbery to which the Congo natives are subjected by the white imperialists. Instead of 'Death to every white man', International Labour Defense puts forward the slogan of 'Death to capitalism'.) In South Africa and Kenya the Negro workers burn their passes which are restrictions on their movements in the country, fight against heavy taxation and low wages, and for the return of their land. In the United States the Negro workers join hands with the whites in strike struggles and unemployment demonstrations and the fight against 'Jim Crowism' and race persecution which finds its echoes in the international struggle of the proletariat of all countries and races for the release of the nine Scottsboro boys. (In the United States nearly a hundred years ago a Negro by the name of Jim Crow entered a tramway which was occupied by white men. They threw him out of the tramway. Since then 'Jim Crowism' has come to be the term used to describe the whole system of social, political and economic discrimination to which the Negroes are subjected, such as special and inferior places in tramways, theatres, schools, etc.)

To this rising wave of struggle the imperialists have only one reply: terror. As the Congress resolution on Negro Work puts it: 'This is a policy of bombs and bullets, machine guns and massacres, of imprisonment, tortures, the burning faggot, the hangman's noose and the electric chair. The MacDonald 'socialist' Government uses soldiers and police to crush strikes and revolts in Gambia and Nigeria, and indulges in punitive expeditions in East, West and South Africa.' *The Times* (London), 28th November 1932, reports great discontent and a movement of revolt in the Gambia district with propaganda circulars urging the people to revolt. The paper (*The Times*) reports that 'The natives have been greatly agitated by this propaganda, and as a consequence it has become necessary to send troops to occupy several districts.' The Anglo-Boer imperialists in South Africa are pursuing the same policy of military suppression of the revolting tribes in South West Africa as the Belgian imperialists. In the United States of America 'Jim Crowism', political and social, lynching, legal and extra-legal methods are the common lot of the Negro toilers.

From these facts it is quite clear that the struggle of the Negro masses against imperialism is an integral part of the struggle of the revolutionary proletariat against capitalism and must not be separated. The facts of white terror against the workers in the metropolitan countries which were revealed by the delegates during the Congress showed the Negro delegates quite clearly that the question of national oppression and exploitation was more economic and social than racial. It is the duty of the revolutionary proletariat of Europe and America to recognize in the Negro toiling masses natural allies in the struggle against imperialism, and remember that Marxian maxim: 'Labour in the white skin cannot emancipate itself while labour in the black skin is branded.' In this spirit and on this basis must the international solidarity of the exploited and oppressed masses grow and strengthen.

## War Ahead

In the present situation when the imperialists are preparing for war and intervention against the Soviet Union, the Congress raised the question of the fight against war as one of the most important questions facing the toiling masses. Millions of Negro toilers will be recruited for the slaughter. 'France is already building her army of blacks and militarizing her African railways; Britain has her "West African Frontier Force" and her "King's African Rifles" in East Africa; Belgium is organizing a tremendous African colonial army while Italy is constructing a military railroad through Libya from the Mediterranean across the Sahara and parallel with the French line.' The imperialists are feverishly preparing for war on all sides and the Negro toiling masses must be won for the struggle against it.

## Soviet Russia, Champion of the Oppressed

It is impossible to discuss the war question without coming up against the question of the Soviet Union and taking a stand on it, either for or against. The victorious Russian Revolution expropriated the expropriators and placed the administration of government and ownership of industry in the hands of the workers and peasants. The history of Russia since the epochal event has been one triumphal march forward. Formerly oppressed nationalities are enjoying complete freedom and are recording with every day new achievements in the spheres of economic, cultural, and social progress. Racial discrimination and oppression have been completely wiped out, and isolated manifestations of chauvinism by counter-revolutionaries are dealt with in a merciless and ruthless manner by the Workers State. The gigantic achievements of socialist construction in the Soviet Union are in striking contrast to the decay and disintegration in the capitalist and colonial world, arousing the fury and hatred of the capitalist class. Therefore the Negro workers and toiling peasants who find inspiration in the achievements of the Russian workers and peasants must put forward in the front rank the slogan: 'Defend the Soviet Union, the fatherland of all toilers.'

## Negro Traitors at Work

In their attacks on the Negro toiling masses the imperialists are supported directly and indirectly by the Negro capitalists and chiefs. It is in recognition of their services as betrayers of their own people that the imperialists promote the West African Negro, Blaze Diagne, and the West Indian Negro, Condace, to positions of 'trust' in their colonial cabinets. In South Africa and West Africa the chiefs are given puppet parliaments (Bunga) and paid salaries; in America the National Association for the Advancement of Coloured People sabotages and hinders the campaign for the release of the Scottsboro boys and, through demagogy, divides the Negro workers from the white workers. In the West Indies the so-called big native leaders are bribed with titles and minor official jobs. The Negro workers must be on their guard against these betrayers of the fight against imperialist terror.

## Tasks of the Masses

The task of educating the toilers of all countries and races in the spirit of international solidarity against race discrimination and chauvinism, against nationalism and the betrayals of the Negro bourgeoisie and chiefs, which the I.L.D. undertakes, makes it the friend of all people.

In South Africa and Madagascar there are already functioning sections of the I.L.D. waging the struggle against imperialist terror, while committees and individual contacts have been established with Senegal, Nigeria, Liberia, Kenya, Sierra Leone, the West Indies and South America. The Scottsboro campaign which has assumed world-wide proportions, almost eclipsing the Sacco-Vanzetti campaign, has brought the whole question of Negro oppression to the forefront and millions of toilers and intellectuals in the fight against the barbarous bloodthirsty lynching by the American imperialists of Negroes in the U.S.A. These are memorable achievements and yet only the beginning of our work.

The I.L.D. is faced with great tasks in the sphere of Negro work. For the achievements of these it will strengthen its Negro Department and as far as possible draw in Negro comrades into the work. This will be connected with the strengthening and closer supervision and assistance of the sections in South Africa and Madagascar which will give us the base for the establishment of sections throughout the Black World. The metropolitan sections can play and must play an increasing role, under the direction of the E.C., in exposing the brutalities of the imperialists in the colonies by means of pamphlets and other leaflets and specific cases of outrages. Finally, the Congress undertook to intensify the Scottsboro campaign emphasizing the forms of terror used against the Negroes all over the world, and to mobilize wider and wider masses of the backward strata in the campaigns against imperialist terror.

## A Friend of the Blacks

The one note of gloom that fell upon the Congress was the death of J. Louis Engdahl, General Chairman of the United States Section of the I.L.D., which occurred on November 21st from an attack of pneumonia. The name of Comrade Engdahl will forever be associated with the struggle for Negro emancipation. His six months tour over Europe with Ada Wright, Scottsboro mother, rousing the toiling masses on behalf of the nine Scottsboro Negro boys, was the greatest factor in compelling the Supreme Court of the United States to reverse the death verdict and order a new trial for the boys. Comrade Engdahl has become the symbol of international solidarity.

The close of the Congress was marked by, among other things, the presentation of a banner, amid scenes of the greatest enthusiasm, to Comrade Hubert Crichlow on behalf of the Negro delegation. A symbolic significant action of international solidarity and revolutionary struggle between the white and black workers of the world.

Organize a branch of the I.L.D. and mobilize to fight for your human rights. Write to the secretary of the International Trade Union Committee of Negro Workers for full information, rules, regulations, etc. Don't put it off. Do so today!

## APPENDIX H

## SOUTH AFRICAN IMPERIALISTS INITIATE NEW TERROR AGAINST NATIVES

The toiling masses of South Africa are the victims of new acts of terror at the hands of British imperialism operating through the Hertzog-Pirow Government of police and hunger. Since the beginning of the economic crisis, the Government has been strengthening the existing anti-native, anti-working class ordinances and adopting new laws restricting the native toilers, imposing new forms of taxation and making the police control over the actions of the Negro masses more stringent.

State police gangs, carrying out the instructions of the Ministry of Justice, engage in mass raids on the Native locations, and mass deportations and banishments are becoming more and more common. The South African bourgeoisie is carrying out a monstrous campaign of chauvinism to create a mob sentiment against the native toilers and at the same time utilize the provisions of the Riotous Assemblies Act in an attempt to crush all resistance to the ruthless offensive.

In November 1932 four leading members of the Communist Party of South Africa were arrested and exiled from Johannesburg, and a number of native and white leaders of the revolutionary trade unions were banished from the mining areas of the Witwatersrand under the far-reaching provisions of the Riotous Assemblies Act.

In August 1932, a punitive expedition equipped with armoured cars, artillery and bombing planes attacked the national liberation movement of the Ukuambi tribes of Ovamboland, South West Africa, with casualties as reported in Johannesburg of several hundred dead, the burning of settlements and the driving of the national revolutionaries into the wilderness.

An enumeration of some of the recent anti-native, anti-toiler ordinances will indicate the terroristic attitude of the Anglo-Boer imperialists:

The Colour Bar Act is a legal discrimination against the Negro workers in industry; the Native Administration Act is a vicious sedition law; the Native Urban Areas Act, as amended in 1930, brings native women within the scope of the pass laws; the Riotous Assemblies Act was especially framed to suppress the revolutionary movement; the Native Service Contract Act ties agricultural labourers and squatters to the big landlords, compelling them to give free labour service for long periods and making them liable to imprisonment and flogging for breaking 'contracts'; the Natal Native Code Act which gives the police power to imprison any native 'agitator' considered dangerous, for a period not exceeding three authority months without any trial whatsoever: the Asiatic Land Tenure Act which segregates Indians and Coloured workers from the industrial areas into the locations, thus 'solving' the unemployment situation in a 'civilized' manner.

The arrests, raids and unbridled reactions of the Hertzog Nationalist Government naturally arouses the deepest indignation and resistance of the toiling masses as is evidenced by growing demonstrations, strikes and peasant revolts, and organized movements for the refusal to carry the obnoxious passes and to pay taxes.

The reply of the Government to the growing revolts and revolutionary upsurge is the most savage terror aiming at the physical extermination of the revolutionary movement. First and foremost the Government directs its attack against the Communist Party of South Africa. The brutal assaults upon the revolutionary workers is instanced in the ambushing, on 12th August 1931, of 12 workers by 150 police thugs in a dark street in Johannesburg; the violent attacks on Negro speakers in the 1st May 1932, demonstrations; the organization of white fascist gangs to attack revolutionaries, as at Germiston in November 1932, and a whole series of similar terror actions that feature the present sharpened offensive of the British imperialists.

There is nothing particularly new about this terror, other than its unprecedented ferocity and savagery. The fierce battles between the native toilers and the police are the inevitable result of the whole situation.

The South African section of the I.L.D. is organizing and leading an energetic mass campaign against the whole regime of white terror and oppression in South Africa. But they must have the loyal support of the revolutionary proletariat and the toiling masses of all countries to expose the terror regime of British imperialism in South Africa. International protest is the great need. The Scottsboro campaign has shown that the toiling masses can make even the strongest of the imperialist powers — America — take its deadly clutch from the throat of the Negro workers.

The International Trade Union Committee of Negro Workers and the Negro Welfare Association of England call on the toiling masses of the world to take up the struggle against the outrages of arrogant chauvinist South African, Afrikaner and British imperialists. Protest against the enslavement of the native toiling masses in South Africa. Protest against the imperialist chauvinist campaign in South Africa to divide the white workers from the native, coloured and Indian toilers under the illusive slogans of 'civilized labour', 'a white South Africa', 'preserve white civilization from the black savages', etc. Expose the rotten lies. Let the white workers know how false and hypocritical these promises are. Support the liberation struggles of the native masses.

Against white terror in South Africa!

Against the whole imperialist slave system of South Africa!

For the solidarity of all toilers with the oppressed people of South Africa in its struggle against imperialist terror and justice.

## APPENDIX I

## THE STRUGGLES OF THE NEGRO TOILERS IN SOUTH AFRICA

EDITOR'S NOTE: With this issue of *The Negro Worker*, we begin the publication of the manuscript of an unpublished pamphlet written by Albert Nzula, a South African Native, shortly before his death last year.

The material is of especial importance because it gives us a clear, though brief, insight into the historic development of the Union of South Africa and the development of the Anti-Imperialist and revolutionary movement.

The fact that it has been written about two years ago and is, therefore, not descriptive of recent events, does not destroy the value of this contribution towards a study and appreciation of the conditions of and the struggles being waged by the Native and white workers against Anglo-Boer Imperialist slavery.

The manuscript will be published in four instalments.

### Historico-Geographical Landmarks

South Africa was discovered to Europe in 1486. The discovery was accidental, and a mere incident in the search for a new sea route to India, by the buccaneering Portuguese navigator, Bartholomew Dias. This was the era of the development of merchant capitalism; and India, with its precious stones and rare spices, was the goal of the pirates and sea dogs of the rising bourgeoisie. The feudal restraints and exactions of the various little states and kingdoms of Europe made the overland trip to India through these states a costly and hazardous one. The open sea, the free highway, where there were no tolls to be paid to avaricious barons and princes, was the ideal thing for our enterprising traders. In those days of sailing ships, entailing long voyages with little fresh provisions, resulting in scurvy for the crew; the southernmost point of Africa (the Cape of Good Hope) by its natural position became the matter of course stopping place, the half-way house, for all ships bound for India. Here they obtained fresh water and fresh meat from the Hottentots.

Finally the Dutch, in 1652, decided to establish a settlement for the purpose of supplying their own ships and those of other nations with fresh provisions. This idea was no sooner conceived than executed. So far as the rights of the Hottentots, the aboriginal inhabitants of the Cape Peninsula, were concerned, they did not matter. The Dutch were prepared to be generous enough to buy the necessary land from the Hottentots and if the Hottentots refused . . . well, the Dutch had learned a few things in the plundering of the natives of India and the Hottentots were, after all, nothing but 'savages'.

The Hottentots did refuse to part with their land and the Dutch were forced to use compulsion to obtain it. Thus began the colonization of Southern Africa three centuries ago.

To understand the remainder of the story we must refer a little to the geography of the country, as the contours of the country played a significant part in the further history of the colony. South Africa consists of a huge and elevated plateau, from 2,000 to 6,000 feet above sea level, sloping gradually towards the west, the Atlantic Ocean; and ending more or less abruptly towards the south and the east, in such a manner as to leave a narrow coast belt on this coast, ranging from 15 to a 100 miles in width. The end of the plateau facing this narrow coast strip forms a sort of high mountain range which constitutes a sort of natural barrier to the hinterland. The few rivers that could be used for travelling into the interior, were, for part of the year (the dry season), practically nothing but shallow streams, while during the rainy season they became raging torrents, full of cataracts and waterfalls which rendered them unfit for navigation. For these reasons the settlers or colonizers confined themselves mainly to the narrow south-eastern coast belt, only a few of the boldest spirits venturing into the interior occasionally.

On the plateau, and further north along the coast belt, were the homes of the Bantu people, as the Negro tribes of South Africa are called. For the next two centuries they were left in peace, the coastal tribes being the only ones forced to retreat before the northerly coast expansion of the Dutch settlers.

One of the results of the 'revolutionary' Napoleonic wars (1795-1815) was the capture of the Cape by the British in 1814. The Dutch were forced to seek for new pastures. This led to what is known in South African history as the 'Great Trek of 1836'. The Dutch, who had increased to thousands since 1652, gathered their belongings and, finding their way through the mountain passes, made their way into the interior. Here they collided with the Bantu tribes who claimed ownership of the land and blocked their further progress. The fight for mastery was severe and bitter and if even today there is no love lost between the Bantu and Boer, it is a legacy of those days which is kept burning by the reactionary schools, churches, press and other vile institutions of the Boer Imperialists. Superior arms and technique decided, however, in favour of the newcomers, and the Bantu were forced to abandon their homes and lands or to become the servants and slaves of their conquerors. The Dutch proceeded to establish two republics in what are today known as the Orange Free State and the Transvaal Provinces of the Union of South Africa. This was not all, however, that they established. They also created a semi-feudal serf state with the Bantu as serfs without land or rights of any kind, the fundamental principle of their constitution being: 'There can be no equality between black and white in either church or state'.

## The Epoch of Imperialism

This brings us to the end of the pre-Imperialist period of capitalist colonial expansion in South Africa. The next period which Lenin, in his wonderful work *Imperialism, the Last Stage of Capitalism*, describes in the following manner: 'The characteristic feature of this period is the definitive partition of the earth — definitive, not in the sense that a new partition is impossible, for on the contrary new partitions are possible and unavoidable, but in the sense that the colonial policy of the capitalist countries has completed the conquest of the unoccupied territories on our planet. For the first time, the world is completely shared out so that in the future territories will only be able to pass from one possessor to another instead of acquiring a possessor for the first time.' Lenin goes on further to quote Supan, a bourgeois writer on Imperialism, as writing: 'the characteristic feature of this period is, therefore, the division of Africa and Polynesia. This was the period of the partition of Africa among the Imperialist powers of Europe.'

The discovery of diamonds at Kimberley in 1867 and gold in the Transvaal in 1886 had led to a great influx of Europeans, mainly Britishers. Railways were built and roads laid into the hinterland. British finance dominated the scene of this expansion. From economic domination arose the necessity for political domination. The result was the Anglo-Boer War of 1899-1902 in which the Dutch republics passed into the hands of the British and were incorporated into the Union of South Africa in 1910.

The Bantu had been driven into small and overcrowded reserves or forced to work on the farms of the Boer landowners, or the mines of the British Imperialists. The great need of those days was labour power. But the natives were not willing to leave their small farms or even their tenancies under the Dutch farmers, which gave them a reasonable living compared to the life of dangerous toil and suffering in the mines at Kimberley and Johannesburg. To persuade them, the slogan of the Imperialists became: 'Tax them and take away more land from them'. Thus began the system of heavy taxation and land expropriation of the natives — a system of low wages, a system of forced labour, a system of cheap, unskilled black labour on which was constructed a superstructure of a 'highly paid, skilled, white labour aristocracy, recruited from Europe and from a section of ruined small Dutch farmers'.

## Agrarian and Industrial Relations

In area, the Union of South Africa is 471,917 square miles, that is, more than five times the size of Great Britain or twice the size of Germany. It has a population of approximately 8,000,000, consisting of 1,500,000 whites and 6,500,000 non-Europeans: 500,000 coloureds, 180,000 Indians and the remainder natives. Though the Indians and coloureds are treated slightly differently and in some respects have a higher status than the natives, their position is bad and for all practical purposes they fall into the same category as the native population.

The Imperialists in South Africa, in their anxiety to 'divide and rule', have evolved a system of race, caste and colour divisions which is the most baneful in the world. From this point of view the whites form the ruling oligarchy, with the natives, coloureds and Asiatics subservient to them in varying degrees.

South Africa is primarily an agricultural and mining country. The agriculture is mainly in the hands of the Boer landowning class, while the mining is the special preserve of British Imperialists. Blessed with a narrow internal market owing to the poverty stricken condition of the native masses, exports play a great part in the economic life of South Africa.

Eighty seven and one-half per cent of the native and coloured population depend for a living upon the land, either as peasants or as agricultural labourers, but we find that a quarter of the population, that is the whites, is in possession of four-fifths of the land, while the natives, who form nearly three-quarters of the population are in possession of only one-fifth of the land, and that, in most cases, the most unfertile and inaccessible. The agrarian native population can be divided into two main sections, those living in the native reserves and those living as tenants, squatters or agricultural labourers on European owned farms.

## In the Native Reserves

The native reserves are those parts of the country which they were allowed to retain after their conquest by foreign imperialists. In extent they are 11,164,484 morgen, (a morgen equals approximately two acres) or 7% of the total area of the Union of South Africa. When it is remembered that most of this land, due to natural causes and also to overcrowding, is barren, it is easy to realize that the majority of the people who occupy it simply cannot make a living. Compare 11,000,000 odd morgen held by the natives the nearly 110,000,000 morgen appropriated by the white landowners. Thus, the land question is the most serious question in the politics of South Africa today.

The system of land tenure under which the natives hold their land is communal. The land belongs to the whole tribe and the chief and his councillors decide how much land each family is entitled to, of course not independently, but with the active interference of the government. The land itself is the property of the government, which reserves to itself the mineral rights and also the right to move the tribe from it at its own discretion and pleasure. Outside of the reserves the natives are not allowed to buy or lease land unless under exceptional circumstances, collectively as a tribe under the chief. The government makes use of these chiefs to collect taxes, to see that law and order is maintained and generally to supervise the petty functions of the tribe. All chiefs who oppose the government soon lose their positions. Thus we find that the chiefs today are the fortress of and the agents of Imperialism in the village. The chiefs, their councillors and the clerks are the young native bourgeoisie which expects to get a share in the imperialist spoliation of the native peasantry on the reserves.

To supervise and assist the chiefs the Imperialists have set up a military machine made up of a bureaucracy of magistrates, police and mobile squadrons (troops) well trained in the art of maintaining 'law and order' and merciless and ruthless in the execution of their 'duty'. One incident in South African history illustrates very clearly what is meant by this. We refer to the Bambata Rebellion of 1906. In 1906 the government, in order to force the natives to leave the reserves to work on European farms and in the mines, imposed a tax upon the Zulu tribes of Natal, the south-eastern province of the Union of South Africa. One of these tribes, under the leadership of their militant chief, Bambata, refused to pay the tax and revolted. The mobile squadron was sent, armed with rifles and machine guns, against the revolting tribe. The tribe was driven out of their homes. Men, women and children were forced into a gorge, the Mamre Gorge, from which there was only one way to escape, and at this exit machine guns were placed and the order given to fire. Unable to defend themselves, hundreds were slaughtered in order to teach 'them and others to respect the white men's laws'. This rebellion, to which Lenin refers in *Imperialism, the Last Stage of Capitalism*, is a record of one of the most shameless massacres of unarmed and defenceless men, women and children by the imperialists in South Africa. But it is by no means an isolated incident.

In addition to being forced to support this bureaucratic state machine, with its chiefs and other petty parasites, another enemy of the natives in the reserves is the European trader and usurer to whom the natives are heavily indebted. This parasite is the main labour recruiting agent for the mines and plantations. Many circumstances have conspired to give him the position that he holds in the native reserves, amongst which are his monopolist privileges, the lack of transport facilities which forbids the personal marketing of the produce of the peasants, and finally, the support which he receives from the government officials.

Because of the absence of transport facilities, for instance there are absolutely no railways on the reserves, the native peasant is at a disadvantage so far as disposing of his stock and grain and the buying of the few necessities that he can afford is concerned. For these transactions he depends entirely on the traders. The system of 'barter' is very widespread, the trader seldom paying in cash for the crops that he buys from the natives, but always gives in exchange his own wares. 'The cheating and chicanery that is connected with these transactions can be more easily imagined than described.' In this manner the produce of the natives soon disappears into the hands of the traders. The native is forced to come to the trader for credit and in a very short time finds himself indebted. Now the trader becomes the labour recruiting agent. The native being unable to pay his indebtedness, the trader forces him to sign a contract to work in the mines, using the threat of arrest and seizure of the stock of the native as persuasion. Thousands of men are thus forced to sign away their liberty for periods of from six to nine months of every year to slave in the mines for the most miserable of wages. The native in these reserves has no rights whatsoever. He cannot leave them without official permission (or passes), his educational requirements are simply ignored, no irrigation schemes are developed for his benefit in spite of frequent drought — and a drought in these reservations is invariably followed by famine and starvation — in a word there is nothing but stagnation and a dead level of poverty.

## The Natives on European Farms: Wage Labourers and Squatters

There are approximately 2,000,000 natives living on European farms as squatters or as wage labourers. The conditions of these people are probably the worst, compared to that of the other sections of the toiling native population of the Union of South Africa. As wage labourers they have to slave for the landowners 12 to 14 hours a day, for a wage as low as 10 shillings a month, the exceptional maximum being 40 shillings on some of the big sugar and wattle plantations. This wage is very often, in fact to a very large extent, not paid in cash but in kind. The labourers are tied on the farms on lengthy contracts and cannot visit even their friends in the neighbourhood without obtaining a written permit or special pass from their employer. To break their contract is a criminal offence punishable by imprisonment or a fine which very often the native cannot pay. Strikes are illegal. On the other hand, the landowner can terminate his part of the contract at pleasure. He can break it without being liable to anything but a theoretical civil prosecution by the native worker, which costs a great deal of money and which the worker is unable to afford. The landowner often uses the lash on the natives and if they defend themselves he can shoot them down with impunity — the charge of murder of a native by a landowner is always changed into a charge of culpable homicide to which a fine is attached. Thousands of natives have been murdered by these slave-drivers on the farms and not one murderer has ever 'swung' for it yet. Should a native, in defending himself, kill one of these bloodthirsty task-masters, the land is filled with howls of rage and cries for his blood by the insatiable bourgeoisie.

The other kind of native labourer on the white landowners' farms is the squatter. The squatter is a native who, for the privilege of remaining on the farm and cultivating a small piece of land and grazing a limited number of cattle, renders without wages three to six months labour service annually for the landowner. To aggravate the oppressive and feudal character of this regulation, the period of service is not consecutive. It leaves to the pleasure and discrimination of the landowner when , and for how long, the labourer must render this service. Thus the native is tied down to the farm for the whole year when he could earn wages on temporary jobs outside of the farm. For the native to break this contract renders him liable to the severest punishment.

Previous to 1913, the squatters were not altogether the exploited class that they are today. We have already referred to the Boers as being the main landowners, while the British are chiefly interested in mining. The Boers had already established semi-slave states in the Orange Free State and Transvaal provinces when they were defeated by the British in 1900. With the foundation of the Union of South Africa in 1910, the landowning class, though defeated, was very powerful and were able to lay down the main lines of policy regarding the natives. One of the very first measures of the new parliament of the Union of South Africa, affecting native interests, was *The Natives' Land Act* of 1913. This act forbade the natives to buy, lease, hire or rent land anywhere in the Union except the overcrowded native reserves or in areas to be provided by the government — these areas have never been set apart. This Act also prohibited any natives from remaining on European farms unless they were employed as wage labourers or as squatters.

What did this mean? It meant that 2,000,000 natives, by a mere flourish of the pen, found themselves faced with the necessity of either submitting to the forced slavery caused by this Act, or revolting. This law caused the greatest sufferings amongst the natives and aroused the bitterest indignation. The movement roused against this Act was only beginning to gain its real momentum when the Great War broke out. About this later.

Thousands left the farms with their stock and families, but as the reserves were overcrowded and employment in the towns limited, they were forced, driven by the pass laws and other discriminatory laws, to accept the slave conditions to which they were condemned by the Act.

## In the Mines and Factories

South Africa, for the last forty years, has been the largest source of gold supply for the world. And also diamonds. Besides, there are important coal fields employing as many as 30,000 native workers. There are also copper, iron, tin and other mines, but these are at present of little significance. The gold mines employ an average of 200,000 native workers and if we include the coal, diamond and other mines, the total number of native miners in South Africa is 311,000.

One of the main difficulties that mine magnates had to face at the beginning was the shortage of labour power. This they tried to overcome at first by following the example of the sugar magnates of Natal who imported Indian labour, by importing Chinese labour. This scheme did not, for various reasons, work too well and it was discontinued. The mines then began to systematically recruit native workers from the native reserves, especially the Transkeian territories, which are extremely overcrowded. In this recruiting, all methods of persuasion are used, from lying promises to coercion. The most effective recruiter who co-operates with the government agents and chiefs is the trader. To this united front of the mine-owners, the government, the recruiting agent and the traders, the native worker is helpless and without much ado is persuaded to sign away his freedom under long-term contracts. The native is not allowed to take his family with him. When a sufficient number of native persons have been secured, they are packed into filthy freight cars, put in charge of police and sent off to Johannesburg, the centre of the gold mining industry. Here they are lodged in compounds, guarded by police, which they can only leave for short periods if they obtain passes or permits.

The compound system keeps the native away from all contact with the outside world while he is in the town, especially from contact with the labour movement. The most elaborate precautions are taken by the mine managers to ensure this.

To realize the slave character of this labour it is sufficient to point out that the wages paid to native miners have never exceeded an average of 50 shillings a month during a period of forty years. The gold mines during this period (1888-1928) have produced precious metal valued at £1,000,000,000 while the wages bill of the native workers, on whose exploitation this industry depends, has only amounted to a paltry £300,000,000 sterling in the same period. They have been a source of profit to the Imperialists, but at what expense! Miner's pthisis (a disease of the lungs caused by rock dust) has destroyed thousands of natives without any compensation being made to their families. Hundreds are entombed, maimed and mutilated annually, and no benefit paid either to them or to their families. According to official figures (these do not include the victims of miner's pthisis) of 1929 and 1930, the numbers are: killed 793, injured 8,356; killed 872, injured 9,253, respectively.

The working day is anything from ten to twelve hours. Underground the men are divided into groups of from ten to fifty under a white overseer and several native boss-boys armed with whips ready to apply them unhesitatingly to any slacker. The very first strike of native miners, in 1913, was against the brutal treatment that they received underground. Things have not improved very much since then. The slave-driving goes on as ruthlessly as ever.

The wages and conditions of mine workers determine to a greater or lesser extent the wages of native workers in other industries. There are 150,000 native workers engaged in industry, mainly of a secondary nature (building, garment, engineering, furniture, etc.), 50,000 in transport and a further 80,000 in commerce and trade. Though the conditions of these workers cannot be compared to the conditions of the miners, essentially they are not very much different. These workers also are persecuted under the pass laws, denied the right to organize and strike, subjected to the colour bar and other 'Jim Crow' laws, forced to live in unsanitary locations and bachelor barracks, in a word subjected to a hundred and one pin-pricks and restrictions that make of their lives an intolerable misery.

## The National Liberation Movement

The conditions that I have described so inadequately cannot but lead to the maximum state of disaffection and dissatisfaction. It is not necessary to recount here all the wars of subjugation and 'civilization' that were carried on by the imperialists against the natives throughout the whole of the nineteenth century. First one tribe was subjugated and then another, the Xhosas, the Basutos, the Zulus, the Bechuanas, the Bapedis. The division of the Bantus into tribes facilitated this preliminary job of the imperialists. It was a realization of the weaknesses that arise out of tribal divisions and differences that gave the very first national movement its character of a striving towards the formation of a great Bantu nation united against the Boer imperialists. This movement came under the leadership of the African National Congress founded in 1912, an organization representing the chiefs, headmen, priests, lawyers and other petty bourgeois elements of the Bantu population. By placing its main task as the fight against Boer Imperialism, failing to see or completely ignoring the role of British Imperialism, it played directly into the hands of British bourgeois liberals whose interests were in some respects opposed to those of the Boer semi-feudal landowners. The British bourgeois liberals desired a free labour market and therefore did not consider such measures as the semi-slave pass laws indispensable. In spite of this African National Congress had the overwhelming support of the native peasantry and a large section of the native workers who did not see through their false programme. The native workers could only be taught by experience that British Imperialism was as much responsible for their position as the more open, brutal and swash-buckling Boer Imperialism. The opportunity for the 'gaining' of this experience was not long in coming.

## Native Resistance

The passing of the Natives Land Act of 1913, the imposition of pass laws on native women, aroused a tremendous movement of indignation and protest. For the first time Zulu, Basuto, Xhosa, Bechuana, Bapedi and Swazi all stood together facing the same enemy. Strikes of the miners in the Rand (Johannesburg), the passive resistance of the native women to the pass laws, the arrest and jailing of them, was leading to a very critical situation. This movement frightened the leaders, who called upon the masses to halt while they sent a deputation to place their grievances before the Imperial Government in London. It is interesting to know that even the more radical elements in the African National Congress were taken in by this manoeuvre, due to their lack of understanding of the role of British Imperialism. We have in mind especially the case of J.T. Gumede (the first native to visit the Soviet Union). Gumede was persuaded to go on this forlorn deputation, which was courteously received by His Majesty's ministers, but received no satisfaction, except the 'assurance' that His Majesty, the King, had the best interests of all his subjects at heart and all reasonable grievances would be remedied.

The Labour Party and the Independent Labour Party locals in England arranged meetings for the deputation and generally did their best to impress the deputation with the 'inborn sense of fair play and justice' of the British people. Then, as now, these slimy hypocrites did their best to hide from the British working class the real nature of British Imperialism. Then, as now, these agents of British Imperialism with their tongue in the cheek were ready with songs of praise of 'liberty and democracy', but always did their best to cover up the oppressive regime of British Imperialism both in England and in the colonies.

War broke out while the deputation was in England. They were persuaded to believe that it was a war of democracy against 'Junker Imperialism' and that out of it would come the liberation of all oppressed nations and peoples. They went back to South Africa convinced recruiters for the war of the Imperialists. With their assistance 40,000 natives under General Botha in German West Africa, and General Smuts, in German East Africa (Tanganyika), thousands in France in the labour contingents, fought and laboured under the leadership of the very same oppressors against whom a few months before they were preparing to revolt. The African National Congress had committed its first act of betrayal to the liberationist struggles of the native peoples. The chiefs and the petty bourgeois native 'good boys' had started on their career of betrayal. The workers and toiling peasants were to learn more about the false promises of chiefs, priests and lawyers; they were to learn more of what imperialists mean by the freedom of nations.

The struggle of the native women, however, continued to grow in scope as well as intensity. The jails were becoming uncomfortably full, it was beginning to lead to a more serious ferment and discontent. The government, to save itself and to hide the treachery of the Congress, repealed the laws against the women in 1916, but not against the men. The masses, however, had not failed to see the passivity of the Congress on the question of the passes as they affected the men. To what extent their faith was shaken was to be seen in the period that followed the war.

## The Post War Period: The Struggles of the Working Class

The high prices and the speculation in foodstuffs and other necessaries during and after the war, and the low wages that native workers received, created a situation of the greatest unrest. The return of thousands of men from the various fronts, France, East and West Africa, only to find themselves confronted with the same oppressive and discriminatory laws that they had been assured would be abolished as a reward for the fight to save the 'Empire and the Union Jack' was exasperating beyond endurance. In this period we see the workers, who were no more as innocent as before, after going through the war, taking the leadership of the struggle and building up the biggest and most popular organization that the native toiling masses had ever had — the Industrial and Commercial Workers Union of Africa.

The brains and moving spirit of this organization was Clements Kadalie, himself not a native of South Africa but of East Africa, who was working in Cape Town. All the rebellious spirits amongst the native intellectuals, especially amongst the teachers, found themselves in the leadership of this organization, but the membership, at one time as high as 100,000, was what the name implies, with strong supporting influence among the native agricultural workers and peasantry. Kadalie was not uneducated in socialist literature, and this was what gave the I.C.U. a distinct working class bias in spite of the petty bourgeois leadership, as opposed to the nationalist character of the African National Congress. The preamble to the I.C.U. Constitution proclaims: 'Whereas the interests of the workers and those of the employers are opposed to each other, the former living by selling their labour and the latter living by exploiting the labour of the workers, depriving the workers of a part of the product of their labour, in the form of profit, no peace can be between the two classes, a struggle must always obtain about the division of the product of human labour.'

This was proclaiming the class struggle, but the I.C.U. also had a national appeal. Its slogan 'Vuka Africa' was often translated to mean 'Africa for the Africans', while the *Workers Herald*, official organ of the I.C.U., called for a 'violent struggle' for industrial emancipation and national liberation.

There were about a dozen native and coloured communists in leading positions in the I.C.U., including the present-day militant fighter, Comrade Gomas, who alone of almost all those comrades has remained true to the working class and is in the forefront of their struggle today. But the Communist Party as a whole did not have much influence over the movement owing to the then opportunist, chauvinist character of its leadership in the person of Bunting and others, now expelled from the Party.

## Strike Struggles

The aftermath of the war brought with it, in South Africa as in other countries, a period of the most severe crisis and suffering for the workers, and many strikes took place. Johannesburg was once more the scene of strike struggles. Several thousand native workers employed by the

Johannesburg municipality came out on strike in 1919 for a six-penny increase in wages. As usual, the strikers were immediately arrested under the Master and Servant Act, for breaking their contracts, and convicted. The magistrate who tried them, in sentencing them, delivered himself of the following diatribe: 'They would go back to their work as soon as the necessary arrangements could be made. They would be placed under a guard, including a guard of Zulus (policemen) with assegais (spears) and white men with guns. If they attempted to escape they would be shot down if necessary and if they refused to obey any orders which might be given them, they would receive lashes.'

The cynical character of this pronouncement, its brutality, and the awesome proclamation of the dire consequences that would follow any resistance to the bidding of these cowardly South African Imperialists, were intended to drive fear into the toiling masses and kill all protests. Actually, it had the opposite effect. It aroused the whole native population to the greatest bitterness and hatred. Protest meetings and demonstrations of unmistakable militancy and revolutionary nature warned the government that the 'patience of even the most patient people has its limits'. The strikers were immediately released. Besides this, the Transvaal night curfew laws and also the one shilling tax for passes were abolished.

At the same time strikes broke out in Bloemfontein and in the coal fields of Natal and in the Messina tin mines in the Transvaal. In Cape Town the strike of the native workers ended in an overwhelming victory for the strikers and did more than anything else to raise the prestige of the Industrial and Commercial Workers Union amongst the native workers. The strikes in Johannesburg, Bloemfontein and Natal were under the leadership of the African National Congress and were notable for the inconclusive and undecisive character of their termination, owing to the treachery of the leaders.

The next important strike occurred in February 1920, at the Village Deep Mine, Johannesburg, involving 42,000 native miners who struck for an increase in wages, better living conditions and treatment. The government decided on stern measures, shooting, killing and wounding scores of native workers, forcing them back to work. Simultaneously with this, another strike broke out at Port Elizabeth under the leadership of the I.C.U. This strike was also for an increase in wages and was led by Masabalala (I.C.U.). In the strike the role of the African National Congress of strike breakers was clearly revealed to the masses. At a meeting of 3,000 workers, held during the course of the strike, Dr Rubusana, a native leader of the Congress, was advising the native workers to go back to work when he was assaulted. For this the police arrested Masabalala. As soon as the native workers learned of this arrest they sent an ultimatum to the police, demanding the release of the strike leader, threatening to storm the jail if this was not done. The native workers armed themselves with such

weapons as they could obtain, mainly sticks and stones, and proceeded to
the jail where they were met by a force of armed police and civilians
(white fascists and ex-servicemen). Mounted police charged into the crowd,
but were pulled down from their horses. The police seeing this, opened fire
into the crowd and killed 76 and wounded scores of others. However,
Masabalala was soon after released.

## Among the Peasants and Agricultural Workers

The peasants were also in a great state of unrest. Here the movement
took the form of a refusal to pay taxes. So strong did this movement
become, that in the Transvaal where the natives were compelled to pay a
tax of 50 shillings a year, it was reduced to 20 shillings. In the Cape
Province we find the first attempt by the peasantry to seize and occupy
land. This attempt occurred in 1921, at Bulhoek near Queenstown. A few
hundred native peasants occupied some vacant government land. When
they were called upon to leave it or pay taxes, they refused to do either
one thing or the other. The story of this action spread to other regions
and soon peasants all over the Cape Province refused to pay their taxes
and the government was faced with the alternative of either abolishing
the taxes or using military measures. It decided on the latter. The mobile
squadron, armed with machine guns, rifles and bayonets was mobilized
against the Bulhoek peasants who were the moving force of the disaffection.
It must be stated here that the leader of these people, Enoch Mgijima, was
a religious fanatic who told his followers that the white man's bullets
would be turned into water. In this way it happened that these people,
without the least fear or caution, opposed their bibles and useless rods to
the bullets of the troops. Three hundred of them were massacred in cold
blood by the troops of the slimy hypocrite and agent of British
Imperialism, General Smuts. This infamous deed won for Smuts the
opprobrious title, 'Bloody Smuts, murderer'. The crushing of the movement
at Bulhoek was the signal for repressive measures against the peasants all
over the country, which was the more easily done, because of their
unorganized state.

The only effective resistance that the forces of reaction met was in
South West Africa, a former German colony, which fell into the hands of
the Union of South Africa through the robber treaty of Versailles. The
Union government, in pursuance of its policy of exploitation and
repression of native people under its rule, immediately started imposing new
taxes on these new native subjects, and to which of course they objected.
This led to the Bondelswarts rebellion — a revolt of one of the native tribes
of South West Africa. The natives armed themselves with all manner of
weapons, including rifles and guns of all descriptions, but these were no
match for the military airplanes and bombs which were brought into play
against them by the Government, in whose trail desolation followed. The

rebellion was suppressed to the greater 'glory' of the British Empire.

## Leading Role Played by Native Women

The only other thing which remains to be said in regard to the struggles of the peasantry at this time, is that of the boycott movement against the traders in the native reserves, of Herschel and the Transkei. If prices were prohibitively high in the towns, they were outrageous in the native reserves and caused the greater dissatisfaction. The interesting feature in this boycott movement was the leading role played by the native women, and it can correctly be called a women's movement. This took place in 1922 and ended in a victory for the women. The organization that was set up during the course of the struggle later in 1926 developed into an anti-tax movement, when the government imposed a new poll tax law on the Cape natives in that year. However, this time the movement was betrayed by its leaders, especially Dr Wellington Butelezi who had played a leading role in the previous struggle.

## Reformist Leadership

The end of 1924 ushered in a lull in the revolutionary movement. Between then and 1930, the Industrial and Commercial Workers Union developed into a reformist organization under the leadership of the Amsterdam Trade Union International. In 1926, Kadalie, the secretary of the I.C.U., under the pressure of the social-fascists and bourgeois liberals who infested the movement as 'sympathizers' and 'advisers', was persuaded to expel the native and coloured Communists from the organization. Very soon after this he received an invitation to join Amsterdam and in 1927 he was in Europe, under the tutelage of the Independent Labour Party of England. Here he also met the English representatives of the Red International of Labour Unions. But, although Kadalie recognized the revolutionary role of the R.I.L.U., (he wrote to this effect in *Labour Monthly*) as opposed to the reformist, imperialist tool of Amsterdam, he refused to have any dealings with the Red International, but rather preferred as his associates the reformist Lansburys, Maxtons and Brockways. These friends of his, on his return to Africa, to make sure that there would be no back-sliding on his part, kindly offered him an adviser, a member of the Independent Labour Party, Mr Ballinger. From this time on, there was a rapid disintegration of the I.C.U. In July of 1928, Kadalie publicly denounced the strike of 18,000 miners on the diamond diggings at Lichtenberg, Transvaal. In December 1928, Kadalie betrayed the strike of 100 agricultural workers at Pretoria. In July 1929, Kadalie split with Ballinger, who had obtained control over the I.C.U. and undermined Kadalie's position. The split with Ballinger did not mean any difference in the policy that Kadalie pursued. Though at the time he tried to convince the native workers that he had discarded the reformist policy for a revolutionary one. In the following months he made a temporary alliance with the Communists and participated in their gigantic demonstrations of that year against the Nationalist Government's pass laws and other anti-native laws.

But this was just a cunning manoeuvre on the part of Kadalie in order to maintain his hold over the native masses. In January 1930, he called a strike of 400 railway workers in the port, East London, which, after three weeks of hard fighting, he betrayed completely, and proved himself to be completely reactionary and a tool of the bourgeoisie. The rapid disintegration of the I.C.U. was astonishing. We must, however, remember the conditions that gave birth to the I.C.U.: its pronounced anarcho-syndicalist tendencies, 'One Big Industrial and Commercial Workers Union of South Africa', and the petty bourgeois character of its leadership, mainly petty bourgeois intellectuals — teachers exasperated by the tyranny of white missionaries, who are in charge of native education in South Africa. Besides these general features was the fact that the I.C.U., organizationally, was neither based on the industry nor still less on the factory, but was mainly a loose organization based on territory.

## The International Revolutionary Movement in South Africa

The expulsion of the Communists from the Industrial and Commercial Workers Union in 1926 resulted in a great deal of dissatisfaction among the rank and file members of the I.C.U., which was crystallized in the formation of the African Federation of Trade Unions in 1928. The Federation was supported mainly by workers in the secondary industries; garment, furniture, laundries, etc. In 1928, it affiliated to the Red International of Labour Unions. Its programme set out to organize all workers, irrespective of colour or race, with the aim of uniting white, coloured, Indian and native workers for the united struggle against capitalism and Imperialism in South Africa. The difficulties to the realization of the goal are great. The bourgeoisie have erected a wall of prejudice between the white and the black workers which is difficult to overcome.

However, signs are not wanting of a better state of things in the future. The crisis in South Africa has led to a broad offensive of the employers against the wages and conditions of the workers. There is a growing volume of unemployment with its misery and starvation. New repressive laws against the revolutionary movement are being introduced by the government. All these things are giving rise to a revolutionary upsurge in the labour movement, amongst both white and native workers, as can be seen from the recent struggles. We have already referred to the strike of the railway and harbour workers in East London in January 1930, in which the Federation participated. This was followed by a whole series of strike struggles among the agricultural workers in the western Cape Province — at Worcester,

Carnarvon, Craddock, Middleburg, Bonnievale, etc. — which have led to
severe clashes with the police forces, especially at Worcester, Craddock and
Middleburg.

## Strike Struggles

In December 1930, we also saw protest strikes and demonstrations
against the government of a militant character, leading in Durban to a clash
with the police, the killing of five native workers, the imprisonment of 33
and the deportations of hundreds to the native reserves.

A characteristic feature of these strikes in 1930 was that they were
almost entirely strikes of native workers led by the revolutionary trade
unions and the Communist Party. In 1931 there was a turn, especially in
Johannesburg and Cape Town. Here it was found that it was possible not
only to win the native workers to the leadership of the revolutionary
movement, but also the white unemployed workers, and sections of the
white employed workers in the secondary industries. The leather workers'
strike at the beginning of 1931 in Johannesburg involved both native
and white workers and gave a great impetus generally to the movement.
This was followed by the joint demonstration of white and native workers
on 1st May 1931, in Johannesburg, when there was witnessed in South
Africa, for the first time in its history, something that made the Imperialists tremble for their future: 8,000 black and white workers demonstrating
and fighting together against the police, something that aroused a howl of
rage from the bloodhounds of Imperialism for the heads of the Bolsheviks.

## The White Terror

The government, frightened by this rising movement, hoped to kill it by
terror: by shooting and jailing, deporting and exiling its leadership. During
the years 1929-31, 43 workers were killed; 100 were imprisoned for
periods ranging from one month to one year and in the case of Buikes, the
leader of the agricultural workers of Worcester, six years. Hundreds have
been deported back to the native reservations, and the leaders of the native
workers have been exiled from their homes and their families.

These persecutions are directed especially against the revolutionary movement and a new feature in this respect is the cowardly attack on small
groups of workers by armed police. We have in mind especially the
ambushing by 150 armed plain clothes constables and police, on 1st
August 1931, of 12 workers, leaders of the Communist Party and the
revolutionary trade unions, in Johannesburg. The Minister of Justice,
Mr Pirow, hoped to strike terror by physical violence and annihilation.
This marks the growth of Fascism in South Africa, the increasing resort to
violence aimed at the revolutionary workers.

Ikaka Laba Sebenzi, African section of the International Labour

Defence, has mobilized the masses in defence of these victims of the terror and in support of their dependents. Not only does it undertake the legal defence in these cases, but mobilizes in demonstrations and protest meetings all the workers against the whole system of terror of the bourgeoisie. Especially active was the I.L.D. In the case of the Durban victims in 1931, where the terror was fiercest, where workers were being arrested in hundreds, and without regard for the safety or comfort of their families deported before they make arrangements, the activity of Ikaka was able, within a very short time, to gain for it the mass support of workers, both white and black, who, whatever their political inclinations may be, always will support the victims of the police terror of the bourgeoisie. Thus we find that, though the Ikaka Laba Sebenzi is a comparatively young organization in South Africa, it has grown rapidly in popularity because even the backward strata of the workers recognize its aims, and grasp its object more easily than that of other organizations.

The growing industrial crisis, coupled with a sharp agrarian crisis, is shaking South African economy to its very foundations. The bourgeoisie is making every attempt to shift the burden of this crisis on to the shoulders of the workers and toiling masses. The attacks on the wages of 90,000 railroad workers, black and white, on the needle workers, miners, etc., are evidence of this, while unemployment has grown to an unprecedented extent. The native peasantry is faced with actual ruin and starvation. The bourgeoisie, as a way out of the crisis, is preparing further attacks on the workers and at the same time supporting the war manoeuvres of British Imperialism in the East and against the Soviet Union. The bourgeois press continuously publishes the most scurrilous attacks and slanders against the Soviet Union in the hope of whipping up an anti-Soviet atmosphere.

But these attacks of the bourgeoisie on the Soviet Union, instead of antagonizing the workers, are arousing the greatest interest of the workers in the land that is building Socialism. Especially is this the case among the native workers and toiling peasants, who are not hoodwinked that there is a worse slavery and oppression than they have to face in South Africa. The screams of the bourgeois press about forced labour in the Soviet Union cannot have any meaning to those who are undergoing such labour. On the other hand, we find that the toiling masses of workers and peasants are astonished at the successes of the Five Year Plan and are showing a great diligence in seeking the truth of what is going on in the Soviet Union. The triumphs of the workers and peasants in the U.S.S.R. who have driven out the capitalist and the landlord, who have solved the national question and given self-determination and the possibilities for development to the national minorities, these are the things that interest the workers, these are the things that are sinking into their consciousness. This is shown by the setting up of sections of the Friends of the Soviet Union in South Africa, at the end of 1931, and the organization of delegations to visit the U.S.S.R.

The growth of the Communist Party, the revolutionary trade unions, coupled with the growth of the Ikaka Laba Sebenzi and the F.S.U., are unmistakable signs of the growing radicalization of the masses and of their determination to follow in the path mapped out by the Russian workers and peasants.

## APPENDIX I

## THE FUSION MOVEMENT IN SOUTH AFRICA

The 'Secessionist' Movement in South Africa has given place to a 'Fusion' Movement. Generals Hertzog and Smuts, after twenty years of apparently bitter and irreconcilable strife and struggle, have embraced each other and decided to be as good friends as they had been enemies in the past — which all decent true South Africans are enjoined to forget and let bury itself.

The Fusion Movement is understood to mean the uniting of the South African and the Nationalist Parties into a National Centre Party under the leadership of the two generals. The Movement has strong support in the Transvaal, Orange Free State and Natal where the leading bodies of the two parties have endorsed the Movement. In the Cape Province, Dr Malan, a former cabinet minister in the Hertzog Government and leader of the Cape Nationalists, has revolted and between him and General Hertzog there is now war to the knife.

The English imperialists are jubilant over the new developments which they claim will lead to the end of 'racial strife' between Boer and Briton, and usher in a new and golden period of prosperity for South Africa. Their optimism has some ground in the fabulous profits they are now making on the gold mines of the Witwatersrand, especially since South Africa abandoned the Gold Standard after a period of — to the British financiers and speculators — criminal vacillation.

The Boer landlords and agrarian capitalists, on the other hand, claim that since the granting of 'Sovereign Dominion Status' to South Africa as a result of the 1926 Imperial Conference, the English have atoned for their sins, have recognized the impossibility of keeping in subjection such a freedom loving people as the Boers.

They claim that 'Dominion Status' as defined by the 1926 and later Imperial Conferences has rendered the issue of a Republic of South Africa obsolete. Thus if we are to believe our South African statesmen, all is set and ready for a real 'love feast'.

Dr Malan and his followers who are making unpleasant references to the past propaganda of the Nationalists are, compared with the Pharisee and his attitude to the publican, people who are to be regarded as a violent pestilence — dull, stupid and bankrupt politicians who are out for mischief for its own sake. Meanwhile the Malanites are making wild and vague charges against the capitalists, imperialists, Hoggenheimers, etc., whose machinations they profess to see behind the Fusion Movement. They claim that South African industry is not as sufficiently fostered as it should be by a system of heavy taxation on the gold mines, that the Fusion Movement will not pay sufficient attention to the interests of white labour, etc.

'There can be no doubt that the Fusion Movement represents quite a new and important, though not unforeseen, development.' The reasons for it, however, are to be sought for behind the wranglings, the charges and counter-charges of the 'politicians' and generals who are very anxious indeed to conceal, by loud and sentimental talk about the evils of 'racial strife', the real causes for their sudden reconciliation.

To more completely encompass the aims of the Movement, a little excursion into the events of the immediate past is not out of place. One of the results of the world economic crisis in South Africa has been its unprecedented severity in the field of agriculture. Continuous and uninterrupted ruin and bankruptcy have been the lot of the farmers in the last four years. The crisis situation has been aggravated by a prolonged drought which has destroyed millions of sheep and other livestock — a situation which continues to the present time. To quote a bourgeois source (*Cape Times*, 30th October 1933) on 'deserted farms' in South West Africa: 'There is still no rain and its continued absence aggravates the position of farmers in many parts, especially in the south. Many farms are deserted, their owners having trekked northwards or eastwards into the Kalahari in search of grazing. On other farms where it was too late to trek, the stock having already died, farmers have also abandoned their farms and gone off in search of work on the roads and railways or are living on charity in the towns.' The same paper, in passing, also informs us that 'natives and wild animals' are also suffering because of the drought.

Speculators have not been slow to exploit its human misery. Thus we are told that there is 'no real shortage of maize', only the farmers — who produced it and lack it now — are re-buying it at enhanced prices from the 'mealie' traders and co-operatives. The co-operatives represent mainly the wealthy farmers.

Other examples of the effects of the crisis could be given to show the seriousness of the situation. A continual and heavy decline in the value of agricultural exports during the whole period of the crisis has taken place year after year. The farmers have been hit severely. During 1932, their discontent with things came out in open revolt against the Hertzog Nationalist Government which had been in power since 1924. This was a new thing for the Hertzog Nationalists who until then had enjoyed universal support among the farmers and landlords, as well as large sections of the urban petty bourgeoisie and white workers.

The propaganda of the South African Party that the root cause of the trouble lay in the obstinacy with which the Hertzog Government adhered to the Gold Standard which Britain had abandoned in the autumn of 1931, began to tell among the supporters of the Nationalist Government. Falling prices of agricultural products were not sufficiently counteracted by the Government policy of export subsidies which mainly benefitted the speculators and agrarian financiers. Leading Nationalists, members of the Nationalist Parliamentary Caucus (like Steytler and Dr Hjannar Reitz) openly opposed the Hertzog Cabinet financial policy.

The finance capitalists, in the latter part of 1932, introduced financial pressure to bear upon the situation. There was a general 'flight' of capital from the country. The Government was being more and more isolated.

Tielman Roos, a leader of the Transvaal Nationalists, then a judge of the Appeal Court, resigned from the bench openly to attack the Hertzog Government's Gold Standard policy and to call 'an end to racial strife'. Hertzog's appeals to Afrikaner solidarity fell on deaf ears. In December 1932, he bowed to the inevitable and South Africa abandoned the Gold Standard. In his New Year's Message (1933) to the people of South Africa, Hertzog declared: 'Financial treason and Afrikaner treachery had forced South Africa off the Gold Standard.' However Tielman Roos, who had forced the Government's pace on the Gold Standard question, did not give it time for self-pity. He immediately set on foot a movement for coalition of the Nationalists and S.A.P. which grew popular overnight and received the support of General Smuts.

At the opening of Parliament in January 1933, Smuts extended the 'olive branch' to Hertzog who scornfully and contemptuously rejected it. But Hertzog had not understood the temper of his supporters. In less than three weeks' time he was forced to appeal to General Smuts to support a coalition, submitting the 'famous seven principles' upon which such a coalition Government should be based. These principles did not present anything new or 'revolutionary', demanding as they did, the maintenance of the *status quo* in the Constitution of the Union of South Africa, measures for the relief of the farmers, agreement on Native policy, special attention for the white workers, bilingualism in Government services, etc. — measures to which the S.A.P. had no objection.

The questions of cabinet representation and division of other spoils of office were amicably settled. Hertzog was to be Prime Minister and Smuts, Deputy Prime Minister and Minister of Justice.

In pursuance of the 'democratic' principles of the South African Constitution, it was decided to appeal to the electorate, the elections being set for May 1933. By electorate is meant the minority of white population. The millions strong native population is not considered.

The result of the elections are complete and universal victory for coalition. The Malanites who demurred at coalition were nevertheless forced to wage their fight for parliamentary honours under the banner of coalition 'with reservations' which they are now revealing. The few Labourites in Parliament were all for coalition. Those who were not were defeated.

The success of coalition led to the Fusion Movement. Its prospects are bound up with the success or non-success of the present Coalition Government. It has already gained firm footing among the 'Nats' and 'Saps' of the Transvaal, Orange Free State and Natal. It is fighting with many factors in its favour in the Cape Province against the Malanite 'diehards'.

As already seen, the revolt of the farmers driven to ruin and desperation by the ravages of the crisis, gave rise to the movement that led to a Coalition Government and its final consummation — the Fusion Movement. The crisis had created a serious situation for the South African bourgeoisie who realized that only a concentration government of bourgeois parties could avoid catastrophe. Questions of minor contradictory interests and policies paled into their proper insignificance in the face of this situation.

Moreover the crisis had solved one of the burning questions between the Chamber of Mines and farmers, i.e. the problem of native labour supply. 'Universal unemployment and the flight of the peasants driven by hunger from the native reserves had created a glut on the labour market; and the farmers and mining magnates had no reason to quarrel with each other.'

Thus, the ground had been prepared by economic factors for a 'rapprochement'. The Coalition Government has already been in power for over six months. The immediate question that faced it and still faces it is the relief of the farmers from the depredations, bond holders and mortgage sharks. The other question is unemployment, which is connected with the first.

It must be admitted that the Government has gone about its job with some determination. To say this, however, does not mean admission of the efficacy of its palliatory methods. On the contrary: the Farmers' Mortgage Act, which reduces interest on mortgages to five per cent and empowers the Land Bank to advance the interest money to the farmers, has been to the advantage of mortgage holders who could otherwise not get the money out of the bankrupt farmers. The inflationist policy has brought about some increase in the export of certain lines of agricultural products (wool, etc.) and a slight rise in prices, but nothing like what is necessary.

To finance its measures the Government has been able to get the Chamber of Mines to agree to a limited taxation on gold-mining profits, not to exceed £6,000,000 annually under the Mining Excess Profits Act. Grain advances, feed for livestock, etc., are other points in favour of the Government. These measures have so far proved of little avail to stem the tide of farm bankruptcies.

The fundamental problem of the situation — the problem of providing the farmers with a market for their products — remains unresolved. No sooner is any attempt made in this direction than a whole line of conflicting interests comes into play. The recent case of the Italian shipping subsidy of £150,000 annually, in return for a contract to supply the Italian army with meat, had thoroughly scandalized British shipping circles and their supporters who cannot understand the necessity for such unpatriotic generosity on the part of the South African Government when English shipping is in the doldrums.

It is clear that the palliative measures of the Government can only postpone for a more or less limited period the inevitable outcome of the present difficulties. With a limited internal market — the standard of living of the native population is being even further reduced — the Government must look outside of South Africa for the solution of its major problem and this is just what every capitalist country is doing !

Thus there can be no hopes of permanent success from the Government's policy. Elements like Malan feel this and . . . their opposition. And hence also their dangerous demagogy. For Dr Malan and his followers, to revolutionaries, are the most cunning supports of the bourgeoisie in South Africa. Dr Malan and his followers realize that such a Coalition Government as the present one serves to teach the masses of poor white farmers and workers the incapacity of a united capitalist Government to solve the crises, a fact which would lead to their disillusionment. As Mrs Jansen, a leading Nationalist and wife of a former cabinet minister, expressed it: 'Coalition will drive our poor classes into the hands of the Bolsheviks' because they will have no other spokesmen.

The Malanites, the Vissers, serve to distract the attention of the poor white farmers and workers from the real issue and thus prevent the genuine elements of revolt among these classes to mature. They have not even a programme, but hope to juggle with the academic questions of Dutch republicanism and South Africa's neutrality in case of war as red herrings.

The boundless, impudent insincerity with which they are raising these barren issues should arouse the ire of all revolutionaries to expose these adventurers. Because the Coalition will be exposed to the South African toiling masses, it will be the future duty of the Malans to divert the anger of the disillusioned masses against the bourgeois system from its proper channels.

The Malanites are nothing but the most cunning supporters of the capitalist system in South Africa, whose job is to keep the white workers especially the Afrikaans speaking section, in bondage to capitalist and semi-feudal politics. This is a task which was entrusted to Hertzog in the past. Dr Malan wants history to repeat itself. Like Hertzog, he chooses the present political wilderness, conscious of his role. He realizes quite clearly that the petty bourgeoisie and large sections of the workers are under the hypnotic influence of the Fusion Movement and that sooner or later there must be a reaction. The parliamentary game must be kept flexible for such an emergency and therefore he goes into opposition.

With Malan must be included the Vissers in the Transvaal, the Mrs Jansens in Natal and the Van der Merwes in the Orange Free State. These people are all agents of the bourgeoisie, the agents of the capitalists in the ranks of the poor white farmers and workers whose reactionary feudalist policies must be thoroughly exposed.

In conclusion, the Fusion Movement marks a distinct step forward in a political sense. It eliminates the racial election cries and replaces them with economic issues. It is a measure of the growing contradictions in the capitalist system and 'marks the sharpening of the class lines, a process which will be highly accelerated by the coalition government'.

Secondly, the most dangerous elements in the present situation are 'left-wing' opposition parties, who cover their treacherous designs under loud-sounding but empty denunciations of the Chamber of Mines, Hoggenheimer, etc., because they prevent the revolutionization of the genuine discontent of the toiling masses.

Finally, we have seen the inadequacy of the measures of the Coalition Government, which are designed only to benefit the rich — mortgage holders, agrarian capitalists, speculators, etc. — while the conditions of the poor continue to worsen. Ultimately coalition will come to mean more and more literally the fusion of Boer landlord and British finance capitalists. It will mean complete political reaction and more bitter exploitation of the native and white toiling masses.

Already the chains have been tightened; the crackling of the *sjamboks* ceaseless; slavery more bitter and galling than in the past threatens the native toiling masses. For the toiling masses the slogan must be for a revolutionary way out of the crises, against imperialist oppression and exploitation.

[This article was written by Comrade Albert Nzula who was on the staff of the *Negro Worker* as a contributing editor, shortly before he passed away. See announcement on another page. — Ed.]

# Africa Series No. 2

Albert Nzula, first African General Secretary of the South African
Communist Party (way back in 1930-31); Ivan Potekhin and
Aleksander Zusmanovich, first Russian Marxists to study Africa in
the freshness of the first decade after the October Revolution —
these are the authors of this book. Nzula, after a brief but intensive
period of revolutionary activity in South Africa, was to die
prematurely in Moscow while Potekhin lived on to become the
grand old man of Russian scholarship on Africa. The authors
embodied a significant juncture of African political struggle and
Russian post-revolutionary Marxism. The editor of this edition,
Dr. Robin Cohen, is a well known sociologist of Africa who has
specialised in research on the African working class. Author and
editor of numerous publications, he is at present a professor at the
University of the West Indies, having previously been attached to
the Centre for West African Studies at the University of
Birmingham.

*Forced Labour in Colonial Africa* was published in Russian over
40 years ago. This — the first English language — edition is being
brought out because the book represents one of the earliest
Marxist analyses of the impact that colonialism had on Africa
during the first half century that followed the Scramble. The
political experience of its African co-author has resulted in a book
whose every page is alight with passion and commitment to the
liberation of the Continent, yet always tempered by an explicit
theoretical understanding of capitalism in its imperialist phase.
The book opens with an outline of Africa's role in the world
economic system. Successive chapters reveal how Western
capitalism conjured up a brutally exploited working class and
dispossessed peasantry throughout the African Continent. Each
major region of Black Africa is analysed. Meticulous information
as to the facts of oppression and many of the early urban and
rural struggles against colonialism before the Second World War
is set out. And important issues which divide Africa today into
radicals and conservatives are raised — notably the limits to
liberation inherent in bourgeois led nationalist movements.
Dr. Cohen's Introduction is a valuable summation of Nzula's
life and of the background to this book. The Appendices bring
together many of Nzula's little known writings.

ISBN Hb 0 905762 30 4
    Pb  0 905762 31 2

Price: Hb £8. 50; $16. 95
      Pb £2. 95; $ 6. 95